Scribes, Printers, and the Accidentals of their Texts

STUDIES IN ENGLISH MEDIEVAL LANGUAGE AND LITERATURE

Edited by Jacek Fisiak

Advisory Board:
John Anderson (Methoni, Greece), Ulrich Busse (Halle),
Olga Fischer (Amsterdam), Dieter Kastovsky (Vienna),
Marcin Krygier (Poznań), Roger Lass (Cape Town),
Peter Lucas (Cambridge), Donka Minkova (Los Angeles),
Akio Oizumi (Kyoto), Katherine O'Brien O'Keeffe (UC Berkeley, USA),
Matti Rissanen (Helsinki), Hans Sauer (Munich),
Liliana Sikorska (Poznań), Jeremy Smith (Glasgow),
Jerzy Wełna (Warsaw)

Vol. 33

PETER LANG

Frankfurt am Main · Berlin · Bern · Bruxelles · New York · Oxford · Warszawa · Wien

Jacob Thaisen
Hanna Rutkowska
(Eds.)

Scribes, Printers, and the Accidentals of their Texts

PETER LANG
Internationaler Verlag der Wissenschaften

Bibliographic Information published by the Deutsche Nationalbibliothek
The Deutsche Nationalbibliothek lists this publication in the Deutsche Nationalbibliografie; detailed bibliographic data is available in the internet at http://dnb.d-nb.de.

Cover design:
Olaf Glöckler, Atelier Platen, Friedberg

Typesetting by motivex.

The publication was financially supported
by the Adam Mickiewicz University, Poznań
and the University of Stavanger.

All books in the series are reviewed
before publication.

ISSN 1436-7521
ISBN 978-3-631-60712-1
© Peter Lang GmbH
Internationaler Verlag der Wissenschaften
Frankfurt am Main 2011
All rights reserved.

All parts of this publication are protected by copyright. Any utilisation outside the strict limits of the copyright law, without the permission of the publisher, is forbidden and liable to prosecution. This applies in particular to reproductions, translations, microfilming, and storage and processing in electronic retrieval systems.

www.peterlang.de

Contents

Acknowledgements 7

    Jacob Thaisen (Adam Mickiewicz University/University of Stavanger)
    Hanna Rutkowska (Adam Mickiewicz University)
    Introduction 9

1. **Javier Calle-Martín** (University of Málaga)
   Line-Final Word Division in Early English Handwriting 15

2. **Larry J. Swain** (Bemidji State University)
   Whose Text for Whom?: Transmission History of Ælfric of Eynsham's *Letter to Sigeweard* 31

3. **David Moreno Olalla** (University of Málaga)
   Nominal Morphemes in *Lelamour's Herbal* 53

4. **Jacob Thaisen** (Adam Mickiewicz University/University of Stavanger)
   Adam Pinkhurst's Short and Long Forms 73

5. **Joanna Kopaczyk** (Adam Mickiewicz University)
   A V or not a V? Transcribing Abbreviations in Seventeen Manuscripts of the "Man of Law's Tale" for a Digital Edition 91

6. **Matti Peikola** (University of Turku)
   Copying Space, Length of Entries, and Textual Transmission in Middle English Tables of Lessons 107

7. **Olga Frolova** (National Library of Russia)
   The "Prologue" to the *Wycliffe Bible* with an English Royal Book Stamp in the National Library of Russia 125

8. **Mari Agata** (Keio University)
   Improvements, Corrections, and Changes in the *Gutenberg Bible* 135

9. **Satoko Tokunaga** (Keio University)
   A Textual Analysis of the Overlooked Tales in de Worde's *Canterbury Tales* 157

10. **Roderick W. McConchie** (University of Helsinki)
    Compounds and Code-Switching: Compositorial Practice in William Turner's *Libellus de re Herbaria Novvs*, 1538 177

Index of manuscripts 191
Index of names 195
Index of terms 201
Notes on contributors 207

Acknowledgements

First of all, we would like to thank all the authors who have contributed their articles to this volume. We are particularly grateful to them for their patience, because the preparation of the volume took an unusually long time due to technical, organisational, as well as financial difficulties. We would like also to thank the reviewers for their valuable comments and suggestions on the organisation and contents of the papers. We are indebted to Professor Jacek Fisiak (Adam Mickiewicz University, Poznań) for his patronage of this project, and to both Adam Mickiewicz University, Poznań and the University of Stavanger for funding the publication of this book. Last but not least, our thanks go to Mr Michał Jankowski and Mrs Ewa Kowalkowska for their editorial work and technical assistance.

Introduction

Jacob Thaisen, Adam Mickiewicz University/University of Stavanger
Hanna Rutkowska, Adam Mickiewicz University

Manuscript culture is often contrasted with print culture. The defining capacity of the latter to produce multiple near-identical copies of a work arrested the textual mobility characteristic of the former. Where every medieval manuscript copy results from a unique instance of transmission of a written work, printing made possible, for the first time, the single canonical text of such a work. However, the year of 1476 when William Caxton set up his printing press at Westminster marks a less abrupt transition in terms of many other aspects of textual transmission. Scribes and their supervisors took decisions about both the visual presentation and content of their products that represent adaptive responses not only to the source materials but also to the intended audience and function. Printers and their compositors made analogous selections when preparing their materials. And both groups additionally introduced various types of mechanical error in the process, the nature of only some of which is medium-specific. The chronological arrangement of the ten essays included in the present collection in terms of their individual subject matter accentuates this continuity across the boundary between the medieval and early modern periods.

All written by students of the transmission history of texts surviving in medieval manuscript or early modern print, several of the contributions also unite in tracing clues found in the material support for the text(s) under study. There is here an implied dismissal of the product of modern editorial intervention as a principal focus of investigation in favour of the historical text itself as it is found in the context of the physical codex (or roll or diptych or other object) that houses it. This concentration could be seen to adhere loosely to the tenets of the New Philology (as advocated by Cerquiglini 1989, Nichols 1990). Many of the clues would be classified as "accidentals" following Walter Greg (1950-51), since they fail to constitute semantic textual differences between the various witnesses to a given text. Yet the essays demonstrate individually and collectively that these clues do form an important basis for puzzling out the transmission history behind the witnesses. Moreover, even a collation focused on the traditional criterion of semantic – "substantive" to use Greg's term – textual difference requires careful manual evaluation, as it is clear that some substantive variants are more substantive than others. Examples are provided by Satoko Tokunaga's discussion of the sources Wynkyn de Worde drew upon for the preparation of his edition of Chaucer's *Canterbury Tales*. The gradualness of the transition from manuscript to print also comes to the fore in her work, as de Worde set his edition partly from Caxton's second edition of the poem (a print) and partly from a manuscript of high textual authority.

Although the claim of the substantiveness of accidentals for textual and editorial purposes by no means originates with the present volume, it can be fairly maintained that accidentals tend to receive limited scholarly attention. An example are the line-final word-division practices in a corpus of Old and Middle English "Fachlitteratur" in manuscript studied by Javier Calle-Martín in the opening essay, since a modern editor rarely records such practices in the apparatus, let alone seeks to preserve it in the critical text. The evidence permits certain generalizations relating to how scribes divided a given word as dictated by its phonology and morphology in combination with the amount of space available at the margin, but also shows idiosyncrasy to be a prominent influence and, therefore, a possible diagnostic of them. The possibility to distinguish one craftsman (or group of them) from another is cautiously addressed by Mari Agata too. Using computerized, photographic techniques, she visually collates copies of the *Gutenberg 42-line Bible*, the first longer work to be printed in Europe, and is able to identify stop-press corrections in them by this means. Despite the cost in labour and time of effecting the corrections, they surprisingly include textually insignificant replacements of one letter-type for another and co-exist with uncorrected textually significant errors. The reason they may prove to be diagnostic of press-crews is that their distribution in the text suggests the individual crews both prioritized non-identically the various types of typographical rule and perceived error.

In contrast to habits of word-division and error correction, it is well-known for the pre-standardization period that iconicity is to be found in the selection between functionally equivalent linguistic forms. John Lelamour's *Herbal*, as witnessed by *British Library, MS Sloane 5*, contains a colophon stating both its date and place of production. The trouble is, David Moreno Olalla argues, essentially that the nominal and verbal morphology supports the "colophonic" localization of the *text* to Herefordshire of 1373, while the orthography of the lexical bases agrees with a much later London placing of the *witness*. The blending of the two systems is ordered, although it is in this case hard to pinpoint exactly the factors which checked the transformative process of linguistic adaptation that is the scribe's copying of the text.

The constraints imposed by the material support itself have sometimes received insufficient attention in the evaluation of a profile of orthographic forms, as Jacob Thaisen demonstrates is the case with the scribe Adam Pinkhurst. From an examination focused on just two manuscripts, the *Hengwrt* and *Ellesmere* copies of Geoffrey Chaucer's *Canterbury Tales*, he generalizes that scribes execute letter shapes by means of a reduced number of strokes when limited time and space are available to them for the copying. While this generalization is perhaps self-evidently valid, this is perhaps less so of his further claim that a comparatively low level of formality of the final product too has a length-lowering effect. The interaction between spatial constraints and the number of letters is a concern also to Matti Peikola. His materials are the manuscripts of the *Wycliffe Bible*, specifically the tables of lessons prefixed to a wide range of them and functioning as an index. The entries in the tables show a progressive shortening through layers of scribal copying, thus seemingly undermining the textual critical principle of *lectio brevior potior*. A suspension of this maxim under a specific set of conditions is, however, a more accurate summing up of the finding, for the length reduction affects the sense of the individual entries to such an extent that it presupposes the intended audience's intimate familiarity with the content, a presumption invalid for countless other texts.

A group of the orthographic forms reviewed by Thaisen differ only in terms of the presence or absence of strokes whose linguistic function is uncertain or even nil; examples include a bar through the back of a word-final <h> or a macron over two consecutive post-vocalic minims in a lexical item like *town* or a derivational suffix like *-ion*. It is interesting to note that these 'subgraphemic' variants nonetheless have diagnostic value in view of the regular practice of modern editors to suppress them in transcription. Nor do such editors fully capture manuscript reality when it comes to the range of superscript marks typically indicating abbreviation, a point demonstrated by Joanna Kopaczyk's survey of seventeen fifteenth-century scribal hands. The individual mark may come in various shapes and sizes in just the same way as a given letter (*littera*) may differ in its graphic manifestations (*figurae*). A mark may expand differently in the diverse contexts in which individual scribes saw fit to insert it, and distinct marks may overlap in their functions. But the distinction between them is usually lost. This loss is a consequence of the standard editorial principle of representing a mark of this type by means of one or more italicized letters of the alphabet placed on the baseline and indicating its hypothesized expansion, that is, its graphemic value.

Nor are editors in the habit of recording variations in the use of white space, although establishing and understanding the conventions of its use in a given incarnation of a historical text may prove key to the accurate decoding of it. In an early printed herbal, William Turner's *Libellus de re herbaria nouus* dating from 1538 and printed by John Byddell, a hierarchy of spaces unconventionally and innovatively serves to separate words as well as to mark switches between languages, such as when the English name of a herb appears in a passage otherwise written in Latin. Roderick McConchie finds no contemporary parallel to this design feature, and he speculates that it may represent an idiosyncratic adaptation of the text to its intended audience.

If accommodation of a text to the target readership shows in accidentals such as typographical and paleographical marking conventions, it is clear that much valuable information may be lost when an editorial process insensitive to these parameters removes a historical text from the contexts provided by the physical medium in which it is housed and transforms it into a modern print or electronic edition. Those contexts may be more peripheral to the medium itself than typography or handwriting, yet speak volumes about the tastes and interests of those who chose to actualize or, literally, objectify a given text and those who later interacted with the resulting object, including the object in its capacity as a witness to the text. A Tudor rose found on a binding in the National Library of Russia thus indicates former ownership by an English monarch, in this case of a printed copy of a title outlawed well into the Renaissance: Robert Crowley's edition from 1550 of the *Prologue to the Wycliffe Bible*. Olga Frolova, who looks at this particular copy in her contribution to the present volume, points out how the adaptation to the readership here includes the conscious preservation of the Middle English of the manuscript Ur-text, which, paradoxically, is a policy at variance with the objective of making the *Bible* and Lollard tracts accessible in the vernacular.

Larry Swain takes the theme of contexts and co-texts further in his lengthy survey of the surviving manuscript and print copies of Ælfric of Evesham's homiletic prose *Letter to Sigeweard*. Although these number few, each incarnation is remarkably different despite the integrated authorial plea to scribes about its accurate duplication. In the case of the twelfth-century *Oxford, Bodleian Library, MS Bodley 343*, for example, the *Letter* appears as a part of a large collection of homilies and texts adapted for homiletic or devotional use, which suggests its compiler(s) enjoyed access, in person or by proxy, to sizeable holdings of this type of religious material such as would be found at a monastic library. The first print edition, William L'Isle's of 1622, appropriates the text for the Protestant aim of justifying *Bible* vernacularization by calling attention to the historical precedent for such activity. Unlike Crowley in relation to the *Wycliffe Bible*, however, he supplies both transcript and translation.

The trustworthiness of editions of historical texts is mostly taken for granted. Roger Lass (2004) warns of the precariousness of proceeding on this assumption, outlining many of the central issues. Philology, in the modern sense of the term, examines those issues in detail. It is a scholarly discipline whose practitioners concern themselves with the establishment of the authenticity and original form of historical texts. As such, the discipline falls in the intersection of several other disciplines, and those who might describe themselves as philologists have often followed quite different educational paths. Indeed, they tend to use other labels themselves: art historian, paleographer, historical linguist, Renaissance scholar, textual critic, historian, Anglo-Saxonist, medievalist, literary scholar, stemmatologist. Few admit to practise philology, and yet its role is difficult to overestimate. Although there will always be a need for scholarly editions of historical texts, it is hoped that the present collection of essays will highlight the multifariousness of the witnesses to them, as revealed by philological research. Doubtlessly, an appreciation of the contexts in which those witnesses are found enriches the experience of working with the evidence they provide.

References

Cerquiglini, Bernard
   1989   *Eloge de la variante: Histoire critique de la philologie.* Paris: Seuil.
Dossena, Marina – Roger Lass (eds.)
   2004   *Methods and data in English historical dialectology.* Bern: Peter Lang.
Greg, Walter W.
   1950–1951   "The rationale of copy-text", *Studies in Bibliography* 3: 19–36.
Lass, Roger
   2004   "*Ut custodiant litteras*: Editions, corpora and witnesshood". In: Marina Dossena – Roger Lass (eds.), 21–48.
Nichols, Stephen
   1990   "Introduction: Philology in a manuscript culture", *Speculum* 65: 1–10.

Line-Final Word Division in Early English Handwriting[1]

Javier Calle-Martín, University of Málaga

1. Introduction

A survey of word separation in early English manuscripts reveals that the phenomenon in most cases depends on the erratic practice of scribes. Even when there are recurrent phono-orthographic environments which may tentatively lead to predict a given word-break, the problem is then to evaluate the level of consistency of the overall practice of a scribe. In Old English (henceforth OE), spaces are prone to occur at a morphological level, separating prefixes, suffixes and the elements of compounds. In Middle English (henceforth ME), an on-going standardization occurs leading to the progressive obliteration of morphological divisions.

Line-final word division, by contrast, is even more controversial to the eye of the modern reader inasmuch as the number of variables increases. A scribe may, in principle, break a word elsewhere and it is therefore dificult to make generalizations. One cannot see the wood for the trees as to the discrepancies which arise when several prose pieces are compared. For instance, line-final division in *Glasgow, University Library, MS Hunter 497* (fols. 1^r–92^v), holding a late fifteenth century translation of Æmilius Macer's *Herbary*, shows a consistent set of rules wherein the phonological outnumbers the morphological, the latter exclusively depending on the room available at the margin of the folio (Calle-Martín 2009: 35-53). *MS Hunter 95* (fols. 82^r–155^v), in turn, housing an anonymous fifteenth century English version of the *Book of Operation*, displays an heterogeneous practice where the number of anomalous divisions is considerable, *i.e. sch-al* (fol. 84^r, 14), *wo-lte* (fol. 86^r, 29), *kn-otte* (fol. 86^v, 6), *etc.*

This apparent chaos has been responsible for the lack of scholarly attention to the topic in the literature. On the traditional side, the foundations of palaeography reveal that line-final division is haphazard in English handwriting, and the only precept "seems to have been that not less than two completing letters could be carried over to the second line" (Hector 1958: 48; Denholm-Young 1964: 70). The modern approaches, on the other hand, have recently rebutted the traditional belief in light of the existence of recurrent patterns behind the scribal hand. This is, however, a moot point as the literature is found to be controversial. In OE,

---

1 The present research has been funded by the Autonomous Government of Andalusia (grant number P07-HUM–2609) and by the Spanish Ministry of Science and Innovation (grant number FFI2008-02336). I am also grateful to the Caledonian Research Foundation/Royal Society of Edinburgh for generous financial support (2006 European Visiting Research Fellowship at the University of Glasgow). These grants are hereby gratefully acknowledged.

Hladký affirms that the main word division principle in the *Exeter Book* is the morphological, including compounds, prefixed and derived words (1985a: 73). One year later, Lutz's analysis of 4,000 instances leads her to conclude that the "scribal division of polysyllabic words reflects their phonological organization into syllables" (Lutz 1986: 193; see also Burchfield 1994: 182). However conflicting, both views are true. The problem here is that the results obtained from a given work cannot be extrapolated to represent a whole period in view of the idiosyncratic nature of mediaeval scribes. Word division practices should then be studied across particular hands so that the conclusions might be eventually compared with other pieces (Calle-Martín 2009: 49).

On an editorial basis, on the other hand, the topic has also been considerably underestimated. As with other palaeographic aspects such as abbreviations and punctuation (Calle-Martín 2004: 407; Calle-Martín – Miranda-García 2005a: 110), word division has not been duly treated, particularly because of the editorial policy of many publishers. There are still voices complaining about this gap since the outcome may not be used as a source for palaeographic research (Burchfield 1994: 187). In my opinion, the scribal practice should at least be made clear in the footnotes or the textual apparatus of the edition.

Under these circumstances, the present paper aims to approach the topic from a multivariate perspective in such a way as to avoid some of the inconsistencies of the previous approaches, such as the lack of representativeness of a single work, on the one hand, and the unitary treatment of different hands, on the other. Even though acknowledging that the phenomenon strictly responds to a palaeographic motivation (*i.e.* handwriting style, manuscript type, script, margin size, *etc.*), this survey is primarily concerned with the written evidence, taken as the input to find the patterns, used by scribes when breaking a word line-finally.

The initial hypothesis for this paper is the so-called transition from morphological division, the prevalent boundary in OE, to phonological division in ME (Hladký 1985a: 73–75). On account of this, the objective of the present paper is threefold: a) to validate or refute the previous hypothesis by using a corpus of OE and ME prose; b) to offer a taxonomy of the word-division rules from a statistical perspective; and c) to characterize the concept of syllable boundary in early English and its orthographic implications. The accomplishment of these objectives will also lead us to conclude whether word-breaking responds to a consistent set of rules or to the idiosyncrasy of mediaeval scribes.

Our study has been accordingly divided into five sections. Section 2 describes the source data and the theoretical framework; sections 3 and 4 present the taxonomy and statistical analysis of the prose works under scrutiny; and finally, section 5 summarizes the conclusions whilst at the same time suggests other future lines of research.

2. Methodology

2.1. The data

The present research forms part of a major project developed at Málaga University that pursues the digital edition of the mediaeval *Fachprosa* housed in the Hunterian Collection at Glasgow University Library (henceforth GUL), a fact which has granted me access to a wide variety of mediaeval prose compositions written by different hands. These range from those texts which display a masterly use of the phenomenon to others whose practice is merely accidental. In order to avoid the bias stemming from the use of a single source, this study is based on several OE and ME texts which have been chosen on account of variables such as their different chronology and the number of word-division instances.

The OE practice, on the one hand, has been investigated through the use of the following sources: a) *London, British Library, MS Cotton Vitelius A.xv* (fols. 94^r–131^v), the *Beowulf* manuscript, housing three other prose tracts elsewhere dated *ca.* 1000 (Rypins 1998): A fragment of the *Life of St. Christopher*, *Wonders of the East*, and *Letter of Alexander the Great to Aristotle* (henceforth abbreviated as *Cot*); b) *Cambridge, University Library, MS Corpus Christi College 140* (fols. 2^r–45^v), containing the Anglo-Saxon version of the *Gospel according to St. Matthew*, from the early eleventh century (henceforth *Mt*); and c) *Cambridge, University Library, MS Corpus Christi College 201* (fols. 131^r–145^r), housing a mid-eleventh century version of *Apollonius of Tyre* (*AoT* for short). The overall OE sample amounts to 37,368 running words, which provide 614 line-final word-division instances.

The ME period, on the other hand, has been based on four sources: a) *London, British Library, MS Egerton 2622* (fols. 136^r–165^v), containing a late ME arithmetical treatise entitled *The Crafte of Nombrynge* (henceforth *E2622*); b) *London, British Library, MS Sloane 340* (fols. 39^v–63^v), holding a ME translation of Corbeil's *De Urinis*, from the second half of the fourteenth century (henceforth *S340*); c) *Cambridge, MS Peterhouse College 118* (fols. 29^v–35^r), housing a mid-fifteenth century version of *The Cure of Enpostumes* (henceforth *P118*); and d) *GUL, MS Hunter 328* (fols. 1^r–44^v), housing a version of the *Treatise on Urines*, from the late fifteenth century (henceforth *H328*). The ME compendium, in turn, amounts to 60,572 running words and 740 instances.

2.2. Rationale

Following the line initiated in a previous paper (Calle-Martín 2009: 35-53), Hladký's approach to the study of word division in English historical texts is partially adopted as a theoretical framework (1985a, 1985b). He proposes a functional classification of the phenomenon in terms of the two basic tendencies for splitting, *i.e.* morphology and phonology. The former recurs to word formation whereas the latter divides words in terms of their actual pronunciation, *i.e. ahyr-ian* (*Mt*, xix) *vs. soþli-ce* (*Mt*, xi). Still, a third group has been added in our case to account for those anomalous divisions which fall apart from this twofold classification, and which seem to escape Hladký's attention, *i.e. mildhe-rtnysse* (*Mt*, v), *mea-hte* (*Cot*, fol. 113^v, 9), *indig-estyon* (*H328*, fol. 5^v, 6), *etc.*

The task is not straightforward as there are cases where the morphological and the phonological overlap, particularly in OE, such as *micel-ne* (*Cot*, fol. 123^r), *yld-ra* (*Mt*, xvii), *etc.* In ME, these cases are yet a minority, as in *grey-ness* (*S340*, fol. 56^v), *need-full* (*P118*, fol. 30^v), *etc.* These instances have been taken as morphological in our study in light of the existence of other breaking possibilities, as the Anglo-Saxon author could have opted for unambiguous phonological divisions like **mi-celne* or **yl-dra*. The conflict, as Powell puts it, is "the disparity between the ear, which divides a word into groups of sounds, and the eye, which perceives its meaningful parts (morphemes)" (1984: 452; see also Massey 1934: 402; Hladký 1987: 124), hence the continuous contention between morphology and phonology in English.[2]

The present paper also discusses the use and distribution of the rules which, both at a morphological and at a phonological level, participate in the breaking of a word line-finally. The former necessarily depends upon processes such as compounding and affixation and the latter is liable to incorporate different rules. In this fashion, Hladký (1985a, 1985b) observes the division after an open syllable (henceforth the CV – CV rule), the division between two consonants (the C – C rule), the division between two vowels (the V – V rule) and the division between the pairs -*st* and -*ct* (the ST rule and the CT rule, respectively). This inventory has been supplemented by mentioning the level of compliance and the exceptions, if any, in each case.

3. Old English

3.1. Form

Word separation is generally dated as a sixth century innovation of Irish and Anglo-Saxon scribes, who made a decisive contribution to the development of the system of *distinctiones*. These scribes were in need of visual cues to understand Latinate texts, most of them written in *scriptura continua*, and recurred to the practice of word separation, spaces and periods normally used therein (Clemens – Graham 2007: 83–84). These separations marked off the genesis of line-final word division in OE, the phenomenon becoming widely spread already in the tenth century.

---

[2] See, for instance, cases like *child-ish* vs. *chil-dren* or *hat-ing* vs. *ha-tred* in present day English. This picture becomes more complicated if British and American dictionaries are compared since the latter divide words phonetically whereas the former are mostly guided by derivation, as in *idio-matic* vs. *idiom-atic* (Powell 1984: 452).

Orthographically speaking, it is elsewhere argued that OE scribes systematically deprecated the use of punctuation to mark off line-final divisions, the hyphen being an exception rather than a rule (Burchfield 1994: 182). This view, however, may be deemed simplistic in light of the picture obtained from the sources under scrutiny, where three different practices are witnessed. Whilst *Cot* ignores the use of punctuation symbols, *Mt* recurs to the hyphen, even though its omission is also found, plausibly as a result of insufficient writing space in the margin. *AoT*, in turn, shows the hyphen both in the outer and the inner margins, the latter at the beginning of the following line.

3.2. Function

This section investigates the phenomenon by using a multifaceted perspective, first using the corpus as a whole and later across the pieces independently, an approach allowing to identify the general trend of the period as well as to explore any likely authorial variation.

Figure 1 below presents the distribution of instances in terms of the particular type of division involved (in absolute figures). As illustrated, the phonological outnumbers the morphological, amounting to 325 and 262 instances, respectively. Irregular divisions, by contrast, are a minority with just twenty-seven instances altogether. These data come to contradict, at least at first sight, the hypothesis that the morphological outweighs the phonological in OE.

The validity of these results is also corroborated by analysing the phenomenon across the different prose works. Figure 2 reproduces the distribution of the instances in each piece and, given that text length is different, the figures have been normalized to a text of 10^3 words for comparison. Two main conclusions can be drawn, one quantitative and the other qualitative. On the quantitative side, the occurrence of word division is found to be at odds in OE texts ranging from *AoT*, with 44.34 instances (every 10^3 words), to *Mt*, amounting to 175,76 examples. *Cot* would be at the top of this continuum with 350.29 tokens. The phenomenon is therefore erratically distributed across the pieces, being therefore more prone to occur when the writer aims at making the most of the writing space at the margin.

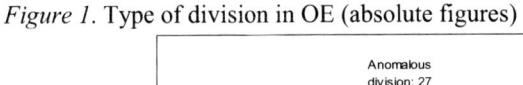

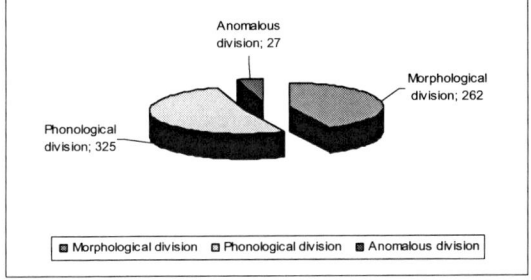

Figure 1. Type of division in OE (absolute figures)

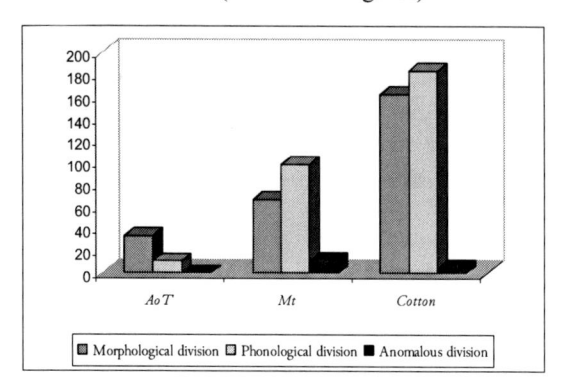

Figure 2. Distribution across texts (normalized figures)

■ Morphological division ■ Phonological division ■ Anomalous division	

From a qualitative standpoint, phonological divisions amount to 98.31 and 183.51 instances in *Mt* and *Cot*, respectively, thus slightly exceeding the morphological, with 66.53 and 162.1 instances. *AoT*, in turn, despite sharing the same dialect and chronology as *Mt*, shows a major preference for morphological divisions, amounting to 33.64 vs. 10.7 instances. Even though morphological boundaries play a significant role, these data cannot validate the tenet that the morphological principle is dominant in OE, as it ultimately depends on the idiosyncrasy of particular scribes.

As regards the distribution of the word-division rules, the level of variation is also significant. From a morphological standpoint, the instances have been classified according to the word-formation processes, *i.e.* compounding, prefixation and suffixation, the latter comprising both derivatives and inflectional endings.[3] Table 1 below summarizes the use and distribution of morphological boundaries in the corpus, where the figures have been also normalized to a text of 10^3 words for comparison. Two conclusions can be drawn, one general and the other particular. One may tentatively affirm that prefixation is the most recurrent morphological boundary, amounting to 94.9 instances, closely followed by suffixation, with 79.3 examples and by compounding (21.6 instances). Compare, for instance, breaks like *ge-hyrsumode* (*AoT*, xiv) and *to-dældon* (*Mt*, xxvi) *vs. cystig-nessa* (*AoT*, x). This evidence may be tentatively rebutted through the analysis of each of the pieces. Even when it is a fact that prefixation outnumbers suffixation in *AoT*, with 22.9 vs. 4.5 instances, the picture observed in the other pieces is more contradictory. Whilst in *Cot* prefixation slightly surpasses suffixation, *Mt* shows exactly the opposite, with 24.3 and 33.7 prefixed and suffixed instances, respectively.

---

[3] Inflectional endings are, by large, preferred – with eighty-five instances, if compared with thirty suffixed instances. These figures are, to a certain extent, expected in a highly-inflected language as OE.

Table 1. Morphological boundaries in OE (normalized figures)

	Cot	Mt	AoT	Total
Prefixation	47.7	24.3	22.9	94.9
Suffixation	41.1	33.7	4.5	79.3
Compounding	10.2	8.4	3.1	21.6

From a phonological standpoint, on the other hand, Table 2 reproduces the rules used by OE scribes. A more homogeneous picture is observed on account of the occurrence of two prevailing rules (the CV – CV and the C – C rules), even though other possibilities emerge depending on the word and the factual space at the margin. Each rule is accordingly dealt with below:

Table 2. Phonological boundaries in OE (normalized figures)

	Cot	Mt	AoT	Total
CV – CV rule	59.8	51.6	1.5	112.9
C – C rule	50.5	42.7	6.1	99.3
V – V rule	0.9	1.9	–	2.8
ST rule	–	1.9	0.3	2.2
CL rule	0.9	–	–	0.9

a) The CV – CV rule: There are 112.9 instances. The preceding syllable consistently shows a consonant plus a vowel as in *cire-niscan* (*AoT*, li), *hla-ford* (*Mt*, xxiv), *unglea-we* (*Cot*, fol. 121^v, 13). Unlike ME, a single vowel does never appear in an open syllable division. The consonant *x*, in turn, falls apart from this rule insofar as it is attached to the preceding vowel, regardless of any other phonological consideration, *i.e. alex-ander* (*Cot*, fol. 129^r, 15).
b) The C – C rule: It is the second top-most rule (99.3 occurrences) and implies the consistent separation of two conjoining consonants, *i.e. nih-tes* (*Cot*, 103^r, 16), *leor-ningcnihtas* (*Mt*, xix), *hear-destan* (*AoT*, ix), *etc.* The objective is twofold: a) to delimit syllabic boundaries in such a way that the first consonant is orthographically left in a closed syllable; and b) to assist in the reading task insofar as it would be misleading for the reader-aloud to find breakings like *mildhe-rtnysse* (*Mt*, v), *mea-hte* (*Cot*, fol. 113^v, 9), *geble-tsod* (*Mt*, xx), *etc.*, which would surely require a pause for a correct interpretation. If three consonants are in a series, the boundary is usually after the second consonant, *i.e. getimb-rigean* (*Mt*, xxv).
c) The V – V rule: This rule implies the separation of two conjoining vowels irrespective of their pronunciation as this practice affects both diphthongs and vocalic graphemes representing separate syllables, such as *anwe-alde* (*Mt*, xx), *farise-isce* (*Mt*, xiv), *olimphi-ade* (*Cot*, 128v, 1), *etc.* This practice is sporadic in OE as it amounts to five instances in the corpus.

d) The ST rule: It may be considered an erratic rule as there is not evidence of a standard practice. *AoT*, on the one hand, as in the *Exeter Book* (Hladký 1985a: 74), presents the systematic preservation of these consonants, as in *arce-strates* (*AoT*, xxii; li), *re-ste* (*Mt*, xi), *mona-sterio* (*Mt*, xxvii), *etc*. The division of these consonants is yet sporadic in *Cot* and, to a lesser extent, in *Mt*, amounting to four and three instances each, as in *wyns-tran* (*Mt*, xix), *belistnodon* (*Mt*, xviii), *fæs-tenu* (*Cot*, fol. 112^v, 17), *wes-tan* (*Cot*, fol. 113^v, 5), *etc*.

e) The CL rule: It implies the keeping together of a consonant and a liquid on condition that both belong to the same syllable. Hladký observes that this rule is almost axiomatic in the *Exeter Book* (1985a: 74). Our survey, however, does not validate Hladký's account because the breaking of these groups becomes a rule rather than an exception. There are fifteen line-final instances of a consonant plus a liquid combination in the corpus, five of which follow the so-called CL rule whereas the cluster is dissociated in the other ten instances, thus considered within the C – C rule. See, for instance, *wun-driende* (*Cot*, fol. 106^v, 9), *ni-cras* (*Cot*, fol. 122^v, 12) or *hreo-fla* (*Mt*, vii) in opposition to *wund-rodon* (*Mt*, xi), *wund-rade* (*Cot*, fol. 118^r, 15), *gad-riaþ* (*Mt*, v), *næd-rena* (*Cot*, fol. 119^r, 5), *etc*.

Finally, the distribution of the anomalous instances is also irregular in the pieces. Leaving aside the *s-t* divisions, these cases amount to twenty instances in the corpus, nineteen of which belong to *Mt* and just one to *Cot*, a fact which corroborates the different level of commitment among scribes. In the majority of cases, these anomalous boundaries stem from a particular space constraint at the margin of the folio, the scribe being somewhat obliged to break the word elsewhere, always on condition that there are at least two letters on the following line, *i.e. tung-el* (*Mt*, ii), *mod-or* (*Mt*, xi), *eald-or* (*Mt*, xxv), *hlafo-rd* (*Mt*, xxvi), *etc*. In other cases, however, the irregularity may be justified in terms of an erroneous interpretation of the inflection/suffix by the scribe himself, as in *heof-enum* (*Mt*, vi), *offr-unge* (*Mt*, xxii), *dys-ige* (*Mt*, xxiv), *etc*.

4. Middle English

4.1. Form

Line-final breaks in ME are formally introduced by means of the colon, the hyphen and the double hyphen, notwithstanding that they can be omitted when there is insufficient space at the margin (Parkes 1992: 304; Petti 1977: 27; Calle-Martín – Miranda-García 2005b: 32). On a chronological basis, as mentioned in Calle-Martín (2009: 38-39), the hyphen is the standard punctuation symbol throughout the thirteenth and fourteenth centuries whilst the double hyphen spread from the latter part of the fifteenth century (Tannenbaum 1930: 146). All these marks of punctuation are met in the corpus inasmuch as *E2622* shows the use of the double hyphen and the colon, though the latter just testimonially; the hyphen is, on the contrary, the mark of punctuation displayed in *H328* and *S340* while *P118* disregards the use of any punctuation symbol.

4.2. Function

As in the OE data, this section approaches the corpus as a whole as well as across the different pieces. Accordingly, Figure 3 reproduces the distribution of the instances in view of the type of splitting, wherefrom two conclusions again arise, one quantitative and the other qualitative.

In quantitative terms, the phenomenon is observed to decrease progressively over the centuries as it occurs in 164.31 instances in OE and in 122.16 cases in ME. It declines in later documents to the extent that in many early modern compositions its occurrence becomes merely testimonial. In *GUL, MS Hunter 3*, for instance, holding a sixteenth century collection of Elizabethan privy seal warrants, the phenomenon is systematically cold-shouldered as it appears in just two cases, *i.e. fur-the* and *ther-with*. If compared with Figure 4 below, a fluctuating level of compromise towards word division is observed across the pieces inasmuch as *S340* and *P118*, with 204.81 and 231.92 occurrences, respectively, considerably exceed those of *E2622* and *H328* (with just 91.2 and 76.38 each). Several variables may be used to account for this fact, *i.e.* the scribe's idiosyncrasy, a major spatial constraint or simply a worry about the visual appeal of the outcome. It is a fact that, if in columns, the phenomenon becomes more widespread not to write beyond the limits of frame ruling, as in the case of *P118*.

Figure 3. Type of division in ME (absolute figures)

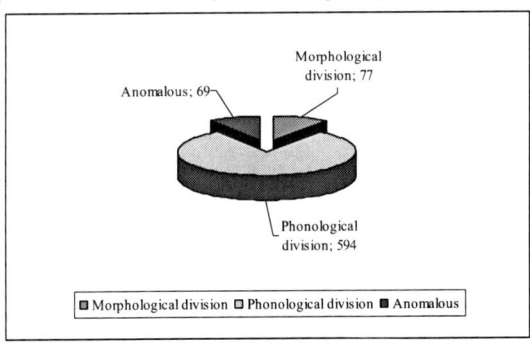

[Pie chart showing: Morphological division: 77; Anomalous: 69; Phonological division: 594]

From a qualitative standpoint, on the other hand, Figure 3 witnesses a major weight of phonological boundaries, with 594 instances. The spread of this principle runs parallel to the progressive obliteration of morphological breaks, which amounts to seventy-seven instances in our data, a negligible figure which comes up to the total of anomalous divisions. The figures for each work also confirm this same tendency insofar as they point to the existence of a consistent practice towards word division in ME.

Figure 4 presents the distribution of morphological and phonological boundaries across the pieces and, given that text-length is different, the figures have also been normalized for comparison. The phonological principle is again the most widespread, whilst the morphological represents less than ten percent. Still, there is room for some level of variation, *P118* in particular, in light of the number of anomalous divisions, which reach 92.32 occurrences if compared with 126.09 phonological instances. Even when one may tentatively say that there are far-reaching dogmatic rules among many scribes, there are also texts like *P118* where word division is subjected to a set of random rules according to which a word is liable to be broken almost elsewhere, such as *m-eddell* (fol. 31^v), *w-omans* (fol. 33^v), *wh-yche* (fol. 31^r), etc. Therefore, word-division practices cannot be extrapolated to represent a whole period on account of the erratic component of the phenomenon across the witnesses.

Next, the instances have been classified in terms of the particular type of rule, either morphological or phonological, to find any likely deviation from the OE practice. At a morphological level, Table 3 summarizes the distribution of word-formation processes in use, according to which it follows that suffixation becomes the most recurrent rule (with 7.59 instances),[4] followed by prefixation (3.96 instances) and compounding (1.15). *E2622* stands apart from this ranking on account of a more consistent use of prefixation, slightly outnumbering suffixation in cases like *for-sothe* (fol. 136^v, 6), *up-warde* (fol. 155^v, 8), *y-do* (fol. 148^r, 10), etc.

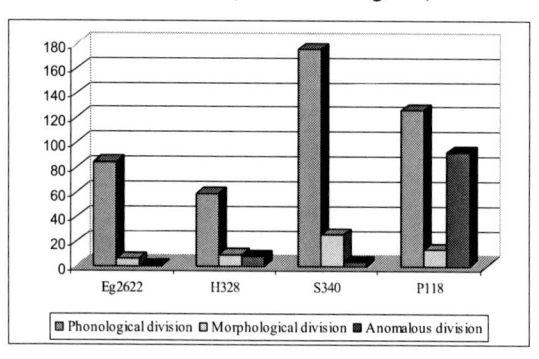

Figure 4. Distribution across texts (normalized figures)

---

4   Unlike OE, derivatives are found to outweigh inflectional endings in the ME sample, amounting to thirty-two and fourteen instances, respectively. As a result of the inflectional weakening occurring after the arrival of the Normans, inflections were progressively cold-shouldered for these purposes and derivatives mostly appear, particularly *-ness(e)*, *-ion*, and *-full(y)*, i.e. *febylnesse* (*H328*, fol. 33r, 21), *adust-yon* (*H328*, fol. 15v, 23), *nede-full* (*P118*, fol. 30v, 1), etc.

Table 3. Morphological boundaries in ME (normalized figures)

	E2622	H328	S340	P118	Total
Prefixation	3.37	1.11	8.96	6.75	3.96
Suffixation	1.35	6.70	15.86	6.75	7.59
Compounding	1.35	1.49	0.68		1.15

From a phonological standpoint, on the other hand, Table 4 presents the rules in ME, both as a whole and in the pieces. It is significant to note that the phenomenon declines sharply throughout this period inasmuch as the figures for the CV – CV rule and the C – C rule are twice and thrice less than in the OE sample, a fact surely linked to the lower frequency of word division in general. The distribution of these rules, on the other hand, does not present significant changes from a historical perspective inasmuch as the CV – CV and the C – C rules consistently prevail, both as a whole and across the pieces. The former reaches 61.41 occurrences as in *oyntementes* (*P118*, fol. 35^r, 14), or of a single vowel, as in *v-ryne* (*S340*, fol. 46^r, 26).

The C – C rule, with the exception of *P118*, amount to half the occurrence of the CV – CV rule (with 27.24 instances in the corpus) and involves the separation of two adjoining consonants irrespective of their factual pronunciation, *i.e.* *hundryth* (*E2622*, fol. 163^r, 26). In some cases, it is more a visual device than a proper phonological division as the consonant is spuriously added in the spelling, as in *vrin-nal* (*S340*, fol. 49^v, 10), *strang-gurie* (*H328*, fol. 26^v, 23), *lak-kyng* (*S340*, fol. 47^v, 8), *etc*.

Table 4. Phonological boundaries in ME (normalized figures)

	E2622	H328	S340	P118	Total
CV – CV rule	56.08	36.52	104.82	87.81	61.41
C – C rule	25.67	10.80	57.24	29.27	27.24
V – V rule	2.70	1.86	8.27	9.06	4.12
ST rule		0.37	5.51		1.48
CT rule		0.37			0.16

Apart from the supremacy of the above rules, if compared with OE, these data point to an on-going specialisation among ME scribes in light of the following evidence. First, there is a slight increase in the use of the V – V rule, always on condition that both vowels are pronounced, as in *ve-ynes* (*S340*, fol. 42^v, 3), *asswaged* (*P118*, fol. 34^r, 15), *tow-ard* (*H497*, fol. 13^r, 29), *etc*. Second, the early instances of the CT rule appear in the history of English handwriting, as in *lac-tea* (*H328*, fol. 11^r, 25). Third, unlike OE, where it is somewhat erratic, the CL rule becomes axiomatic as no counterexample is found, *i.e.* *multi-plicacion* (*E2622*, fol. 153^r, 18), *du-placion* (*E2622*, fol. 148^r, 11), *dou-blet* (*E2622*, fol. 148^r, 24), *etc.*[5] The ST rule, in turn, is also broken at the end of a line in the corpus, as in *was-tyng* (*S340*, fol. 49ʳ, 24), *dyges-tyon* (*S340*, fol. 40ᵛ, 24), with the only exception of *wa-styng* (*H328*, fol. 8ʳ, 15).

5. Conclusions

In the present paper scribal word division has been investigated in early English handwriting in order to conclude whether there is a theoretical basis behind the scribal usage. The topic has been vaguely dealt with in the literature, to the extent that the analyst cannot often see the wood for the trees as to the number of contradictions which arise when different texts are surveyed. In order to avoid the shortcomings of these early approaches, this study has been based on a corpus which contains 97,940 running words and 1,354 word-division instances, a sizeable input to explore the phenomenon, not only across centuries but also across particular hands. The following conclusions may be accordingly drawn.

The first objective of this paper is to investigate the use and distribution of word division in early English to corroborate or disprove the hypothesis of a transition from the morphological to the phonological in early English handwriting. The results suggest that this tenet must be discredited both diachronically and synchronically. On the one hand, the phonological criterion is found to be the leading principle in both periods as it occurs in 52.93% in OE and 80.27% in ME, whilst the morphological reaches 42.67% in OE, and dwindles to 10.4% in ME. From a synchronic standpoint, on the other hand, pronunciation is also claimed to be the leading force for splitting across the pieces, notwithstanding the room for a possible variation, which may ultimately stem from the choice of the morphological criterion (as in *AoT*) or from the erratic and haphazard practice of a given scribe (as in *P118*). In light of this, it follows that the phenomenon must be analysed in independent manuscripts, so that the results may be subsequently used as the input to survey the topic in other texts of the same or of a different chronology.

The second objective of this paper is the offering of a taxonomy of the underlying rules to cast light upon their level of standardization in the periods. Morphologically speaking, there is ground to hypothesize the existence of a transition from prefixation to suffixation, the former as the most widespread rule in OE (with the exception of *Mt*). Some centuries later, both prefixation and suffixation were progressively cold-shouldered as a guided principle for word division, thus reflecting an intrinsic development of English derivational morphology in the periods under scrutiny. Pronunciation was thereafter used to fill the gap left by morphology, becoming the standard word division principle from the early ME period.

From a phonological perspective, the outstanding use of the CV – CV rule and the C – C rule is observed, followed by the V – V rule. However, the data also

---

5   They have been accordingly classified within the CV – CV rule.

point to a progressive specialisation of the CL rule, the ST rule and the CT rule over the centuries, culminating towards the end of the fifteenth century.

Finally, this issue leads us to deal with the concept of syllable boundary among mediaeval scribes and its orthographic implications when breaking a word at the end of a line: A word is taken to contain as many syllables as vowel sounds and, in principle, it may be broken elsewhere on condition that a) there are two or more letters at the beginning of the second line; b) the second part is pronounceable; and c) the boundary does not affect two letters forming one same sound (with the exception of OE diphthongs like *anwe-alde*). Minor differences arise, however, when comparing OE and ME as the former excludes the standing of one letter at the end of the first line, which is a frequent practice in ME, *i.e. v-ryne* (*S340*, fol. 46^r, 26).

These orthographic requirements, together with the space constraints at the margin of the folio, are therefore the key elements participating in the choice of a particular word break. We may further hypothesize the existence of a continuum which scribes apply depending on the particular constraints at the margin. On a statistical basis, the sequence would therefore begin with a) open syllable division; b) close syllable division; c) morphological division (prefixation and suffixation in particular); and d) vowel – vowel division (leaving also room for the anomalous cases). The ST, the CL, and the CT rules would therefore be at the bottom of this continuum on account of their scarce occurrence and their erratic component, OE in particular. Bearing this in mind, the modern reader is then in a position to predict any likely boundary of a word with a mere glance at the writing space available at the margin. A verb form like *andswarode* may, in principle, be broken in OE texts as *andswaro-de* (*Mt*, xiii), *andswa-rode* (*Mt*, xiv) or *andswarode* (*Mt*, xi). Likewise, the word *multiplicacion* would offer the following breaking possibilities in ME: *multipli-cacion* (*E2622*, fol. 159^v, 4), *multiplica-cion* (*E2622*, fol. 161^v, 12), *mul-tiplicacion* (*E2622*, fol. 162^v, 7) and the like. All in all, the data obtained from this study may redefine some of the tenets published in the literature in the sense that line-final word division is not subjected to the particular idiosyncrasy of mediaeval scribes but to the existence of a preconceived set of rules, plausibly derived from the teaching of particular scriptoria, which the writers consciously manipulate according to the spatial requirements at the margin of the folio.

References

Burchfield, Robert
    1994   "Line-end hyphens in the *Ormulum* manuscript (*MS Junius I*)", in: Malcolm Godden – Douglas Gray – Terry Hoad (eds.), 182–187.

Calle-Martín, Javier
    2004   "Punctuation practice in a 15th-century arithmetical treatise (*MS Bodley 790*)", *Neuphilologische Mitteilungen* 4: 407–422.
    2009   "Line-final word division in late Middle English *Fachprosa*: *GUL MS Hunter 497* (V.7.24)", in: Javier Díaz-Vera (ed.), 35–53.

Calle-Martín, Javier – Antonio Miranda-García
    2005a   "Aspects of punctuation in the Old English *Apollonius of Tyre*", *Folia Linguistica Historica* 26, 1–2: 95–113.
    2005b   "Editing Middle English punctuation: The case of *MS Egerton 2622* (fols. 136–152)", *International Journal of English Studies* 5, 2: 27–44.

Clemens, Raymond – Timothy Graham
    2007   *Introduction to manuscript studies.* Ithaca: Cornell University Press.

Denholm-Young, Noël
    1964   *Handwriting in England and Wales.* Cardiff: University of Wales Press.

Díaz-Vera, Javier (ed.)
    2009   *Textual healing: Studies in medieval English medical, scientific and techical texts.* Frankfurt: Peter Lang.

Godden, Malcolm – Douglas Gray – Terry Hoad (eds.)
    1994   *From Anglo-Saxon to Early Middle English.* Oxford: Clarendon Press.

Hector, Leonard C.
    1958   *The handwriting of English documents.* London: Edward Arnold.

Hladký, Josef
    1985a   "Notes on the history of word division in English", *Brno Studies in English* 16: 73–83.
    1985b   "Word division in Caxton and Dryden", *Philologica Pragensia* 28: 135–141.
    1987   "Word division and syllabification in English", *Brno Studies in English* 17: 123–130.

Lutz, Angelika
    1986   "The syllabic basis of word division in Old English manuscripts", *English Studies* 67, 3: 193–210.

Massey, Bernard W. A.
    1934   "The division of words", *Modern Language Notes* 49, 6: 400–404.

Parkes, Malcolm B.
    1992   *Pause and effect: An introduction to the history of punctuation in the West.* Aldershot: Scolar Press.

Petti, Anthony G.
    1977   *English literary hands from Chaucer to Dryden.* Cambridge, Mass: Harvard University Press.

Powell, Marcy S.
    1984   "Word division", *English Studies* 65, 5: 452–458.
Rypins, Stanley (ed.)
    [1924]
    1998   *Three Old English prose texts in* MS. Cotton Vitellius A xv. (Early English Text Society OS 161.) London: Oxford University Press.
Tannenbaum, Samuel A.
    1930   *The handwriting of the Renaissance.* New York: Columbia University Press.

Whose text for whom?: Transmission history of Ælfric of Eynsham's *Letter to Sigeweard*

Larry J. Swain, Bemidji State University

Ælfric of Eynsham was born in the middle of the tenth century during a period of comparative peace. Little is known of his life. He informs us in his *Excerptiones de arte grammatica anglice* – his *Grammar* – that he studied under St. Dunstan, who also ordained Ælfric, and later under St. Æthelwold. Both of his teachers were major architects of the Benedictine Reform in England, and both were influenced by the Benedictine Reform movement occurring on the continent. These teachers brought the reform to England and taught it to their students. Ælfric seems to have absorbed his lessons well; in 987, he became a monk at Cerne Abbas. Within a few years he established himself as a major literary figure.

In 1005, Ælfric was named abbot of the newly established monastery at Eynsham. While there, Ælfric composed his last works, including the *Letter to Sigeweard*, also known by the title it bears in one of the manuscripts, *Libellus de Veteri Testamento et Novo*.[1] This text is Ælfric's response to a request from an Anglo-Saxon nobleman to provide texts from Ælfric's pen. The letter is in part a review of Christian doctrine and in part a review, book by book, of the Christian *Bible*, its meanings and its contents.

This letter is one of Ælfric's last known works. During the course of the letter Ælfric often makes reference to other works he has written, as well as to multiple sources from which he borrows. The *Letter* is in many ways a capstone to Ælfric's teaching program that saw a substantial number of Christian texts come from his pen. As such, the letter informs us a great deal about Ælfric, his library, his chief concerns, his sources and other related issues.

The *Letter to Sigeweard* begins with an exhortation to good works, proceeds through a meditation on the Trinity, and then relates the hexameral tradition. This is followed by a discussion of each biblical book, its contents, and meaning. Ælfric next mentions the three estates, and ends the letter with a final exhortation against drinking. Along the way Ælfric discusses various literal and typological meanings of Biblical figures, making use of a variety of exegetical techniques as well as material not in the biblical text. As an example of this last point, when discussing the *Acts of the Apostles*, Ælfric does not summarize the book but relates what subsequently happened to each of the twelve apostles, none of which is actually included in the biblical *Acts*, seemingly drawing on the Old English poem

---

1   I have followed the tradition of referring to this text as the *Letter to Sigeweard* rather than *Libellus* since the topics covered in the letter are much more than simply the discussion of the books of the *Bible*. The title *Libellus* disguises this fact.

Fates of the Apostles by Cynewulf or its sources.[2] The *Letter*'s chief concern seems to be the instruction of Sigeweard in *Heilsgeschichte*, in holy history, and as such gives Ælfric an opportunity to look back over his own career as he mentions his own works on various subjects.

The transmission history of Ælfric's *Letter to Sigeweard* is a case of a medieval prose text that was intended for and used by different audiences in many different ways and whose transmission, not including nineteenth and twentieth century editions, spans some six hundred years. It is an interesting case to study the interactions of multiple audiences with a medieval text over a long span of time.

The *Letter* survives in four manuscripts. A complete text appears in one manuscript, *Oxford, Bodleian Library, MS Laud Misc. 509*. A second manuscript, *Oxford, Bodleian Library, MS Bodley 343*, contains approximately half of the text, the *Old Testament* portion of the *Letter*, though even here there are gaps where the redactor has excised material. Two other manuscripts have been thought to contain longer or shorter excerpts: *London, British Library, MS Cotton Vitellius C.v* and *London, British Library, MS Harley 3271*.

What has been seldom commented on in what little study has been done on this text is the intended audience at the various levels of editing and textual transmission. From Ælfric's pen to the present, each incarnation of the text or portion of the text preserved for us, addresses a different audience, sometimes rather creatively so.

The first audience that Ælfric had in mind is the addressee of the *Letter*: Sigeweard. Apart from the *Letter*, nothing is known of Sigeweard. His name appears on no other charters of the period beyond *S911* for the "foundation" of Eynsham (Sawyer 1968). On this charter, if it is in fact the same Sigeweard, he is only a signatory, and so the charter itself tells us nothing about him either. No other text mentions him or refers to him. All that it is possible to glean about him comes from the *Letter* itself.

Ælfric tells us that Sigeweard is at East Halon, east of Eynsham. He further tells us that Sigeweard had often requested from Ælfric some text; Ælfric relates that he was reluctant, but was won over by Sigeweard's good works. At the end of the work Ælfric turns again to addressing Sigeweard directly and chastises him for trying to persuade Ælfric to drink too much; in the same breath, however, Ælfric addresses Sigeweard as *leof man* 'dear man' and with this exhortation on drinking, the *Letter* closes.

A few inferences may be made. Ælfric tells us directly that he had been at Sigeweard's home; he also tells us that he had observed Sigeweard enough to be convinced of the latter's good works. One might infer from Ælfric's comments that he was concerned that Sigeweard was asking for Ælfric's works for nefarious

---

[2] In source critical work on the text, I believe that a strong case may be made that Ælfric knows Cynewulf based on shape, content, and context.

reasons. One reason might be a kind of prestige that the possession of Ælfric's writings might bring. Æthelmær was a patron and probable friend of Ælfric and was responsible for having Ælfric appointed abbot at Eynsham as the charter makes clear. There is also some evidence that Æthelmær and his family were instrumental in the compiling of the *Exeter Book* (Conner 1975: 23; Flower 1933: 83–90). If so, it would seem that having Ælfric and Æthelmær in the neighborhood heightened the local nobility's desires for literary works of their own. Likewise, the letters written to Sigefyrth and to Wulfgeat both seek to fill pastoral gaps in the environs of Eynsham. The letter to Wulfgeat in fact seems similarly concerned with catechesis and morality. Thus, it would seem that as Ælfric's career began to become more prominent, his works were in higher demand, possibly fueled by Æthelmær's patronage.

This impression is strengthened by observing that Ælfric references his own works in both this letter and that to Wulfgeat. The purpose of these references seems to be to point the recipients to further works on specific topics, indicating that the works in question were available to be copied for Wulfgeat and Sigeweard should they desire to commission copies or purchase them. It is already well known that Ælfric was very aware of and, in fact, participated in his own "success" in this regard: he often left instructions to scribes copying his work and, at least in the homilies, continued to work on revising the collection, as he does at the end of the *Letter*. That he did these things for altruistic and pastoral reasons is the most probable explanation, but one result is that he drew attention to his works, which in the economy of prestige in a society like the Anglo-Saxons' would make them the more desirable. That Ælfric was the friend of Æthelmær who until 1005 at least was very close to the king did not hinder that desirability or demand.

A final inference that may be drawn is that literacy in the vernacular at least among the nobility seems fairly widespread. In addition, it would seem that at least some noblemen beyond Æthelwold and Æthelmær were interested in developing personal libraries. Sigeweard, as mentioned, was probably a minor nobleman; he does not sign any other charter than *S911*, the foundation charter for Eynsham. Since the form of his name on the charter, "Siward", is different from in Ælfric's address, there is some room to doubt whether the two are the same person, because in neither text are there any other identifying features (Keynes 1980: 162, 192, n. 143).[3] It is from this position that he requests not only the presence of the abbot in his home, but speaks of the acquisition of Ælfric's works, including the *Letter* itself. He presumably is able to read the *Letter*. These facts confirm what is already known of late Anglo-Saxon England: it was a highly literate society in the vernacular language, at least at the top two layers – nobles and churchmen.

---

3   Keynes (1980: 162, 192, n. 143) notes that
    a) the identifications are uncertain and
    b) interestingly this foundation charter has a large number of Scandinavian names in the witness list.

More importantly, perhaps, it is apparent that Ælfric's essential concerns in writing this letter are catechetical. He is imparting the essentials of Christian doctrine and knowledge to Sigeweard, a program that the Benedictine Reform generally and Ælfric in particular seemed to be highly concerned with. It is tempting to conclude that even a nobleman in England was in need of basic instruction. In any case, the original audience seems to be a rather limited one, one which may have needed, in Ælfric's view, fundamental Christian education. The tone and overall information is pastoral and seems to be the local abbot instructing one of his charges, a role Ælfric was very familiar with by this point in his career. It is not known how Sigeweard reacted to the letter.

The *Letter* is preserved in its entirety in *Oxford, Bodleian, MS Laud Misc. 509*. This is an octavo manuscript consisting of 141 folia and overall is written in a very nice, smooth and clear hand, nearly all by a single scribe. The manuscript was constructed in the second half of the eleventh century, determined on paleographical and phonological grounds.

The manuscript contains the Old English translation of the first six books of the *Bible*, the *Hexateuch*, preceded by Ælfric's preface to the *Book of Genesis*. This is followed by Ælfric's homily on the *Book of Judges*, which is in many ways a summary of the book rather than either a translation or homily. The fact that the scribe has left a blank leaf between *Judges*, which begins at fol. 108^r, and the end of *Joshua*, ending on fol. 107^v, may indicate that the scribe considered the sermon on *Judges* to be a separate work from the translation of the *Hexateuch*. The *Judges* paraphrase is often included with the *Hexateuch* and titled the *Old English Heptateuch*. Ælfric himself translated *Genesis* and summarized *Judges*, but someone else rendered the remainder of the Biblical books into Old English (Marsden 1991: 319–58, 2000: 41–89). Together, these texts include fols. 1–115^v of the manuscript. Ælfric's *Letter to Wulfgeat* (fols. 115^v–120^v) and the *Letter to Sigeweard* (fols. 120^v–141^v) follow. The Old English translation of Felix's *Vita sancti Guthlaci* on fols. 18–40 of *London, British Library, MS Cotton Vespasian D.xxi* also once belonged to this manuscript.

Nothing is known of the origins of the manuscript or of its history before the sixteenth century. It would appear that neither *Laud 509*, nor the other copy of the *Old English Hexateuch*, is close to the original, composed around 1020 (Crawford 1922 [1997: 3]). Titles in *Laud 509* are rubricated. The beginning of Biblical sections is often marked by a capital letter in green ink. The text is written by a single scribe except for sections on fol. 15^r, lines 8–21 and fol. 15^v, lines 1–10. A third hand wrote fol. 17, lines 11–23. The writing space is generally about twenty-six lines per page.

As with the contents of the *Letter*, there are some clues as to whom the manuscript's audience might be. First, the manuscript apparently has access to Ælfrician texts: the collection of just these texts together does not exist otherwise. The *Heptateuch* in whole or in part survives in eight other manuscripts, the

Letter to Wulfgeat exists in two other manuscripts where it has been adapted to be a sermon, neither of which manuscripts contains the *Heptateuch* in its entirety but only short sections. Thus, it would seem that *Laud 509* was put together deliberately to include at least some of Ælfric's specifically Biblical materials and in a locale where there was access to these materials. This certainly suggests a scriptorium attached to a monastery rather than a lord's house.

Further, though, the *Letter* begins in the manuscript with a rubricated line that states that although this letter was written for one man, yet many could benefit from it. This line suggests that the intended audience of the manuscript and its recasting of Ælfric's letter is the larger community of the monastery. The manuscript was probably designed, then, for private reading or reading in the refectory. In any case it was not a manuscript meant for proclamation or preaching or even teaching lay or young men. The *Letter* has changed slightly from a didactic letter to a devotional text meant to aid a monastic community in its contemplation of divine things.

There is some evidence of later, medieval use of *Laud 509*, however. In the early twelfth century, or possibly very late eleventh, a hand has added a Latin gloss to ninety-three of the 144 pages of the *Hexateuch*, and to three of the pages in the *Letter*.[4] In reference to the latter, the gloss begins on fol. 137, where three words of Old English are glossed with Latin equivalents. In the *Letter*, at least, the glosses are of a lexical nature. Another glossator of the late thirteenth or early fourteenth century made some marginal glosses, largely marking omissions in the Biblical translation with the word *oblitus*. This glossator does not seem to have worked in the *Letter*.

One of the more interesting places that the twelfth century glossator has acted in the *Letter* is in the listing of Christ's disciples, where the glossator has first numbered Ælfric's list, and then added to it. Ælfric lists the disciples, in large part though not entirely following *Matthew* 10: Peter, Andrew, James, John, Thomas, the "other James", Phillip, Bartholomew, Thaddeus, and Paul, making a total of ten disciples. To this list the Latin glossator has added Matthew and Simon the Canaanite and numbered them all, one to eleven. He does not, however, number Paul. Neither Ælfric, apparently, nor the glossator found it fit to include either Judas, or Judas's official replacement in the *Book of Acts*, Matthias. It is an interesting piece of Christian lore that the glossator has decided to fix in the text and to enumerate the apostles.

More interesting, however, are some other glosses that correct the Old English text of Ælfric's letter. For example, where in the text Ælfric is discussing Lot from the *Book of Genesis*, Ælfric describes Lot as fleeing from Sodom and Gomorroah with three *hiwan* 'three household members'. The glossator has corrected this to read more specifically, and more in line with the Biblical account, three *wifum* 'three women'. It is an interesting correction given the probable reason that Ælfric had *hiwan* there in the first place.

---

4 For a fuller examination of this gloss, see Marsden (2005: 147).

In his preface to *Genesis* Ælfric informs us that he was reluctant to make the translation of *Genesis* in part because later in the Biblical book some of the figures in the book had practiced polygamy (Crawford 1922 [1997: 49]). Ælfric did not wish his readers to therefore think that it was acceptable to marry multiple wives, even if one wife should die, then to go on to marry another. Although he maintains in his translation the Biblical account of Genesis where Lot flees with his wife and two daughters and later has sex with his two daughters, in the *Letter* he omits all of that rather unseemly material. In the *Letter*, Ælfric draws a distinction between the *fulan mennisces Sodomitisces* 'evil men-lusting Sodomites' and Lot who is led by God because of Lot's righteousness... – an attribute that the Biblical account certainly does not ascribe to Lot, who would have given his daughters to be sexually assaulted by the crowd to save his own skin. Later, Lot drunkenly commits incest. It is my contention that in his *Letter to Sigeweard*, Ælfric deliberately cleansed the story of Lot along the lines outlined in the preface to *Genesis* so that his audience should not consider Lot's actions appropriate. As such, and to deemphasize the relationship, he chose the word *hiw*. The interactive audience in this case has changed Ælfric's word by crossing out *hiw* and replacing it with the more accurate *wif*, which at least in a small way militates against Ælfric's pastoral concerns, but at the same time reflects a different audience with different concerns than Ælfric's original audience.

At least in these two examples, we have an interactive audience, not simply a passive reader. They confirm that the manuscript was likely associated with a monastic library, and that it was in fact read. Unlike Sigeweard, who Ælfric at least thought needed some education, these readers have added to and corrected Ælfric's text as they read. This suggests both a level of sophistication to these readers and knowledge of the *Bible* as detailed as Ælfric's own. While Ælfric was concerned that monks and lay alike needed catechetical knowledge, it would seem that in the ensuing years that at least in some monasteries the need for education was met and mastered, as evidenced by the knowledge of the *Bible* in both Latin and Old English demonstrated by the readers of *Laud Misc. 509*.

The next manuscript is of a much different character. *Oxford, Bodleian Library, MS Bodley 343* was copied in the latter half of the twelfth century somewhere in the West Midlands as indicated on fol. iii which contains a rhymed poem to St. Wulfhad, and from the dialect and orthography of the text (Ker 1957: 368; Irvine 1993, 2000: 55). There is on fol. 173 an image of a bishop with an inscription that likely refers to Wulfstan of Worcester, though whether this denotes Wulfstan the Homilist or Wulfstan II, is indeterminable (Irvine 1993: xix). All considered together, this indicates that the manuscript was compiled in the West Midlands, possibly at Worcester, but more likely nearby.[5]

---

[5] This is the stated opinion of both Ker (1957) and Irvine, in contrast to Pope (1967: 82–83), who suggests that the manuscript was southern, even south-eastern before moving to the Midlands.

The manuscript is by and large a collection of homilies, though a few other items are interspersed and some materials, such as the excerpt from the *Letter to Sigeweard*, which were not originally homilies, seem to have been adapted for homiletic or devotional use. Of the eighty-five homilies in the manuscript, forty-eight are by Ælfric and come from the *Catholic Homilies* series (Ker 1957: 368). The vast majority of the texts in the manuscript are in Old English, adapted to late twelfth-century orthography, though there are a number of Latin pieces included as well. Additional short Latin pieces were added later in the fifteenth-century (Irvine 1993: xvii).

Irvine has detected that the texts fall into seven main sections in two scribal hands (Irvine 1993: xx*ff*). The first section contains four items, all from one of the *Catholic Homilies* series by Ælfric. The second section consists of sixty-seven short Latin homilies; Irvine describes these homilies as short and fairly simple both in terms of syntax and content (Irvine 2000: 56). The third section is a collection of homilies, six by Ælfric, and a text titled by modern editors *History of the Holy Rood Tree*. The fourth section has nineteen items, thirteen sermons by Ælfric from the *Catholic Homilies* series, three from Ælfric's *Lives of Saints* series, two anonymous homilies, and a narrative on the nativity of St. Mary. The next section contains some thirty-three items, the majority homilies by Ælfric, though among the other interesting items included in the section is an Old English retelling of the *Visio Sancti Pauli* oddly titled *De Doctrina Sancti Gregorii* that includes, in addition to the *Visio*, injunctions to do good works and abstain from evil. The sixth section includes an adaptation of the *Letter to Sigeweard* among other texts and will be dealt with in more detail below. The seventh section consists of nine pieces, four by Ælfric, three anonymous homilies, a Latin exegesis of the *Lord's Prayer* which also doubles as a colloquy, and a verse fragment titled by modern scholars *The Grave*. The Ælfrician homilies come from various stages in Ælfric's own development of the *Catholic Homilies* and from different textual traditions, suggesting some access by the compiler to a large library or the ability to borrow manuscripts from such a library.

The sixth section of the manuscript is unique, a fact not noticed by Irvine in her otherwise excellent analyses of this manuscript. It contains twelve pieces. Four are by Wulfstan: a sermon on baptism, a copy of the *Sermo Lupi ad Anglos*, a Latin homily and an English homily. The remaining works of the section are works by Ælfric. The *Letter to Sigeweard* adaptation comes first in the section; two other letters for Wulfstan follow and were adapted as sermons. Two of the items are homilies from the First Series of the *Catholic Homilies*. Then follow the last three items in the section: a copy of the *De Septiformi Spiritu*, a homily on St. Michael, and three lines about Mary.

What makes this section different from the others in the manuscript is the inclusion of material adapted from letters, and not all of them didactic or homiletic in nature. In contrast to *Laud 509* which places the *Letter* in the context of discussions of the *Bible*, *Bodley 343* places an adaptation of the *Letter* in and among materials largely associated with Wulfstan. In addition to the four homilies by Wulfstan and the two adapted letters for Wulfstan on church polity, two of the homilies and the *De Septiformi Spiritu* were rewritten by Wulfstan in other contexts, making a total of eight of the twelve items specifically associated with Wulfstan. All the homilies and associations are discoveries by later scholars; the compiler or redactor(s) of the texts have thoroughly anonymized the contents so as to make the texts "catholic". But the adaptation of these letters does raise some interesting questions about the transmission of the text.

In terms of the *Letter* specifically, the redactor has made some changes to the text, or at least his exemplar has. The most apparent and obvious is that the redactor has shortened the letter considerably, leaving out the prologue information, which includes not only Ælfric's greeting to Sigeweard but the exhortations to good works. The *Bodley 343* version begins with the creation of the angels. The redactor has also left out the second half of the *Letter*: the portion where Ælfric discusses the *New Testament*, the story of John, his mention of the Jews and their fate, and the other materials after line 396.[6] In between, the redactor has excised any mention on Ælfric's part of Ælfric's other works.[7]

The purpose behind such redacting is difficult to perceive. For example, while it seems that he may have intended to include Ælfric's discussion of both testaments judging from the *incipit* which mentions both testaments, he only includes the discussion on the *Old Testament*. At least that has been the typical understanding of his purpose.[8] However, the section that includes the *Letter* is on average the same length as the other sermons in the manuscript – averaging approximately two–three leaves each. The redactor has also made the text a unit: excising seemingly unrelated material at the beginning and ending precisely where the *Old Testament* material ends. The *343* redactor has included the title *De Ueteri Testamento et Novo*, but it is easier to explain the inclusion of *et Novo* as a scribal oversight than to explain the absence of half of the text of the *Letter*, some 400 lines, as being due to the same scribal oversight, particularly since the length is approximately the same as all the other single texts in the manuscripts, give or take a leaf.

Nor does our redactor's editorial activity end with merely adapting the text to fit a good sermon length. The redactor edits out Ælfric's address to Sigeweard, and any personal statements about Sigeweard, such as his request for Ælfric's works, which is entirely befitting a text intended to be a sermon, homily, or devo-

---

6 Line number references refer to my edition of the text.
7 At line 370 the redactor apparently overlooked one of Ælfric's self-referential remarks and failed to edit it out.
8 Clemoes, Pope, and following them, Irvine, all assume that the redactor has made an error. Clemoes ([1959] 1980: 24), Pope (1967: 142), Irvine (1993, xlv).

tional reading. This careful redactor then begins his homily appropriately with "the almighty creator who shaped the angels..." and ends equally worshipfully with "...to the glory of God".

There are other changes as well. At line 61, when describing Satan's choice not to follow God, Ælfric likely said that "He nolde þa habban his scippend him to hlaforde ne he nolde þurhwunian on ðære soðfæstnisse ðæs soðfæstan godes sunu". The Bodley redactor changed *soðfæstnisse* 'faithfulness' to *softnysse* 'softness, comfort, ease'. While possibly a scribal error, such a change would indeed be aimed at a monastic reader to remain in God's comforts, lest he become like Satan. Another and perhaps clearer example of change is at line 91 where Ælfric likely wrote "Eua getacnode þe of Adames sidan God silf geworhte Godes gelaðunge þe of Cristes sidan siþþan wearð acenned". *Bodley 343* adds "...acenned his sylfes agen bryd mid his blode aðwogen" 'Eve who God himself made out of Adam's side, signifies the church of God which was brought forth from Christ's side... his own bride washed clean with his blood.' The latter phrase, emphasizing as it does the salvific event of Christ, would certainly add a more devotional element to the already devotional context of the original *Letter*.

The question is what is meant by "homily" in this context. The manuscript bears no indication of having been used for preaching and no preacher's marks (Irvine 2000: 59). Originally homiletic material is then juxtaposed with other non-homiletic materials, whether the letters for Wulfstan or the exegesis of the *Lord's Prayer*. Nonetheless, the contents are largely homiletic, with subsections of the manuscript even showing some design in choosing homilies that follow the church year, even if the whole manuscript does not display such a design. Most of the contents are treatments of saints or of basic Christian doctrines. Irvine argues that the Latin inclusions in the manuscript argue against *Bodley 343* being an "antiquarian" collection preserving Old English materials and adds further that the inclusion of non-homiletic material indicates that the manuscript was not a homiliary (Irvine 1993: li–liii). The best suggestion then, and one that surprisingly Irvine steers clear of, is that the manuscript was compiled as more of a teaching or devotional text from largely though not exclusively homiletic materials. The redactor was less interested by and large in the personalities of the Anglo-Saxon past and so has edited out any direct references to Ælfric and Wulfstan and other known figures in favor of essential Christian teaching. This suggests that the redactor had limited access to his materials, and that he chose them deliberately and carefully, being cautious not to repeat or overlap material. He expected from himself or other readers at least basic Latin, but nothing too extraordinary in terms of syntax or word choice.

Before leaving this manuscript, there is one other consideration. Susan Irvine, who has studied this manuscript and published the anonymous homilies, suggests that it was a previous scribe or manuscript that excised the text. She, however, does not give any reason for this conclusion. I would suggest that the observable methods of the *Bodley 343* redactor in adapting sermons and texts as sermons, anonymizing them, and creating a manuscript for the preacher, make it most likely that the *343* redactor is the editor of the *Letter*, transforming it into a different genre of text. It is the redactor himself who is selecting the materials rather than others who are redacting Ælfric and Wulfstan's letters.

That is one level of audience for the form of the *Letter* in *Bodley 343*. The other question to address is to whom would such a collection of sermons that includes the *Letter of Sigeweard* be of use. The language of the text generally has been updated, but certainly does not reflect twelfth-century Middle English, though the early eleventh-century English of the original author has been updated to reflect late twelfth-century orthography. The material in the manuscript is not organized so as to be effective as a source for preaching, and certainly not even all the adapted texts are really suitable for preaching, such as the letters for Wulfstan, which would not be the material most preachers would choose for a Sunday sermon. This suggests that though the *343* redactor has compiled his collection with some care and deliberation, he does not have in mind a wider audience such as one would preach to, but rather a devotional audience. It is likely, then, that the manuscript, probably composed in the West Midlands in the twelfth century, is meant to fill a void in a monastic foundation's library, used for devotion and the establishment of faith. Interestingly enough, then, we have material adapted and anonymized to be not sermons, but easy-to-read devotional texts, fitting easily into a single reading period allowed by the Rule. The audiences of the *Letter* are multiple and varied, but all approach the *Letter* as a piece of literature, a written text. It is intended to be a read text to Sigeweard in origin, as also in *Laud Misc. 509*, and in *Bodley 343*.[9]

Thus far, then, the text of the *Letter to Sigeweard* has been adapted for three different audiences, with overlapping, but not identical, needs and purposes spanning the eleventh and twelfth centuries. The two other manuscripts mentioned above, *London, British Library, MS Cotton Vitellius C.v* and *London, British Library, MS Harley 3271*, each present an interesting problem for discerning the issues of audience and reuse of the text. Each of these manuscripts contains a homily about the apostle John and a young thief whom the apostle returns to the Christian fold. This story is also part of the *Letter to Sigeweard* and appears after Ælfric has discussed the apostle in relation to the biblical *Book of Revelation*. It originates in Eusebius's *Historia Ecclesiastica* III.26 and came to Ælfric from two sources: one is Rufinus's Latin translation of Eusebius, but Ælfric translated the piece not from Rufinus, but from the influential homiliary of Paul the Deacon from the late eighth century. The story of John and the young thief as a separate

---

9 When this paper was first proposed, I held the common view that the *Letter to Sigeweard* had been adapted to a homiletic use and the portion on John excised from the *Letter* for that purpose in these two manuscripts. I no longer hold that view, but rather think that Ælfric prepared the John story as a homily, translated from Paul the Deacon's homiliary, and attached it to the *Letter*. More on this below.

unit is a polished piece of writing. It is, further, a translation of a Latin text. There is also a homily about the Jews that matches a portion of the *Letter* that is heavily dependent on Rufinus's translation of Eusebius's *Historia Ecclesiastica*, in part translation, in part paraphrase. This would suggest that Ælfric prepared some translation at least for inclusion in the letter. Such, in fact, is the position of both Clemoes and Pope (Clemoes 1959 [1980: 28]; Pope 1967: 17).

There are several reasons to reconsider the position of Clemoes and Pope regarding this selection about John the apostle. Clemoes makes some points regarding its inclusion and being specially prepared for the *Letter*. First, he thinks it is too short to be considered a homily in its own right. Second, the summary of John's life with which it opens does not mention John's authorship of the *Apocalypse*, mentioned by Ælfric just previously. Third, Clemoes believes that it is not Ælfric's usual practice to repeat material in one homily that he has already given in another homily, pointing to *Catholic Homilies* I.4 on the Assumption of John.

Regarding Clemoes's first objection, it should be noted that the story of John is now known to have been a homily in its own right, something that Clemoes did not know in his original article published in 1959. Cyril Smetana in an important article demonstrated Ælfric's dependence on the homiliary of the late eighth century Paul the Deacon, a member of Charlemagne's court. As mentioned above, among the three sermons for 27 December, the feast of St. John, is a selection from Rufinus's translation of Eusebius's *Historia* (Smetana 1959: 167). There the homily is attributed to Chrysostom, but Ælfric undoubtedly recognizing it as from the *Historia* corrects it to Jerome, since Rufinus's translation often went under Jerome's name.[10] The homily and the excerpt in the *Letter* appear to match otherwise, including in the preamble that is not included in Eusebius's original telling of the tale.

Thus, the story's inclusion in Paul the Deacon's influential homiliary demonstrates that it was indeed a sermon in its own right. Further, though, it should be noted that Ælfric has short sermons as well. In published editions, the following sermons are close to the length of this homily from Paul the Deacon's homiliary. In my edition of the *Letter*, the story of John occupies lines 541 through 652, or 111 lines. In Crawford's edition, the story occupies lines 1015 through 1154, or 139 lines (Crawford 1922 [1997: 61–68]). Comparing these two editions with, for example, the printed edition of the *Lives of Saints* edited by Skeat, yields some interesting results (Skeat 1881–1900). The homily on St. Lucy, *Lives of Saints* I.9, is 152 lines, St. George, *Lives of Saints* I.14, is 184 lines long, *Lives of Saints* II.24 on Abdon and Sennes, on its own is eighty lines long, and the addition of the *Item Alia* to this sermon, the apocryphal *Letter of Christ to Abgar*, adds an additional 109 lines in the printed edition. The homily on one of the few Anglo-Saxon saints, St. Æthelthryth, *Lives of Saints* I.20, is 135 lines long. Turning to the *Catholic Homilies*, I.3 on St. Stephen, is just 201 lines long in the printed edition, and the homily

---

10 See Smetana (1959: 167).

on *Natale Innocentium Infantum*, I.5, is 189 lines. As an example of a homily that deals with something other than a saint, I.17 on the Second Sunday after Easter is only 89 lines long. Admittedly, line numbers in printed editions are not the best indicator of the actual length of the sermons, but the foregoing should be sufficient to demonstrate that there are other homilies by Ælfric that certainly are on the brief side of things, and a few that are even shorter than the story of John included in the *Letter*. Clemoes's first objection, that the story of John in the *Letter* is too short to be a homily, may thus be safely discounted.

Clemoes's second objection may also be set aside. Knowing that the passage originates in Eusebius's history and comes to Ælfric by way of Paul the Deacon's homiliary, one need simply compare Ælfric's translation with the two sources mentioned. In neither source is John's authorship of the *Apocalypse* mentioned or in view. In fact, although Ælfric and the Christian West accepted Johannine authorship of the final book of the *New Testament* canon, any reader of Eusebius's history is aware that Eusebius reports some questioning of John's authorship of that book, and does not mention it as having been composed by John in his history, book III.25, where the passage originates. Likewise, the preamble in the homiliary does not include that piece of information. There seem to be no grounds to argue against the John story not being an independent sermon included in the letter on the basis of the absence of any mention that the *Book of Revelation* was written by John. It is not in the source texts; it should not be expected here.

Lastly, Clemoes believes that it is not Ælfric's practice to repeat in one homily what he has already covered in another. He points to *Catholic Homilies* I.4 on the Assumption of St. John to illustrate the point. This homily does deal in large part with the life of John and the stories told about him during the period from the end of his exile by Domitian to his death. It does not, however, include the story here of John and the young man, and so Ælfric is not repeating himself or even reusing the same material. Further, according to Godden, Ælfric's principal sources in that homily are Haymo, Bede, Augustine, and chiefly a passion of St. John that lies behind the Cotton Corpus legendary, a different source than that which Ælfric draws on here (Godden 2000: 28–29). So once again this objection may be safely disregarded.

All this, however, still does not demonstrate that Ælfric did not prepare the story of John specifically for the *Letter to Sigeweard*. Its appearance in other manuscripts simply illustrates that it was an easy and popular passage to excerpt. It is further known that Ælfric often used and reused materials to produce new homilies, and likewise that Ælfric's works were excerpted and used for new works by later audiences.

There are several points here, however. First, and foremost, Ælfric did often prepare materials for his Old English works. It is not known, however, that in any of his letters, particularly his three letters to laymen that he specifically translated and prepared Latin works in Old English for those audiences! Generally, where

Latin works are his source and he translates them, those prepared materials are for other monks and a wider audience such as in the homilies. The argument that Ælfric prepared this sermon for inclusion as part of the *Letter* seems to go against Ælfric's normal custom.

If Ælfric did prepare this piece for the *Letter*, then the transmission history of the story of John becomes somewhat problematic for both the *Letter to Sigeweard* as well as for the tale as a separate text. It must be asked why a certain portion of the *Letter* was excerpted but not other parts that actually would have fitted the manuscript contexts better.

For example, *London, British Library, Cotton Vitellius MS C.v* is close in origin to Ælfric himself, containing a copy of the *Catholic Homilies*, and is from the late tenth and early eleventh centuries. While nothing is known of the origin or pre-modern history of the manuscript, it did become part of Sir Robert Cotton's collection, as the shelf mark makes clear, in the sixteenth century, and from there became part of the foundation of the British Museum. The manuscript unfortunately was damaged by the Ashburnham House fire of 1731 that damaged so many of the Cotton manuscripts. Fortunately, nevertheless, this one was only smoke damaged, making many of the leaves hard to read, but was not significantly burned in that fire.

Seventeen homilies are interpolated into the manuscript of which the portion about John is one. These homilies are considered part of the "third stage" of the manuscript's production and seem to be within twenty-five years or so of the origin of the manuscript in the late tenth century, or very early eleventh. The manuscript is one of the chief witnesses to the *Catholic Homilies*, containing almost all of the first series, the first stage, with two sets of additions. The second stage, nearly contemporaneous with the origin of the manuscript, adds five sermons for Fridays during Lent. The third stage occurred within twenty–twenty-five years of the origin of the manuscript, still quite close to Ælfric's lifetime, when a scribe interpolated those seventeen sermons. Among these sermons were seven from the second series of the *Catholic Homilies* and the addition of ten others. One of those ten is the excerpt of the story about John and the young thief. Others are *De Sancta Trinitate et de Festis Diebus per Annum*, one on the nativity, five on various church dates, and *De Sancta Virginitate*.

The composition of this collection is odd if the John sermon is adapted from the *Letter*. Gneuss posits the origin of the manuscript to be possibly Tavistock, not one of the primary centres (Gneuss 2001: 73). Thus, on the model proposed by Pope and Clemoes for the John story, the *Letter to Sigeweard* must have traveled and been disseminated widely in order for it to make it to Tavistock in order to be excerpted and included in this manuscript. And yet, while the *Letter* does seem to have enjoyed some circulation beyond Sigeweard, there is no evidence that it was disseminated so widely, as widely in fact as Ælfric's *Catholic Homilies*, as to be available for this process of adaptation so early in the text's history.

Further, it would be a unique example of a homily constructed out of epistolary contents in this time period.[11] While there is a possibility that another sermon has been constructed out of Ælfric's works by a later redactor, perhaps even the third scribe of this manuscript, this possibility is created out of "topical" sections of Ælfric's works, not narrative sections, and not sections translated from another source. And so this leaves this excerpt as a unique piece if it is excerpted from the *Letter to Sigeweard* by a later redactor.

In addition to this consideration, others of the interpolated sermons also are related to saints' days. The sermon on the nativity, *De Virginitate*, and a new, revised version of *Catholic Homilies*, II.24, *De Assumptione Mariæ*, are among these. Clemoes further dates the *Letter* between Ælfric's completion of the first series of *Temporal Homilies* and a second series of *Temporal Homilies* (Clemoes 1959 [1980: 32]). Even if Clemoes is incorrect about this, it is known that Ælfric updated, revised and added to his homily collections, and it would seem that the majority of these homilies were intended to be part of such an addition. In fact, Clemoes identifies most of these sermons as belonging to the *Temporal Homilies*, second series.

On a final note, the John story as it is included here lacks Ælfric's statement in the *Letter* that he would say something about John and begins precisely where the homily from Paul the Deacon's homiliary begins. This suggests that if excerpted, the author knew Paul's homiliary. A better explanation, though, since such "paragraphing" is not indicated in medieval manuscripts, would be that Ælfric sent out a copy of this translated homily without his comments to Sigeweard being included, and this as part of a series of sermons rounding out the *Catholic Homilies*. It would thus be the natural conclusion that Ælfric prepared a third sermon for a popular Saint John in the Christmas octave from a popular, influential collection of Latin homilies that also included three sermons on John. Ælfric, then, simply included his translation of the sermon as part of the *Letter* since it is unlikely that Sigeweard would receive a copy of the homily otherwise and as the homily fitted some of the concerns that he was outlining in the letter. There is no reason why he would have taken the effort to prepare the homily specifically for Sigeweard, but, as can be seen, there was at least some reason to do so for the *Temporal Homilies*, second series.

The fact that this excerpt is not unique also tells against the excision theory. Another manuscript also contains this homily. *London, British Library, MS Harley 3271* is an odd manuscript. It contains both Latin and Old English pieces, theological or devotional, and grammatical and scientific pieces. The manuscript

---

11　There is one other possible example: *De Sancta Trinitate*. Pope (1967: 453–461) believes that this homily is a construct out of Ælfrician writings by a later redactor. Clemoes ([1959] 1980: 3, 37) believes this is Ælfric reusing his own materials. In my view, the reasons Pope gives for later compilation may all be duplicated in Ælfric's own writing, save one: the argument that this is a unique sermon in this one single manuscript.

was possibly produced in Mercia, and was copied in the early eleventh century, the third and latest hand believed to be dated to approximately 1032 (Ker 1957: 309). This places production of the manuscript to within thirty years of Ælfric's death and the *Letter*. The manuscript contains several Ælfrician texts: the initial sermon to the *Catholic Homilies*, *De Initio Creaturæ*, plus Ælfric's *Grammar*, his work on the Holy Spirit, exerpts from his translation of Alcuin's *Interrogationes*, plus two short passages that match portions of the *Letter*. The presence of these other works in the collection suggest that the pieces were chosen for reasons that are now not recoverable but that the compilers found to be useful and helpful.

A number of the texts are related to the church year: the *computus* notes, office for invention of St. Stephen, which may be enough to suggest the John sermon, and both together with the problem of the Jews, are among these. The appearance of the John story here in conjunction with other *Catholic Homilies* pieces, however, does suggest that the story as an Old English translation of a Latin homily was disseminated independently of the letter. It would be unusual that two scribes working in two different places should both excerpt the same material, word for word, with essentially no differences in copying. It is more likely that both copies are close to an exemplar, if not at only a single remove, that was penned and sent by Ælfric himself.

The evidence is admittedly slight. On the other hand, the evidence for the belief that the John story was prepared specifically for the *Letter* and later excerpted independently by two different scribes in an out-of-the-way scriptorium, has been shown above to be non-existent. This suggests that the John story, and possibly the material about the Jews, were materials that Ælfric was preparing for wider dissemination and use and simply included in the *Letter* because they were at hand.

If, then, Ælfric was in the process of translating other homiletic material from Paul the Deacon's work and from other sources into Old English in order to expand the *Catholic Homilies*, and we know that he was doing that, it would seem best to explain the three copies of the story of John and the young thief as one of these homilies. Ælfric, as he was simultaneously writing to Sigeweard, was reminded of this homily as he wrote about John and the *Book of Revelation* in the *Bible*, and included it in the letter. For this one story, then, there are four simultaneous audiences.[12]

The first audience is Ælfric himself. This is just one example of many in his overall design: to produce in English a collection of homiletic texts for the edification and education of lay and monk alike, as he informs us in his preface to the *Catholic Homilies*. This lesson regarding John, though it comes late in Ælfric's career, if it was meant to be included in the *Temporal Homilies* sequence as seems

---

12 The same might be said of the material from Rufinus regarding the fall of Jerusalem and the Jews, which seems to be a sermon in preparation in its two surviving contexts (the *Letter* and the manuscript, *Harley 3271*), but not one that seems to have been popular. The focus of this work has been on the more frequently commented upon story of John.

apparent, is a case of Ælfric doing just as he said, translating Latin texts into English for the benefit of a somewhat uneducated audience.

Ælfric then does what he said he would. He publishes his translation along with the other sermons in the *Temporal Homilies* series; seemingly designed more for monastic hearers in this case as most lay people would not be observing these days with regularity. Simultaneously, however, he includes it not as a homily but as a narrative in the *Letter to Sigeweard*, using the text in two very different ways to achieve very similar ends. By doing so, Sigeweard becomes an audience for this story as well, in a context not of the church year, but in a context dealing with the books of the *Bible*. Specifically, the tale comes after discussion of the *Book of Revelation* stating more about the hero of the story, John, who is also the author of that final biblical book. Regrettably we do not know what Sigeweard made of the text.

The other audiences of this homily on John are the creators and readers of the manuscripts that contain this homily shared with the *Letter*. First, *London, British Library, MS Harley 3271* is a miscellany. But this manuscript escapes the scholar's eye in determining anything regarding the audience. The only helpful remark that could be made is that the manuscript also contains a Latin sermon on St. Stephen; in the Christian calendar Stephen and John are celebrated on 26 and 27 December. This association may explain the inclusion of Ælfric's homily on St. John, matching a portion of the *Letter to Sigeweard*. But the two homilies are separated by a number of leaves and so this justification may not have any basis.

This manuscript does seem to have been intended for homiletic use, not simply devotional use, and there are a few signs of just such use. At least in the early eleventh century the texts gathered there continued to be preached, and it was thought important enough to update the collection with homilies that Ælfric sent after his original collection. It is known that Ælfric continued to correct, expand, and add new homilies to the *Catholic Homilies* through the rest of his career.

The original audience of *Cotton Vitellius C.v* may be dealt with quickly. This manuscript is one of the earliest and most important copies of Ælfric's *Catholic Homilies*. Ælfric tells us in the previously mentioned preface that his intent was to provide a collection of homilies for the education and edification of both monk and layperson alike. Thus, the dissemination of the homily of John and its later addition to this manuscript appears to be in fulfillment of Ælfric's wishes, to use this additional homily as part of a program of Christian catechism.

There are many layers of transmission of this story regarding John included in these two manuscripts. It seems to have first been an oral tradition, becomes included in written Christian texts in Greek, one of them a history, and is translated into other languages including Latin. The story then becomes a Latin homily in Paul the Deacon, and finally a homily in Old English in Ælfric. Ælfric did not stop there, however, but included this homily as a part of a didactic letter to Sigeweard. The process of transmission to the *Letter* illustrates multiple genres, one might even say multiple media, and multiple audiences: learned monastic audiences, lay audiences for homilies, a laymen as part of a letter. Ælfric used the text in two different but very interesting ways.

The story does not quite end there. As things worked out, *Oxford, Bodleian Library, MS Laud 509* also was a manuscript that was collected by Robert Cotton. During the late sixteenth and early seventeenth century, the Protestant Reformation in England continued to feel uncertain on its feet as witnessed by the reign of Mary Tudor, the difficulties under Elizabeth and works written for her such as Spenser's *Faerie Queene*, and on into the era of Cromwell. The first modern Anglo-Saxon scholars happened to be men like Cotton, Matthew Parker, and the like, who were interested in supporting the new English church's doctrines with evidence from the Anglo-Saxon past. A sermon by Ælfric on Easter was the first piece of Old English literature ever printed and it was printed to justify Protestant theology (Parker 1566).

L'Isle was interested in compiling a complete *Bible* in Old English and compiled a notebook of Biblical references in Anglo-Saxon manuscripts.[13] As part of that program he borrowed from Robert Cotton the manuscripts *Laud 509* and British Library, *Cotton Claudius B.iv*, both containing Ælfric's translations of the *Heptateuch* (Graham 2000: 288).[14] The latter manuscript is of interest since it is also illustrated. Of course, as he read through *Laud 509* he discovered the *Letter to Sigeweard* with its summary of the Biblical books.

In 1622, L'Isle published his edition of the *Letter* with some other materials, in part to show the continuity of the Protestant English church with the Anglo-Saxon church as against the developments in Roman Catholicism. One of his chief concerns, as it was for much of English Protestantism, was to justify the possession of the Bible in the vernacular. He states his purposes at the very beginning, in the title to the work:

> A Saxon Treatise Concerning the Old and New Testament. Written about the time of King Edgar (700 yeares agoe) by Ælfricvs Abbas, thought to be the same that was afterward Archbishop of Canterbvrie. Whereby appeares what was the Canon of holy Scripture here then receiued and that the Church of England had it so long agoe in her Mother-tongue.

He continues in the preface to say:

> Lo here in this field of learning, this orchard of the old English Church, haue I set my selfe on worke, where though I plant not a new, I may save at least a good old tre or two, that were like to be lost: now, for a triall, this remnant of the learned Ælfrikes writing; as I meane to doe ere long (if it may be accepted) a part of the Bible which our Saxon Ancestors left vs in their owne tongue...

---

13 The *Hexateuch* L'Isle mentions is *Laud 509*, the manuscript discussed above.
14 This and much of what follows comes from Graham (2000: 287–313). Helpfully, the article contains as much information regarding L'Isle's use of *Laud 509* as it does of *Claudius B.iv*.

Further on he states, "And the rather because it hath beene slandered for heresie and new doctrine... to haue the Scripture in vulgar" (L'Isle 1622, b1 and d1). There follows a lengthy defense of translating the Bible into the vernacular, something that he claims the ancient church of England had done. As is well known, this point had become a significant issue in the Protestant Reformation movements. Even as the Reformation in England approached its centenary, the issue of vernacular translation of the Bible remained an important enough issue that L'Isle thought it significant to reproduce this "monument" of the ancient English church in order to bolster the practice current in England. It is inviting to see L'Isle undertaking this task in part to defend the King James Version of 1611, though he does not explicitly mention such practices in his preface. He repeats also some of Parker's points from Parker's preface to *A Testimonie...*, namely the translation in the Vulgate about the nature of the Eucharist. L'Isle sees himself as defending the doctrines of the Church of England.[15]

L'Isle used *Laud 509* for his edition of the *Letter*. His method was straightforward. He transcribed the text and published it for the most part as it now is. L'Isle has earned a reputation for changing or altering the texts he worked on.[16] However, the works which he allegedly altered were materials on which he worked in the 1630s, more than a decade after he had worked on the *Letter*. His emendations in those years were for altruistic reasons, the recovery of the Bible in Old English.[17]

L'Isle did make marks in the manuscript. The majority of these, at least in the *Letter*, are guides for L'Isle. That is, he marks the topic matter of the letter, not unlike a sixteenth century book put the topic matter as guides to the reader in the outside margins. L'Isle followed the same practice in the *Letter* in *Laud 509*, marking various topics, particularly the Biblical books and subjects, generally in the outside margins, though sometimes in the upper or lower margins. A further comparison between L'Isle's working habit and early print practices occurs on the bottom of fol. 132^r. At some point in its history, *Laud 509* was misbound and the quire from fol. 133^v to fol. 138^r was placed after the quire which began with fol. 139^v. At the bottom of this leaf is written the first word of what should be the following leaf, *sacerde*, and a page number, *26*. The leaf that should follow is also marked. Early printed books often placed the first word of the following page at the last line of text in order to collate a volume accurately. L'Isle seems to be following this practice in his emendations to *Laud 509*.

L'Isle's translation is for the most part accurate as well, though there are certainly errors. One such error occurs during the discussion of David where L'Isle translates *ceaflas* as 'whelps' rather than 'jaws', a translation he repeats

---

15 He even begins the *Preface* with a defence that though he is not a divine, a clergyman, yet he is justified in taking on these matters.
16 Lee has a full discussion and bibliography on L'Isle's reputation.
17 See Lee's conclusion for the evidence of this procedure.

a line later for the same word. A few lines after this, he translates the line "...mid his liðeran ofwearp þone geleafeasan ent þæt he læg geswogen and sloh him of þæt heafod..." as "...and with his sling overthrew the huge Infidel dead to the ground and cut off his head..." rather than "...and with his sling slew the unbelieving giant so that he lay in a swoon and he cut off the giant's head...". There are other such errors where L'Isle seems to perceive the sense of the phrase but not necessarily the precise meaning of all the elements in the phrase. Overall, however, L'Isle's translation is an amazing piece of work for the tools he had in the early 1600s.

Much more could be said about L'Isle and his work, but the point here is that he, like his medieval forebears, excised the text of the *Letter* and introduced it to a new audience for a new purpose. In contrast to the medieval audiences, however, the purpose to which L'Isle applied Ælfric's words was a purpose that Ælfric could never have foreseen. The intervening centuries saw the birth of attitudes and theology that had not even been on the horizon in Ælfric's day. At the same time, Ælfric and his program of Christian education and Biblical translation have more in common in many ways with the modern Protestant movement than with the activities of Christendom on the continent contemporaneous to Ælfric. Men like Parker and L'Isle were quick to seize on those similarities while minimizing or even overlooking the differences.

The *Letter to Sigeweard*, then, takes many shapes and has many audiences between Ælfric's autograph and modern editions and scholarly study. These different audiences, and what can be discovered of their different reactions to the text, illustrate several points.

First, when we study the tales of the medieval period and note the creativity of a Chaucer who draws on stories like that of St. Anne and recasts them into something else, or Malory and his *Morte d'Arthur*, we note the interweaving, the ring compositions, the use and reuse of stories ever taking on new form and new shape while retaining enough as to be recognized as a part of the larger tale. By contrast, however, scholars seldom, if ever, note that it is this same mindset that operates in medieval approaches to non-literary, and even homiletic, material. The transmission history of the *Letter to Sigeweard* demonstrates this very clearly. In this one prose text we have a letter to a lay audience, a text housed with Biblical translations interacted with by a learned, monastic community, a devotional text for a monastic community, and the reuse of a Latin homily as an illustrative story and as a homily in the vernacular, and as a Protestant tract. While perhaps not as dramatic or as varied as the Matter of Britain or the Matter of Troy, nonetheless, it is the same approach to the text.

Second, this *Letter* inhabits the interesting space between the oral and the written, and it straddles the lines between several genres and between periods. Interestingly enough, while Ælfric requests that any future scribe of the piece be accurate and render his words carefully, it would seem that perhaps even as early as his own lifetime this instruction by the author is ignored, as the text is reshaped and reused in new and interesting ways by subsequent audiences.

Finally, a little more specific to the text in hand, it is to be noted where possible that there is evidence of the audiences of Ælfric's letter through time, from the interactive glossing in *Laud 509* to L'Isle's Protestant tract. These audiences are interesting in their own right. In the end, though, they remain shrouded in mist behind the centuries and only guesses about them may be made on the basis of their interactions with the *Letter to Sigeweard*.

References

Barnhouse, Rebecca – Benjamin C. Withers (eds.)
    2000   *The Old English "Hexateuch": Aspects and approaches*. Kalamazoo: Medieval Institute Publications.

Chambers Raymond W. – Max Förster – Robin Flower (eds.)
    1933   *The "Exeter Book" of Old English poetry*. Exeter: Exeter University Press.

Clemoes, Peter A. M.
    [1959]
    1980   *The chronology of Ælfric's works*. (Old English Newsletter Subsidia 5.) Binghamton: CEMERS, State University of New York. [Reprinted with corrections from: Peter A. M. Clemoes (ed.), 1959, 212–47.]

Clemoes, Peter A. M. (ed.)
    1959   *The Anglo-Saxons: Studies in some aspects of their history and culture presented to Bruce Dickins*. London: Bowes & Bowes.

Conner, Patrick W.
    1975   A contextual study of the Old English *Exeter Book*. [Unpublished Ph.D. dissertation, University of Maryland.]

Crawford, Samuel John. (ed.)
    [1922]
    1997   *The Old English version of the "Heptateuch", Ælfric's "Treatise on the Old and New Testament" and his "Preface" to "Genesis"*. (Early English Text Society OS 160.) London: Oxford University Press.

Flower, Robin
    1933   "The script of the *Exeter Book*", in: Raymond W. Chambers – Max Förster – Robin Flower (eds.), 83–90.

Godden, Malcolm
    2000   *Ælfric's "Catholic Homilies": Introduction, commentary, and glossary*. Oxford: Oxford University Press for the Early English Text Society.

Gneuss, Helmut
    2001   *Handlist of Anglo-Saxon manuscripts: A list of manuscripts and manuscript fragments written or owned in England up to 1100*. Tempe, Ariz.: Arizona Center for Medieval and Renaissance Studies.

Graham, Timothy
    2000   "Early modern users of Claudius B.iv: Robert Talbot and William L'Isle", in: Rebecca Barnhouse – Benjamin C. Withers (eds.), 271–316.

Graham, Timothy (ed.)
    2000   *The recovery of Old English: Anglo-Saxon studies in the sixteenth and seventeenth centuries.* (Publications of the Richard Rawlinson Center.) Kalamazoo: Medieval Institute Publications.

Irvine, Susan (ed.)
    1993   *Old English homilies from MS Bodley 343.* (Early English Text Society OS 302.) Oxford: Oxford University Press.
    2000   "The compilation and use of manuscripts containing Old English in the twelfth century", in: Mary Swan – Elaine Treharne (eds.), 41–61.

Ker, Neil R.
    1957   *Catalogue of manuscripts containing Anglo-Saxon.* Oxford: Clarendon Press.

Keynes, Simon
    1980   *The diplomas of Æthelred "the Unready" 978–1016: A study in their use as historical evidence.* Cambridge: Cambridge University Press.

Lapidge, Michael
    1993   *Anglo-Latin literature.* Vol. 2: *900–1066.* London: Hambledon Press.

Lee, Stuart
    2000   "Oxford, Bodleian Library, MS Laud Misc. 381: William L'Isle, Ælfric, and the *Ancrene Wisse*", in: Timothy Graham (ed.), 207–209.

Marsden, Richard
    1991   "Ælfric as translator: The Old English prose *Genesis*", *Anglia* 109, 319–358.
    2000   "Translation by committee? The 'anonymous' text of the Old English *Hexateuch*", in: Rebecca Barnhouse – Benjamin C. Withers (eds.), 41–89.
    2005   "Latin in the ascendant: The interlinear gloss of Oxford, Bodleian Library, Laud Misc. 509", in: Katherine O'Brien O'Keeffe – Andy Orchard (eds.), 132–152.

O'Brien O'Keeffe, Katherine – Andy Orchard (eds.)
    2005   *Latin learning and English lore: Studies in Anglo-Saxon literature for Michael Lapidge.* (Toronto Old English Series 14.) Toronto: University of Toronto Press.

Parker, Matthew
    1566   *A testimonie of antiquitie, showing "the ancient faith of the Church of England touching the sacrament of the body and blood of the Lord... above 600 years ago".* London: John Day.

Pope, John C.
    1967   *Homilies of Ælfric: A supplementary collection.* Vol. 1. Oxford: Early English Text Society.

Sawyer, Peter H.
    1968   *Anglo-Saxon charters: An annotated list and bibliography.* London: Royal Historical Society. (http://www.anglo-saxons.net/hwaet/?do=get&type=charter&id=911) (date of access: 15 Aug. 2008).

Skeat, Walter William (ed.)
  1881-1900   *Ælfric's "Lives of Saints"*. (Early English Texts Society OS 76, 82, 94, 114.) London: Early English Texts Society.
Smetana, Cyril
  1959   "Ælfric and the early medieval homiliary", *Traditio: Studies in ancient and medieval history, thought, and religion* 15, 163–204.
Swan, Mary – Elaine Treharne (eds.)
  2000   *Rewriting Old English in the twelfth century.* Cambridge: Cambridge University Press.

Nominal Morphemes in *Lelamour's Herbal*[1]

David Moreno Olalla, *University of Málaga*

> The results of... dry enumerations are often interesting and surprising. No one knows whether statistics will be dry and barren or not, until they are collected and classified.
> (W. W. Goodwin, *Syntax of the Moods and Tenses of the Greek Verb* (1889), vii)

Lelamour's Herbal (*LH* for short) is the name given to the version of a Middle English herbal contained in London, British Library, MS Sloane 5, fols. 13ra–57ra (*S* henceforth). It records the healing qualities of 214 species, some of them repeated, arranged in an imprecise alphabetical order following their English names. Neither the presentation of the scientific facts nor the selection of sources makes this manuscript particularly remarkable by any modern standard. It does not offer any of the plant drawings that are sometimes found in this kind of work and, though its main hand is competent and may be indicative of a professional scribe, the choice of colours and the overall decoration are unimpressive.

Nevertheless the text has attracted the attention of scholars, probably because it is one of the few examples of botanical *Fachliteratur* in ME giving a precise composition place and date as well as a definite author: Information to that effect is consigned in its colophon (see Rohde 1922: 42–43; Talbot 1967: 187). It is claimed there that the text was a translation into ME of a popular Middle Latin text, Macer Floridus's *De Viribus Herbarum*, made in the year 1373 by a certain schoolmaster from Hereford, called John Lelamour. The *LALME* team validated Herefordshire as the composition area for the manuscript, assigning it the Linguistic Profile 7361 (McIntosh – Samuels *et al.* 1986, 1: 199), and this was reassured in Black 1997: 81–90.[2] The validity of these scribal statements has been discussed in Moreno Olalla 2007, where the suitability of *S* as a trustworthy witness for the particular purposes of *LALME* was called into question as well.

Although *Lelamour's Herbal* was once edited as an MPhil thesis (Whytlaw-Gray 1938), the transcription and solutions offered there to several problematic readings were either dubious or demonstrably mistaken, which makes it all the more regrettable that it was later employed as a primary source of information by

---

[1] Research for this study received financial support from the Autonomous Government of Andalusia (grant P07–HUM02609). Its final version also benefited from the comments and suggestions made by an anonymous reviewer; thanks are also given herewith.

[2] Black's study is for the most part a reassessment of the Hereford materials analysed by the *LALME* team by using roughly the same methodology, which in practice has meant the rearrangement of several of the dots presented in the appropriate sections of McIntosh – Samuels *et al.* (1986), and the rejection of four of the LPs used in the *Atlas* (7290, 7362, 7402, 7482), which are reconsidered as unsuitable dialectal evidence. The rationale and the new dot-maps are given in Black (1997: 237–248).

the compilers of the *MED*.[3] The text was re-edited and annotated following more modern criteria some years ago (Moreno Olalla 2002), but this edition and its accompanying study are not yet published.

Lack of real interest in this manuscript, notwithstanding its frequent mentioning in scholarly literature, has meant that most of the ideas put forth in the colophon have been accepted almost without further ado. But palaeographical analysis has disclosed that the paper and the hands in *S* cannot be possibly ascribed to the fourteenth century as stated in the colophon, but rather to a year *ca.* 1460 (Moreno Olalla 2004: 90–91). We must assume that this is a copy of a previous manuscript, and that at least the date recorded in the *explicit* does not apply to *S*, but rather to an earlier version of the text. Research on the current whereabouts of this hypothetical exemplar has proven a fruitless task so far.

Inferences on the existence of a manuscript serving as basis to the *Sloane* version can also be drawn from a strictly linguistic analysis, using – and transcending – the *LALME* methodology. The evidence unearthed through this type of research is equivocal but suggestive of several dialectal layers blended together in the final product. Although there is still work to be done, I think that MS *S* represents one of the latest witnesses of a textual tradition that probably had its ultimate origin in the North or North Midlands area, then spread to the adjacent regions until it finally found its way to London, where the *Sloane* version seems to have been actually written. During its journey south, the initial text was enriched with major additions in a desire to turn it into a more comprehensive treatise (see Moreno Olalla forthcoming for details).

Since the scribe of *S* kept the date appearing in his exemplar's colophon but mentioned nothing about his own work being a copy, a logical question arises as to the degree of exactitude that this text maintains to its exemplar: Is *LH* a mere transcription, one we can accept as a more or less faithful mirroring of a text composed at Hereford in 1373 as its colophon suggests, or not? The issue can be reformulated from a linguistic perspective: Does *LH* keep the same *état de langue* as the text from which it stemmed? Direct comparison between both versions of the text is of course impossible at the moment since the exemplar of *LH* is missing; but there are other means whereby information might be gained.

A study of the nominal morphology can be used for the purpose, paying especial attention to the behaviour and grammatical values of *–e*, which is one of the salient features to tell a fifteenth century text from one written at an earlier date. If the data fit in with those that we hold to be true for a Hereford dialect during the fourteenth century, then we can probably trust the *explicit*. The contrary indicates a mismatch that can be explained in a number of ways, ranging from textual con-

---

[3] The inescapable result of such a policy was the population of the dictionary with a collection of ghost words (see fn. 15 for an example of this), showing that a careful selection of the editions used (or, as in this case, a thorough double-checking of the readings contained therein against those in the manuscript) should always precede any lexicographical enterprise.

tamination to alterations due to the fifteenth century copyist, who not only transcribed but also adapted the exemplary readings to his idiolect.[4]

To do this it would be necessary to check, for instance, whether there are any traces of the old dative case, which many scholars take to have survived, if faultily, in the works of Chaucer and fellow Ricardians (cases like *to bedde, on fire, with childe*, etc.; see the remarks of Davis 1988: xxxi), but which seems to have disappeared soon in the fifteenth century, being regarded as an archaism already by Lydgate's time (Samuels 1972: 447), or the use of *-e* with many adjectives to mark the plural. A survey of the whole treatise has yielded no clear-cut cases of the keeping of *-e* in those environments where it would be expected. For demonstrative purposes the following excerpt (the initial lines of the entry devoted to Betony, fol. 15rb, line 28–fol. 15va, line 14) is representative of the spelling habits of the scribe of *S*:[5]

> Betayne is *colde*, and makiþ | to pisse and brekiþ þe *stone*. ‖ Betayne, hony and *wyne* drow|ith þe *dropesye* and helpiþe þe | empetik. Stampe þe leuys and | make a *plastre*; hit heliþ þe *dente* | of þe eye. The juis þ[er]e-of and *oyle* | of rose in erye a-batiþ *akynge*. | Þe poud[er] of betayne and hony | sod to-ged[er] is *gode* **for þe cogh**, | and a-batith þ[e] kyng[re] and diu[er]se | **akyng** of þe stomake. And drinke | hit in wyne; hit helpiþ for feu[er]. | The levis **with salt** in man[er] **of a** | **plaster**, hit helpiþ newe wou[n]dis | and brokyn hedis.

Note *wyne, oyle* (acting as subject, therefore in the nominative), or *dente, stone, dropesye, plastre* (in the accusative, as direct object) and conversely the lack of *-e* in heads of prepositional phrases like *for þe cogh, with salt*, rather than *coghe, *salte. In a similar vein, check also the appearance of *colde* and *gode*, with *-e* in a singular context; *cold, *god would have been expected if actually written by a fourteenth century Herefordian. The use of *-e* in this context, then, casts doubt on the assumption of *newe* as a morphologically plural form. A revealing word is *plaster*, which seems to have the ME usage of *-e* reversed: *make a plastre* (expected

---

4   Laing (2004) provides us with a good introduction to scribal ethology expanding on McIntosh (1989: 92). Using their terminology and although the dialect used in *LH* is, as expected, not totally coherent, the scribe of MS *S* is best regarded as a B-type, or translator, with minor literatim spells due either to pen lapses, constrained selection (see Benskin and Laing 1981: 72–75 about this concept), or else to simple lexical deficiencies, rather than to any conscious design of accuracy towards his exemplar.

5   This text, as the rest of examples, is quoted by folio, column and line as they appear in the manuscript, since the 2002 edition is as yet unpublished and Whytlaw-Gray's is not easy to get – besides, its readings are unreliable. It has been punctuated and capitalized according to modern usage for convenience. Editorial expansions are indicated in square brackets: Note that the figures given in the following pages for *-e* would be greatly altered if, for example *poud*[*er*] or *toged*[*er*] were transcribed *poud*[*re*], *toged*[*re*] instead; the same is valid in the plural and the genitive for *-is* vs. *-es*. In the edition that served as source, suspension marks were expanded according to the most frequent form when written in full.

zero ending) next to *of a plaster* (head of a prepositional phrase; hence *-e* would be expected).[6] The clearest case of the non-distinctiveness of *-e* in the fragment, though, is *akyng*, which appears both with and without *-e* in virtually the same environment: *a-batiþ akynge* and *a-batith þ[e] kyng[re] and diu[er]se akyng*.[7]

It seems advisable to compare the behaviour patterns of *-e* in a suspicious Ricardian text such as *LH* with those in another text composed in the same area but which can be safely dated '1300s'. Out of the texts selected in Black 1997 as representative of the Hereford dialects, the *Harley Lyrics*, the miscellany of ME poems recorded on *London, British Library, Harley MS 2253* and copied sometime *ca.* 1340 (see Revard 1979: 199–200 relying on external evidence, and Ker 1965: xxi using information taken from the manuscript), seem chronologically the most appropriate for the purpose.[8] The relevant results are presented as an appendix. Being of secondary importance to the present article, the data from the poems were collected in a less thorough manner than that used for *LH*, but the conclusions, provisional and all, will show the different behaviour patterns of this letter in both texts.

1. Nouns

1.1. Core case

As seen from above, it seems evident that *-e* is used randomly with any word in any syntactic environment and this would be a clear case for a fifteenth century date. But this would be but half the truth: If the appearance of this marker is studied more deeply, a certain pattern emerges. There are 845 noun lexemes in *LH* offering instances of the core case, *i.e.* not in the genitive or the plural; they have been split into: (a) lexemes that *always* end in *-e*, (b) lexemes that *never* do so and, (c) lexemes with an unstable *-e*, that is, alternating in its use. The result of this simple distribution is given in Table 1:

---

6   Note that in both cases the word is spelt in full in the manuscript.
7   This is a rare word meaning 'asthma' or 'sighing'; I take it to be a scribal mistake for '**kink*'.
8   I am aware that comparing verse language with scientific prose is not the best procedure, as the former tends to be more conservative – if only to achieve poetic goals. Moreover, it is very likely that the text was copied at Ludlow in southern Shropshire by Richard Hurd, a legal scribe, and that some of the poems display noticeable non-Herefordian features, like *-s* as the ending for the third singular present indicative (see Black 1997, 235). Nonetheless, this manuscript remains the best witness at our disposal, if only because it would be near-contemporary to *LH* and since it was ratified as valid North Leominster evidence in Black (1997: 232–233), drawing from evidence given in Samuels (1989). Poems in the *Harley* manuscript will be quoted according to the number given in Brook (1968).

Table 1. Final *-e*

	# lexemes	%
(a) + final *-e*	383	45.33
(b) – final *-e*	323	38.22
(c) ± final *-e*	139	16.45

But there are words, like *ende* or *side*, where *-e* was part of the lexeme (cf. OE *sīde*, OF *peine*) and which could, if only for argument's sake, be taken as displaying -Ø rather than *-e* in opposition to, say, *annete* (OF *anet*) or *merke* (OE *mearc*) where *-e* is etymologically intrusive. Consequently, the information under Table 1 was refined by checking the etymology of each item. The results are the following:

Table 2. Final *-e* (refined)

	# lexemes	etym. *-e*	%	etym. ≠ *-e*	%
(a) + final *-e*	383	203	53.00	180	47.00
(b) – final *-e*	323	116	35.91	207	64.09

As for cases with ± final *-e*, the first step was to split the results presented in Table 1 into two groups, according to the presence or absence of an etymological *-e*, just as in the previous chart. But these data had to be sifted again to check which one of the two allomorphs is more frequent in the corpus, or whether there is roughly the same number of cases for both (equipollence):

Table 3. Unstable *-e*

	+ final *-e*	– final *-e*	equipollence
etym. + final *-e*	18 (13.67%)	22 (15.83%)	16 (11.51%)
etym. – final *-e*	35 (24.46%)	31 (22.30%)	17 (12.23%)
total	53 (38.13%)	53 (38.13%)	33 (23.74%)

An initial reaction might conclude that the usage of *-e* is unbalanced and unpredictable. These figures are yet misleading, as seen from the following example: Both *man(ne)* and *fenigrek(e)* are words that tend not to show *-e*, in keeping with their etymological forms; but while *man(ne)* appears seventy-one times altogether, *fenigrek(e)* is recorded only three times. This means that we are taking *fenigrek(e)* to be as representative of a tendency as *man(ne)*, which belongs to the same subgroup but which has a far greater frequency. This causes a deviation that must be rectified taking into consideration a new variable: We have to attend not only to *absolute frequency* (i.e. which of the allomorphs is hegemonic as a whole), but also to *relative frequency* (*i.e.* the number of times that a certain lexeme is recorded in the corpus). In this manner, the information retrieved from the most frequent lexemes will be more representative than the data offered by those items of scarce apparition, in the hope that the general use of *-e* by the copyist will become more transparent.

Sieving the most frequent lexemes of *LH* that display unstable *-e* through this filter alters the picture. It becomes evident that there is predilection for one spelling throughout the whole text. With the following, *-e* is very much preferred: *childe* 35× : *child* 1× (97.22% : 2.78%); *grece* 23× : *gres* 3× (88.46% : 11.53%); *here* 13× : *her* 1× (92.86% : 7.14%); *mylke* 47× : *mylk* 4× (92.16% : 7.84%); *mo(u)the* 40× : *moþ* 1× (97.56% : 2.44%), *oyl(l)e* 57× : *oyll* 1× (98.28% : 1.72%); *se(e)de* 97× : *sed* 1× (98.98% : 1.02%); *stomake* 62× : *stomak* 8× (88.57% : 11.43%); *stone* 27× : *ston* 2× (93.1% : 6.9%); *wyne* 189× : *wyn* 12× (94.03% : 5.97%) and *wo(u)nde* 13× : *wo(u)nd* 2× (86.67% : 13.33%).

Conversely, low occurrence of the *-e* allograph is noticeable among the following: *co(u)gh* 36× : *coghe* 1× (97.3% : 2.7%); *day* 12× : *daye* 1× (92.31% : 7.69%); *jaundys* 20× : *jaundyce* 1× (95.24% : 4.76%); *juis* 274× : *juise* 10× (96.48% : 3.52%); *lyuer* 25× : *lyuere* 3× (89.29% : 10.71%), *maner* 57× : *manere* 1× (98.28% : 1.72%); *man(n)* 70× : *manne* 1× (98.6% : 1.4%); *plaster* 57× : *plastre* 3× (95.24% : 4.76%); *sauo(u)r* 23× : *sauo(u)re* 2× (92% : 8%); *venym* 29× : *venyme* 5× (85.29% : 14.71%); *vertu* 87× : *vertue* 14× (86.14% : 13.86%).

If we take into account that, apart for the items just given, most cases of ±*-e* are provided by pairs such as *bak* : *bakke*, *dronknes* : *dronknesse*, etc., where each variant appears only once (twenty-seven words, almost twenty percent of the words displaying an unstable *-e*), or in ratios such as 1 : 2, 3 : 1, and the like, being hence of lesser statistical consequence, the alternation is really substantive only in relatively few words. These are, in alphabetical order: *betony(e)* 6 : 8;[9] *bren(n)yng(e)* 10 : 8; *brest(e)* 12 : 14; *drop(e)sy(e)* 12 : 12; *mylt(e)* 7 : 6; *stop(p)ing(e)* 10 : 7 and *tisik(e)* 4 : 4. To the aforementioned *swellyng(e)* 30 : 18 and *vyneg(e)r(e)* 9 : 19 should perhaps be added, even though a preference for a single spelling could be posited for these as well.

The quantities proposed in Table 3 should then be reconsidered since, in the scribe's actual practice, words such as *childe, grece, here, mylke, mo(u)the, oyl(l)e, sede, stomake, stone, wyne, wo(u)nde* and some others are best regarded as part of (a) in Table 1, while *cogh, day, jaundys, juis, lyuer, maner, mann, plaster, sauo(u)r, venym, vertu*, etc., which normally do not display *-e*, should be taken as a subgroup within (b). Only 16.45% of the nouns in the core case can actually be said to present a similar percentage of occurrences with and without *-e*.

---

9   The variant displaying final *-e* is placed first in the following list.

2. Genitive

In comparison with the core case, the picture for the synthetic genitive is clearer. The following endings are employed in the treatise: *-ys*, *-is*, *-es(s)*, *-s* and *-ese*. The use of one or the other is not easily predictable from a morphological or phonological point of view, cf. *manys* (fol. 13[vb], line 11), *manis* (fol. 32[va], lines 21–22), *mans* (fol. 30[vb], line 20), *mannes* (fol. 34[ra], line 21). They stand in free variation although *-is/-ys* is by far the preferred morpheme (115 out of 145 instances, 79.31%); *-es(s)* follows (23×, 15.86%), while the *-s* variant is rarely attested (6×; 4.14%).[10] Finally, *-ese* is recorded just once (0.69%: *eyese rennyng* fol. 15[va], line 18).

Zero genitives appear sometimes: *modir wombe* (fol. 17[vb], line 25), an *r*-stem; *cowe mylke* (fol. 14[rb], line 16), *gose gres* (fol. 18[ra], line 1) and *oke treise* (fol. 24[ra], line 5), which are athematic stems etymologically. The following could be taken to maintain weak forms: *eye liddys* (fol. 27[rb], line 28), *lady day* (fol. 38va, line 11), *sparowe tonge* (fol. 50ra, line 23) and *wesill bitt* (fol. 46va, line 20).[11]

Still, all or most of these zero genitives may be cases of premodification, to be paired with examples like *mayden pappis* (fol. 23va, line 12), where an *s*-genitive is expected (OE *mægdenes*), and with such Romance etyma as *confery flour* (fol. 28rb, line 15), *erbe stalke* (fol. 27ra, line 29–fol. 27rb, line 1), *grommyll sede* (fol. 17ra, lines 22–23), *molayne leuys* (fol. 27vb, line 2–3), *mostarde sede* (fol. 35rb, line 17) or *paynter oyll* (fol. 25rb, line 17). *s*- and zero genitives alternate in *hownde bitte* (fol. 16[ra], line 28), *nadder stynggynge* (fol. 19[rb], line 25), *shepe blode* (fol. 34[ra], lines 11–12) and *woman flouris* (fol. 18[vb], line 20) vs. *houndys bytinge* (fol. 37[vb], line 20), *naddyris hole* (fol. 47[vb], line 6), *schepis tallowe* (fol. 17[ra], line 1) and *womanys flouris* (fol. 21[rb], line 12), but the former prevails (6 : 1; 2 : 1; 8 : 1; and 31 : 2, respectively).

---

10 Theoretically at least, a word like *houndes* could be split *hounde-s*; I have yet reserved *-s* for cases where the ending is preceded by a consonant; only two such cases have been detected: *manns* (fol. 13[rb], line 7; fol. 15[ra], line 17), also spelt *mans* (fol. 30[vb], line 20; fol. 33[rb], line 19), and *womans* (fol. 25[vb], line 2; fol. 33[ra], line 17). Even so, in fol. 33[rb], line 19 and fol. 25[vb], line 2 the scribe wrote the second leg of *-n* with a raising stroke, a modest flourish that normally marks the end of a word, which suggests that he added the *-s* only on second thoughts. Maybe they were zero genitives in his exemplar, like *mayden pappis* (fol. 23[va], line 12)?

11 Arguably, *bene hyve* (fol. 35vb, lines 5–6) also belongs here if from OE *bēon-hȳf*, where *-n* may have been kept because of phonotactic criteria, to avoid collision between vowels (*h*- is phonetically irrelevant since the syllable only bears a secondary stress); cf. OE *bēo(n)brēad* 'bee-bread', *bēon-broð* '?mead' and the appearance of *ben* in the plural (see below), which gives some weight to the idea that this could be a weak form here, *bene* being a plural form. *Prima facie*, *otyn malt* (fol. 17ra, line 13) should also be included here, as it could be taken to be heir to OE *ātan mealt*. But I think that it is safer to assume that *otyn* is an adjective here (PDE 'oaten').

3. Plural

The plural markers are virtually the same as the genitival ones and again the election of one or other variant is apparently free: *berys* (fol. 28ra, lines 22–23) : *beryis* (fol. 31ra, line 23) : *beryes* (fol. 29va, line 11); *flouris* (fol. 13vb, line 4) : *floures* (fol. 18va, line 4) : *flours* (fol. 22rb, line 21); *maneres* (fol. 18ra, line 26) : *maners* (fol. 18vb, line 23) : *manerys* (fol. 27vb, line 27).[12] The most frequent ending is *-is/-ys* (831 out of 1,042 instances, 79.75%), followed by *-es* (186×, 17.85%) and *-s* (20×, 1.92%). *-is(s)e* and *-esse* are seldom found: Three instances of *-esse* (0.29%: *medycinesse* fol. 16ra, line 1, *reynesse* fol. 30va, line 20, fol. 38va, line 27), and two of *-is(s)e* (0.19%: *levisse* fol. 27rb, line 26, *treise* fol. 24ra, line 5); the figures are therefore strikingly alike to those for the genitive. Interestingly, the copyist attaches the same ending to a given word with an astonishing consistency: *lefe* 'leaf', the most frequent word in the plural, shows *-is/-ys* almost unexceptionally (132 out of 136 instances, 97.06%), while a few items (*medicine* 11×, *gardyne* 5×) prefer *-es*.

Apart from this, and from regularly umlauted plurals (*fete, geese, lyse, (sek)men, myse, teþe* and *women*, totalling eighty-six instances), weak forms frequently occur (*eyne*, 44×, *eyen*, 5×, *tone* 2×; also *childryn*, 9×, and *housyn* 1×), the last two being remnants of an earlier reaction against the preponderance of the strong declension.[13] Sometimes old, weak plurals coexist with new, strong reformulations: *askyn* (fol. 54ra, line 5) : *askys* (fol. 20rb, line 13); *ben* (fol. 35vb, line 10) : *beeys* (fol. 56ra, line 7); *cromyn* (fol. 46rb, line 28) : *crommys* (fol. 35rb, line 19); *eryn* (fol. 21vb, line 26) : *erys* (fol. 13va, line 26). The strong variant normally prevails: *erys* is chosen in fifteen out of twenty cases (75%), and similar figures can be posited for *askys* (four out of six, 66.7%) and *crommys* (five out of six, 83.3%). *Beeys* and *ben* appear only once each. The case of 'flea' is dubious, as the text displays both the weak *flene* (fol. 14ra, line 10) and the strong *fleys* (fol. 54rb, line 11); in OE a similar dichotomy existed between *flēah* and *flēa*. Unfortunately, the word is recorded just twice, making it impossible to know which of the two was unmarked in the scribe's dialect.[14]

---

12 This particular word frequently alternates with a form in the singular when after a numeral, as in *ij maner* (fol. 18rb, line 23); this is normal in ME for this type of nouns (Mossé 1968: §60.2).

13 *Maythen* (fol. 27ra, line 20), a synonym for the Stinking Camomile (*Anthemis cotula* L.), does not belong here: Though etymologically plural (OE *magoða*, pl. *magoðan*), it is singular by sense; a parallel case is PDE *mallows*. The existence of an analogical singular *childire* (fol. 35va, line 24) suggests that *-en* was not a remnant of OE morphology in the idiolect of the copyist but a normal device, if seldom used, to build the plural form; but since *LH* is a compilation from several sources, the possibility of diverse dialectal realizations cannot be easily ruled out. As for *housen*, dialectally well attested in the early twentieth century (Wright 1896–1905: s.v.), the form was first recorded ca. 1550 *pace* OED (s.v. 'house' n. 1) but its appearance here shows that the earliest date can be pushed back to *ca.* 1460 – and arguably even to 1373, if the form reproduces an exemplary reading.

14 This word was originally strong (cf. OHG *flōh*, ON *fló*) but this variant is sparsely found in

Next to these, there is a word that offers an intriguing plural ending: *bayith* (fol. 33vb, line 23).[15] Although a dental morpheme is used in several languages to mark the plural (for example, Arabic), this is best understood as a case of hypercorrection. As already stated at the beginning, *MS Sloane 5* is not a holograph by Lelamour, but a copy made *ca.* ninety years later. Its scribe, reading the exemplary *bayis 'berries', erroneously took it as third singular present form, assuming that -*s* was the marker for this verbal form that – we can assume – was the current ending to be found in his exemplar. Probably driven by a desire to iron out dialectal features, he then proceeded to turn what he regarded as an alien form into his own, changing the original morpheme into its Southern equivalent, -*th*.

There is external evidence supporting this assumption. *LH* is a compilation from Latin and Middle English sources, most of which have been unearthed (Moreno Olalla forthcoming). The entry devoted to *lvnary*, where the awkward reading appears, was translated from the Middle Latin entry in *Agnus Castus*. This text has never been edited, to my knowledge, but a ME translation has (Brodin 1950), and the passage reads as follows there: *qwo-so ete of þe bayis of þis herbe in the wanynge of þe mone quanne it is in the sygne of virgine* (fol. 166^r, lines 24–26); cf. *LH* fol. 33vb, lines 22–26: *who-so etith of | his bayith oþer else of the erbe | in the wanyng of the mone | whan he is in the synge vir|ginis...*

4. Adjectives

As for adjective analysis, the list of items in the corpus must be broken down into two main groups: Monosyllabic and non-monosyllabic adjectives, since it is on the former that a distinction 'weak : strong' could still be maintained. A second classification is then made between those non-monosyllabic adjectives that dis-

---

OE while the weak one is amply attested – to judge from the quotations in Bosworth and Toller *et al.* 1972: *s.vv.* '*fleá*' and '*fleah*' [*sic*]; see the corresponding entries in Toller's *Supplement* as well. Most instances of the weak variant in the *English Dialect Dictionary* (Wright 1896–1905: *s.v.*) belong to the West Midlands (Hereford, Worcester, Staffordshire, Shropshire and Worcester); though a form *fleen* was recorded in Wexford County (South-East Ireland), its testimony can be safely ignored here. It may be possible to argue, therefore, that *flene* is an exemplary reading, all the more so since the word is recorded early in the treatise, when the scribe was still sounding out his exemplar; *fleys* at the end of the treatise may in turn represent the idiolect of the scribe of the *Sloane* version, used when he was more at ease with his exemplar and bolder – or more careless – in his choices.

15 Following the explanation first suggested in Whytlaw-Gray 1938: i and maintained in the MED, a mysterious *adeleth* (apparently, from OE *ādela*) was taken to represent a plural form in Moreno Olalla 2007: 128, n. 48. I have discovered since then that this is in fact a copy mistake for an exemplary *anleth, 'face' (< ON *andlit*), cf. *Þe juis and hony | to-gedir doþe a-way þe schalis | of the adeleth* (fol. 19ra, lines 4–6) with the original Latin text: *squamas de vultibus aufert / Si tritam apponas solam mellive iugatam* (*DVH* 570–571; Choulant 1832: 51).

play an etymological *-e* and those with an intrusive *-e*. This was done because several adjectives in *LH* are heir to the OE **ja-/jō-* declension, where strong singular forms could occur hypothetically displaying *-e*; the dropping or maintenance of *-e* in those cases will also be informative. Finally, the usage of *-e* in plural forms, as well as synthetic gradation, will also be attended to.

4.1. Singular

An analysis of the adjective in the singular is important since it was there that the strong : weak distinction was maintained for longer in ME. Out of the 1,958 occurrences of adjectives in *LH*, 1,511 (77.17%) refer to singular nouns; and 60.82% of them (919×, fifty-nine lexemes) are adjectives susceptible to show strong : weak distinction, *i.e.*, monosyllables ending in a consonant. Only forty-seven examples (5.11%, twenty-one lexemes) have been found in weak contexts, thirty-six of which display the expected *-e* (76.6%). This first piece of information would suggest that *-e* still held quite well in *LH*.

Nevertheless, this has to be analyzed more deeply before reaching any firm conclusion; it seems logical, at least, to double-check it with a similar comparison with the occurrences of the strong adjectives and see whether in these cases the contrary, *i.e.* zero ending, appears. The results obtained change this view completely:

(a) Out of the twenty-one lexemes that ever appear in weak contexts (*beste, black(e), blew(e), clere, cold(e), dede, foule, gret(e), halfe, hard(e), hote, longe, olde, quy(c)k, rede, right, rounde, seke, sore, tame* and *wise*), fourteen use *-e* as the only possibility *in both weak and strong contexts alike*. In four other lexemes, moreover, the allomorph showing *-e* is the most frequent of the two (*blewe* 5× : *blew* 1×; *colde* 41× : *cold* 4×; *grete* 20× : *grett* 1×; *harde* 9× : *hard* 3×).
(b) Three of these four last cases (all but the first one) display doublets with and without *-e*: Cf. *gode for þe colde spasom* (fol. 28vb, lines 6–7) : *gode for the cold spasum* (fol. 28va, lines 11–12); *þe grete flewme* (fol. 45va, lines 11) : *þe grett wombe* (fol. 42rb, line 11); *the harde postem* (fol. 49va, line 2) : *the hard swellyng* (fol. 48va, lines 12–13).
(c) In one of the three lexemes where *-Ø* appears oftener than *-e*, 'black(e)', the preferred spelling in weak contexts is *black* (5 : 1), while in the other two (*qui(c)k* and *right*) the form without *-e* is the only possibility, *in both strong and weak contexts alike*.

These new data, and especially (a), seem to prove that *-e* forms do not possess morphological value in the adjective any longer, since they do not stand in opposition to *-Ø* allomorphs anymore. Thus, there is no *de facto* weak : strong distinction in the author's idiolect but the usage of *-e* serves other purposes. It does not seem wise, therefore, to affirm that those forms where -*e* appear are vestiges of the old system while those allomorphs not displaying -*e* present us with the late ME picture: Both forms, those with and those without -*e*, are allomorphs – or, rather, allographs.

Other factors are against any morphological value for -*e*. On the one hand, ±-*e* swings in polysyllables: At least in theory, non-monosyllabic adjectives presented an unchangeable form in all contexts from a very early date (Mossé 1968: §74.2). But this idea clashes with such "aberrant" doublets as *flewmatike* : *flewmatik*; *holsome* : *holsum*; *yelowe* : *yelow*; *jren* : *yrne*, etc. Examination of the seventy-seven polysyllabic adjectives recorded in the corpus produced the following:

(a) Fifty-three lexemes never display -*e* (68.83%), while fifteen always show one (19.48%); the remaining nine lexemes (11.69%) display an unstable -*e*.
(b) The appearance of the mark does not follow an etymological criterion: Although it represents the OE-OF spelling in forty-four out of the fifty-three cases without -*e* (83.02%), the opposite (maintenance of -*e* since OE-OF times) is not true. Only one lexeme (*profitable*) consistently displays an etymological -*e* (6.67%). In other words, almost thirty percent of the polysyllabic adjectives (29.87% exactly) do not keep an etymological ending: Nine lexemes display an unhistorical -*e* while fourteen do not display it though it is expected etymologically.
(c) The instances of unstable -*e* are revealing since they ignore the above rule: In three of the nine cases the preferred form displays -*e* (*femalle* 4× : *femall* 1×; *yelowe* 11× : *yelow* 3×; *souerayne* 6× : *souerayn* 3×) while the opposite happens in another three lexemes (*colouryd* 2× : *colourde* 1×; *cotidian* 4× : *cotidiane* 1×; *venym* 14× : *venyme* 2×). The remaining three offer pretty much equal figures (*flewmatik* 1× : *flewmatike* 1×; *holsom* 5× : *holsome* 4×; *purpur* 2× : *purpure* 2×).

On the other hand, the presence/absence of -*e* becomes vital when dealing with adjectives from the OE **ja-/jō-* declension, and with many Romance loans. Within this group twenty-five lexemes are available: Fifteen of them always offer -*e* (60%), while seven never do (28%); three display it only occasionally. Final -*e* is more stable in Gmc etyma within this group: Thirteen of the fifteen words showing -*e* have Anglo-Saxon (*clere, drye, grene, ilke, kene, neshe, ripe, softe, swete, unkynde, wilde, wlake*) or Scandinavian (*same*) origins, and only two lexemes, *leper* and *þi(c)k* (OE *līðre, ðicce*), have lost theirs. On the other hand, it has a tendency to disappear in bisyllables with a /KR(ə)/ coda: *febill* (OF *feble*), *nobill* (OF *noble*), *tendir* (OF *tendre*). The behaviour of -*e* in old trisyllables is unforeseeable: Cf. *mery* (OE *myr(i)ġe*), *savery* (OF *savouré*), but *flewmatike, female* (next to *flewmatik, femall*; *vid. supra*). On the other hand, *moist(e)* dropped -*e* only once (fol. 50vb, line 28), but kept it in the remaining eleven occurrences (91.67%).

4.2. Plural

The plural of the adjectives in *LH*, just as in the singular, characteristically displays an unstable *-e*. According to the classical explanation, *-e* was the marker of plurality here (Mossé 1968: §74; Davis – Gray *et al.* 1979: xvi), but by the last years of the fourteenth century, with the general drop of *-e*, adjectives became virtually invariable (Brunner 1963: §43; Lass 1992: 116). Out of the 447 plural occurrences recorded in *LH*, *-e* appears 218× (48.77%) used with eighty-four lexemes; of these, only thirty offer *-e* consistently (35.71%), while forty-four never show it (52.38%). We need not infer from this that *-e* is maintained (even if faultily) in *LH*; we should rather suppose that the the opposition 'singular -Ø : plural -e' is obliterated. Indeed there are cases of the contrary situation, like *fyrst(e)*, showing *-e* 6× out of the fourteen appearances before a singular noun, but displaying -Ø after a plural noun: *þre of þe fyrst daies* (fol. 30ra, line 16).

5. Gradation

There are few examples of synthetic gradation in *LH*. The morpheme used for the comparative is *-er*, *-ir* (< OE *-ra*): **depe* : *deppir*, *white* : *whitter*, where gemination probably implies shortening of the preceding vowel, see Lass 1992: 116; cf. yet *grete* : *greter*. The ending is normally used with Romance loanwords as well: *to febler... men* (fol. 32ra, lines 15–16), also in the *þe* + comparative construction: *[hit] bryngeþ oute the hastier borthen of a womann* (fol. 14ra, lines 21–22).[16]

A single case of umlauted comparative has been detected: *that is more strenger in medicyne* (fol. 17va, lines 28–29), maintaining OE *strengra* (Gmc **strang-iz-az*, Lass 1994: 150);[17] note the double comparative here as well, again the sole instance in *LH*.[18]

Only irregular superlatives occur in *LH*, *tendyrst* (fol. 56rb, lines 21) being a probable *lectio facilior* for **tendryns* 'sprouts'. For the record, they are offered in Table 7 below with the corresponding comparative forms:

---

16 *The hastier borthen* could be a noun phrase, but then *hastier borthen* is meaningless while *borþen of a woman* as 'foetus' is well attested in *LH*; a possible translation is 'it causes abortion very quickly'.

17 Campbell 1962: §658 contends that "e" is not due to Umlaut, but that *strengra* is related to *strenge* (Gmc. **strangjaz*, cf. OHG *strengi*), while *strangra*, *strangost* would answer to OE *strang*. Compare yet the parallel *lang* : *lengra* (**langaz* : **langizaz*); note moreover that *strenge* is seldom attested in OE, whereas *strengra* is frequent.

18 Analytic comparatives with *mor(e)* are sometimes found in the text (8× in six lexemes: *white* fol. 21rb, line 23, fol. 23rb, line 7; *bustous* fol. 22va, line 9; *large* fol. 24ra, lines 20–21; *prety* fol. 32vb, line 4; *violent* fol. 33vb, line 15, fol. 54ra, line 26; *black* fol. 50vb, line 20), but synthetic ones outnumber them (26× in nine lexemes).

Table 4. Anomalous adjectives

positive	comparative	superlative
gode	*better* (5×), *bettir* (4×)	*beste* (2×), *best* (1×)
evill	—	*worste*
litell	*lasse* (9×), *less* (1×)	—
mekill	*more* (13×), *mo* (1×), *mor* (1×)	*moste*

6. Conclusions

All things considered, *LH* displays a remarkable stability in the use of *-e*. But the choice seems to be motivated neither by grammatical nor etymological conditions, and that sets it apart from earlier usage as exemplified by the *Harley Lyrics*, where those criteria seem critical (see Appendix for details). Rather, *-e* is expected in *LH* in the following environments: (1) after a long-vowel syllable followed by a single consonant; (2) after a short-vowel syllable followed by two consonants, especially with /RK/ clusters (liquid+stop, particularly voiceless ones such as *ng, lk, mp, rk, rt*), while it is absent in the opposite, stop+liquid clusters; and (3) after those superheavy syllables due to homorganic lengthening. Spellings without *-e* are the rule otherwise. Generally speaking, then, the scribe of *S* uses *-e* as a diacritic, very much in the same way as the Chancery English practice (see Fisher – Richardson *et al.* 1984 for details);[19] this suggests that, as far as this feature goes, it is unlikely that *Lelamour's Herbal* carried over spellings from its assumed fourteenth century exemplar.

It is yet noticeable that the scribe disregarded so many of the other features of the *Schriftsprache*, and above all those concerned with verbal morphology: The endings are not the expected East Midlands ones, which turns *LH* into a peculiar text. As far as spelling habits go, it is close to the contemporary Chancery English standard, but its grammatical system offers some features that are not concomitant: *-eþ, -iþ* both for the third singular and the plural present forms or the extensive use of the marker *y-* (Burrow – Turville-Petre 1997: 33; Mossé 1968: §95, IV); the use of the forms *wote* (third plural present of **wit* 'to know') and *wolle* (third singular present of *wille*) may be added if they represent a pronunciation */wʊt/, /wʊl/* (see Brunner 1963: §72).

The reasons for this mismatch are not totally clear. Perhaps the scribe, trained in the Chancery tradition (see Fisher 1977: 894 about trainees working as professionals outside government circles), found the exemplary text – written in a different dialect, possibly a South-West Midlands one – incomprehensible at times,

---

19 Although its use was evidently far from standardized in the period, I remain unconvinced about an alleged "cavalier treatment" of final *-e* in Chancery (Fisher 1977: 884), particularly in a text this late.

and thought it wiser to alter its grammar as little as possible lest his client would not approve of such changes as could jeopardize its perfect sense. Could this concern be construed as supportive evidence to demonstrate that the person who copied *S* was a professional scribe, rather than a specialist in botanical matters?

Regarding the plural, *bayith* is a key spelling for tracing the textual transmission of *LH*: Either its exemplar or some previous version of the text was written in a dialect where *-s* was normally used as the mark for third singular present verbal forms – alone or in conjunction with *-th*. This suggests a North Midlands or Northern origin for that early version. The extremely rare appearance of a third singular present *sleys* (fol. 23va, line 7) should then be interpreted in this context, and explained not as an allomorph next to the much more frequent *sleyth*, but as a slip that passed unnoticed to the Southern copyist, who had an evident preference for the *-iþ* ending (877 out of 1,085 instances; 80.83%); for comparison, *-is* for this person is recorded just 11×, slightly over 1%, while *-es* is recorded just twice (0.18%).[20]

References

Benskin, Michael – Margaret Laing
    1981   "Translations and *Mischsprachen* in Middle English manuscripts", in: Michael Benskin – Michael L. Samuels (eds.), 55–106.
Benskin, Michael – Michael L. Samuels (eds.)
    1981   *So meny people longages and tonges: Philological essays in Scots and mediaeval English presented to Angus McIntosh.* Edinburgh: Middle English Dialect Project.
Benson, Larry Dean (ed.)
    1988   *The Riverside Chaucer.* (3rd ed.) Oxford: Oxford University Press.
Black, Merja Riitta
    1997   Studies in the dialect materials of medieval Herefordshire. [Unpublished Ph.D. dissertation, University of Glasgow.]
Blake, Norman. (ed.)
    1992   *The Cambridge history of the English language. Volume II: 1066–1476.* Cambridge: Cambridge University Press.
Bosworth, Joseph – Thomas Northcote Toller – Alistair Campbell
    1972   *An Anglo-Saxon dictionary based on the manuscript collections of Joseph Bosworth: Enlarged addenda and corrigenda.* Oxford: Clarendon Press.
Brodin, Gösta (ed.)
    1950   *Agnus Castus: A Middle English herbal, reconstructed from various manuscripts.* Uppsala: A.-B. Lundequistska Bokhandeln.

---

20 Similarly low figures can be quoted for the plural, where *-is* appears only twice in a corpus of 113 examples (1.76%); again, *-iþ* is hegemonic here (79×).

Brook, George L.
   1968   *The Harley lyrics: The Middle English lyrics of MS. Harley 2253.* (4th ed.). Manchester: Manchester University Press.
Brunner, Karl
   1963   *An outline of Middle English grammar.* Cambridge, Mass.: Harvard University Press.
Burrow, John Anthony – Thorlac Turville-Petre
   1997   *A book of Middle English.* (2nd ed.) Oxford: Blackwell.
Campbell, Alistair
   1962   *Old English grammar.* Oxford: Clarendon Press.
Choulant, Ludwig (ed.)
   1832   *De viribus herbarum: Una cum Walafridi Strabonis, Othonis Cremonensis et Joannis Folez carminibus similis argumenti, quae recensuit et adnotatione critica instruxit Ludovicus Choulant; accedit anonymi carmen Graecum de herbis quod edidit Julius Sillig.* Lipsiae: Sumptibus Leopoldi Vossii.
Davis, Norman
   1988   "Language and versification", in: Larry Dean Benson (ed.), xxv–xli.
Davis, Norman – Douglas Gray – Patricia Ingham – Anne Wallace-Hadrill
   1979   *A Chaucer glossary.* Oxford: Clarendon Press.
Dossena, Marina – Roger Lass. (eds.)
   2004   *Methods and data in English historical dialectology.* Bern: Peter Lang.
Fisher, John H.
   1977   "Chancery and the emergence of standard written English in the fifteenth century", *Speculum* 52, 4: 870–899.
Fisher, John H. – Malcolm Richardson – Jane L. Fisher
   1984   *An anthology of Chancery English.* Knoxville: The University of Tennessee Press.
Ker, Neil Ripley (ed.)
   1965   *Facsimile of British Museum MS. Harley 2253.* London: Oxford University Press.
Laing, Margaret
   2004   "Multidimensionality: Time, space and stratigraphy in historical dialectology", in: Marina Dossena – Roger Lass (ed.), 49–96.
Lass, Roger
   1992   "Phonology and morphology", in: Norman Blake (ed.), 23–155.
   1994   *Old English: A historical linguistic companion.* Cambridge: Cambridge University Press.
McIntosh, Angus
   [1973]
   1989   "Word geography in the lexicography of mediæval English", in: Angus McIntosh – Michael L. Samuels – Margaret Laing (eds.), 86–97. [Reprinted from *Annals of the New York Academy of Sciences* 211: 55–66.]
McIntosh, Angus – Michael L. Samuels – Michael Benskin, with the assistance of Margaret Laing and Keith Williamson (eds.)

1986   *A linguistic atlas of late mediaeval English.* 4 vols. Aberdeen: Aberdeen University Press.

McIntosh, Angus – Michael L. Samuels – Margaret Laing (eds.)
1989   *Middle English dialectology: Essays on some principles and problems.* Aberdeen: Aberdeen University Press.

Mitchell, Bruce
1985   *Old English syntax.* 2 vols. Oxford: Clarendon Press – Oxford University Press.

Moreno Olalla, David
2002   Lelamour's *Herbal* (*MS Sloane 5*, fols. 13–57): Critical edition and philological study. [Unpublished Ph.D. dissertation, Universidad de Málaga.]
2004   "A manuscript life: *BL, Sloane 5* from a physical perspective", in: Alicia Rodríguez Álvarez – Francisco Alonso Almeida (eds.), 89–98.
2007   "'The fautys to amende': On the interpretation of the *explicit* of *Sloane 5*, ff. 13–57, and related matters", *English Studies* 88, 2: 119–142.
forthcom.   "Reconstructing John Lelamour's herbal".

Mossé, Fernand
1968   *A handbook of Middle English.* Baltimore: John Hopkins Press.

Mustanoja, Tauno F.
1960   *A Middle English syntax.* Part 1: *Parts of speech.* Helsinki: Société Néophilologique.

Revard, Carter
1979   "Richard Hurd and *MS. Harley 2253*", *Notes and Queries* 26, 3: 199–202.

Rodríguez Álvarez, Alicia – Francisco Alonso Almeida (ed.)
2004   *Voices of the past: Studies in Old and Middle English language and literature.* A Coruña: Netbiblo.

Rohde, Eleanor Sinclair.
1922   *The Old English herbals.* London: Longmans, Green and Co.

Samuels, Michael L.
1972   "Chaucerian final *-e*", *Notes and Queries* CCXVII: 445–448.
1989   "The dialect of the scribe of the *Harley Lyrics*", in: Angus McIntosh – Michael L. Samuels – Margaret Laing (eds.), 256–263.

Talbot, Charles H.
1967   *Medicine in medieval England.* London: Olbourne.

Whytlaw-Gray, Alianore
1938   John Lelamour's translation of Macer's *Herbal*. [Unpublished M.A. dissertation, University of Leeds.]

Wright, Joseph (ed.)
1896–1905   *The English dialect dictionary.* 6 vols. London: Henry Frowde.

Appendix

-e in the *Harley Lyrics*

Nouns

Just like in *LH*, the usage of final *-e* in this environment is almost predictable in the *Harley Lyrics*. Here as well a single spelling is normally employed regardless of whether a noun is syntactically the head of a prepositional phrase or stands as the subject or direct object of a sentence. But the appearance of the final letter in the poems seems to answer to an etymological criterion; the grammatical criterion (*i.e.*, that *-e* is still kept as a dative marking in fourteenth century texts) can only be assumed at times, *-e* being added or dropped according to the poet's particular rhyming needs.

Out of the 464 instances recorded as head of a prepositional phrase in the singular,[21] which could theoretically keep the dative case, 320 (68.97%) still maintained an etymological spelling, while 117 offered an intrusive *-e* (25.21%); an etymologically correct *-e* was dropped in thirteen cases (2.8%). Finally, fourteen cases (3.02%) could answer to doublets in OE (*cropp* : *croppa* or *hell* : *helle*),[22] where the actual origin of the mark could be arguable.

The usage follows no strict rule though, and there are case of unstable *-e* as well; but even here a single spelling, normally the etymological one, is clearly hegemonic for all positions. The case of 'blood', a word appearing twenty times in the poems, is illustrative of the trend. It is spelt *blod* in all cases but three (Poem 15, line 31; Poem 22, line 24, and Poem 28, line 29). In all these cases 'blood' stands at the end of a line, and in two of them (Poems 15 and 28) it rhymes with *fode*, where *-e* is etymological (< OE *fōda*). Only once (in Poem 22) does *blode* rhyme with another word displaying an unetymological *-e*, *rode* (< OE *rōd*): *þou hengest al of blode / so heȝe vpon þe rode*. Note that both words function here as heads of prepositional phrases and the *-e* here could be understood as a remnant of the dative case.

It is to be noted that, irrespective of the syntactic value of the word in the sentence, *-e* always appears with some particular words where it would not be expected etymologically: *lore* (< OE *lār*), *mede* (< OE *mēd*), *toune* (< OE *tūn*) and *nede* (< OE *nēod*), and it is normally found, moreover, with the percentually important word *rod(e)* (< OE *rōd*, spelt *rode* fifteen times out of eight-

---

21 Proper names such as *Alysoun* (fol. 4ʳ, line 11) or *Catenas* (fol. 23ʳ, line 33) were discarded from the list. The following prepositions were used to extract the data: *at, be-bi, for, from, in* (locative sense), *mid, of, on* (locative sense) and *to*. They were chosen because they overwhelmingly governed the dative case in OE (see details in Mitchell 1985: §1178, and the subsequent discussion on the rare instances with other cases in some of them, such as *be* or *to*). The nouns were then doublechecked with the spellings used in the manuscript when the words were not being used as head of prepositional phrases to spot any divergence.

22 While in OE there was an opposition *heofon* (str. m.) : *heofone* (wk. f.), the word consistently used in the manuscript for 'heaven', *he(o)uene*, is taken to be heir to the latter, as this seems to have been the preferred form in Southern texts (*vid. OED, s.v.* 'heaven').

een, 83.33%). Of course the presence of *-e* could be easily taken to represent an initial stage of this letter as a diacritical. But this would be exceptional in a work where etymological *-e* still held quite good and was still pronounced, and would moreover leave some questions unanswered, *inter alia* to explain why there is the different behaviour in the respective heirs of so similar OE words as *rōd* and *blōd*. Although this point certainly wants deeper research, it is perhaps not idle to note here that, *toune* excepted, all the words quoted above were *'ō'-stems in OE, and that *toune* might have undergone some influence from the French equivalents *cité* or *ville*, which are feminine (see Mustanoja 1960: 43–48 for other examples of this trend). Could it be that in these particular words the letter was carried over to the nominative from the rest of the cases in the singular, and *-e* was thus considered a feminine marking?

Adjectives

Adjectives appearing three or more times in the *Harley* poems have been collected to form a representative collection of fifty-three lexemes (475 occurrences). The analysis of final *-e* in these items suggests that, in opposition to its usage in *LH* as a mere diacritical, the letter was still pronounced and retained grammatical value.[23]

First of all, it is noteworthy that all old **ja-/jō-* stems (126×) carefully preserved their etymological *-e* and are therefore unchangeable: *suete/swete* (< OE *swēte*, 61×); *trewe* (< OE *trēowe*, 11×); *derne, milde* (< OE *dierne, milde*; 8×); *grene, wilde* (< OE *grēne, wilde*; 7×); *bliþe, stille* (< OE *blīþe, stille*; 6×); *breme, newe, shene* (< OE *brēme, nīwe, scīene*; 3×).[24] In the same vein, bisyllabic adjectives – *muchel* (9×) and *mony* (4×) excepted – are also invariable: *semly* (9×); *eny* (7×); *lutel/lvtel* (5×); *comely, hendy, holy, lefly, middel* and *worly* (3× each). These facts are only to be expected in a fourteenth century text, in accordance with Mossé 1968: §74.2.

On the other hand, *-e/-Ø* alternates for monosyllabic adjectives that followed the **a-/ō-* declension or were naturalized into it as with OF *fol, fals* (280×). 'Bright', for example, appears sixteen times (*bryht* 11×, *briht* 3×; *bryhte* 2×). All spellings without *-e* are singular adjectives in a strong environment (*e.g. hire bleo ys briht* [poem 27, line 8]), while the two instances of *bryhte* are once in the vocative (*bryhte & shene sterre cler lyht þou me & lere* [poem 22, line 17]) and once in the plural (*wiþ eyȝen bryhte bo* [poem 22, line 22]); the same happens to 'white' (*whyt* 4×, *whit* 1×; *white* 3×, *whyte* 1×), which appears all five times without *-e* in strong singular positions, while the form with *-e* is either plural (poem 3, line 12; poem 7, line 40; poem 9, line 50) or weak singu-

---

23　It must be remembered that *-e*, probably an instrumental ending, was used in OE to create adverbs from adjectives (Campbell 1962: §661); the *Harley Lyrics* maintain this feature in sentences like *me reoweþ sore* (fol. 15, line 33; fol. 25, line 7, *etc.*) 'I repent bitterly'. Those cases have ignored from the present list, notwithstanding the fact that in such cases no clear line can be drawn between adjectives and adverbs: The ME text could be also translated as 'I, aching, repent'; cf. *woundes fele sore* (fol. 24, line 30), where *sore* could be taken as an adverb or as a predicate adjective to the semi-copulative verb 'fele'.

24　The evidence provided by the twelve instances of *fre(o)* 'free' (< Gmc **frijaz*) and the six appearances of *mo* (< OE *mā*) is of course irrelevant here.

lar (poem 7, line 50). Not all adjectives are yet so regular as *bryht* or *whyt*, as demonstrated by *god*. This appears eleven times (*god* 6×, *gode* 5×). All six instances without *-e* are singular in number and set in a strong context (for example, *þat art so god* [poem 26, line 15]; *of fol god bous* [poem 30, line 29]), while forms displaying *-e* are to be split as follows: 2× as adjectives in weak environments (*by gode miht* [poem 29, line 34]; *my gode luef* [poem 32, line 31]), 2× as adjectives in the plural (*werkes buen bo suete & gode* [poem 15, line 30]; *my gode deden* [poem 29, line 10]) and once (poem 14, line 18), at line end as a singular adjective in a strong position, with *-e* probably added since it rhymes with *hode* and *rode*, both of them being heads of prepositional phrases: *eye grete ant gode : vnder hode : on þe rode*.

Table 5. -*e*/-Ø in monosyllabic adjectives

	-*e*	-Ø
Weak	12 (13.04%)	—
Strong sg.	19 (20.65%)	184 (97.87%)
Strong pl.	53 (57.61%)	3 (1.60%)
Line end	8 (8.70%)	1 (0.53%)
Total	92	188

Full figures regarding the alternation -*e*/-Ø in monosyllabic adjectives are given in Table 5; note that figures under 'Line end' represent the unetymological presence of -*e* in a singular context and a missing final letter in a plural context. All in all, there seems to be enough evidence to suggest that -*e* was still maintained to mark the plural number as well as being the ending of the weak declension, while at least in line end position it could have been added unetymologically sometimes for poetic purposes. The regular absence of -*e* with singular adjectives set in strong contexts (184 : 19, *i.e.* more than 90% of the cases), and conversely its total absence in singular weak positions – which stand in clear opposition to the usage in *LH* – are points to be particularly noted. The exact functions of -*e* are numerically less defined. While evidence is strong concerning its value as a plural marker, and the scarce number of weak examples is perhaps to be safely explained as due to the nature of the text (note that all twelve cases found regularly display -*e*), the apperance of unetymological -*e* in a substantial number of instances (27×, 29.35%) is a factor to be reckoned with. This may be taken as evidence to assume that loss of -*e* had already begun but was not yet a strong trend, as seen by the low number of -*e* dropping in the plural (4×, 2.13%).

Adam Pinkhurst's short and long forms

Jacob Thaisen, Adam Mickiewicz University/University of Stavanger

1. Introduction

Few historians of the English language would be surprised to see the spatial, temporal, and functional constraints of working in the written medium listed among the possible influences on a mediaeval scribe's selection of orthographic form. After all, scholars know that professional scribes had a hierarchy of scripts available to them that permitted them to adjust their handwriting as those constraints dictated, and they also know that early modern printers at times inserted a final *-e* to justify their margins. Yet, the topic tends to be touched upon only in passing in discussions of other matters; few studies specifically address it.

Furthermore, scholars can easily lose sight of the codicological and palaeographic context for the occurrence of a given orthographic form. In semidiplomatic editions of mediaeval manuscript texts, abbreviations may be silently expanded, otiose strokes suppressed, superscript graphs transposed to the baseline, and a line added on the margin restored to its intended place. Forms may be extracted from the transcribed text and arranged into a profile, with the scholar in the process perhaps recording the syntactic environment or the position in the verse line, but rarely the codicological attributes or the palaeographic details. At the same time, the influential theoretical orientation of material philology calls upon scholars to take the historical artefacts themselves as the starting point for their enquiry.

In what follows, I evaluate the distribution and relative occurrence of certain orthographic forms in the full text of *Aberystwyth, National Library of Wales, MS Peniarth 392 D* and *San Marino, California, Huntington Library, MS El.29.C.9*; these are the well-known *Hengwrt* [*Hg*] and *Ellesmere* [*El*] manuscripts of Geoffrey Chaucer's *Canterbury Tales* respectively. Scholars have traced differences between these two manuscripts from similar data before and have taken the contrast to be indicative of a chronological shift in their shared scribe's orthographic habits. However, Ian Doyle (1995) appears to assume without any further ado that the differences can be attributed to the physical characteristics of the manuscripts themselves. The present evaluation agrees with that attribution before turning to a discussion of the iconicity of the language of their shared scribe.

2. Previous scholarship

That a single scribe is responsible for *Hg* and *El* appears to have been first suggested in published writing by John Tatlock (1935: 128, 133–134). John Manly and Edith Rickert concurred with him with the support of unnamed palaeographers (1940, 1: 148, 268, 2: 477, 479), and Anthony Petti deemed the suggestion justifiable (1977: 47). Ian Doyle and Malcolm Parkes (1978, 1979: xx n. 2) definitively confirmed the attribution and added further texts to the scribe's corpus: Quires 2–4 of *Cambridge, Trinity College, MS R.3.2* of John Gower's *Confessio Amantis* [*Tc³*] and a damaged two-leaf fragment of Chaucer's *Troilus and Criseyde, Hatfield, Marquess of Salisbury's Library, Cecil Papers, Box S/1* [*Sa*]. The scribe has recently been identified, again by palaeographic means, as Adam Pinkhurst from the oath and declaration to the metropolitan Scriveners' Company he entered on page 56 of *London, Guildhall Library, MS 5370*, and further non-literary texts in his hand have come to light (Mooney 2006).

In the face of the inherent variability so characteristic of late Middle English orthographies, a few scholars have maintained that scribes, especially professional scribes, would develop fixed orthographic habits over time as a result of the mechanical nature of their work. Any substantial sample of the output of a single scribe would consequently be found always to contain the same forms used in the same proportions. Vance Ramsey (1982, 1986) thus bases his argument for separate scribes being responsible for *Hg* and *El* on certain common form pairs such as *atte* vs. *at the* 'at the', and *þ[a]t* vs. *that* 'that' being used in non-identical proportions in these two manuscripts. He attributes the identical palaeographic profiles of these two scribes to their having shared the same professional training. This view has found little scholarly favour, as it takes no account of the many and varied influences on a scribe's selection of form at any given position of the text he is copying.

In a response to Ramsey, Michael Samuels (1983a) shows that the various orthographic forms used by Pinkhurst for a range of lemmata are practically identical between *Hg* and *El*. Their profiles are closer to each other than to other texts written in the metropolitan area at approximately the same date, leading to the conflation of their linguistic profiles in *A linguistic atlas of late mediaeval English* (McIntosh – Samuels *et al.* 1986).

In another response to Ramsey, Samuels (1983b) argues that the Pinkhurst orthography not only is inherently variable like that of any other late mediaeval English scribe, but also exhibits a chronological shift analogous to shifts that were ongoing in the language of the London-Westminster area around 1400, such as *þ[a]t* falling out of use. Based on data collected from Fragment A of the *Canterbury Tales* – the "General Prologue" and the links and tales of the Knight, Miller, Reeve, and Cook – Samuels notes a decrease in the relative occurrence of the former form in the following thirteen pairs in *Hg* relative to *El*: *y* vs. *i*, *ay* vs. *ey*, [*and*] vs. *and* 'and', *town* vs. *toun* 'town', *-[er]*(*-*) vs. *-er(-)*, single vowel graph vs. double vowel graphs, *thow* vs. *thou* 'thou', plain *h* vs. crossed *h*, *þ[a]t* vs. *that* 'that', plain *d* vs. tailed *d*, *-on* vs. *-oun*, *-ogh* vs. *-ough*, and *w[i]t[h]* vs. *with* 'with'. It is this decrease that reflects a chronological shift in Pinkhurst's orthographic habits, so a comparison with the relative occurrence of these same forms in the other two then-known texts written by Pinkhurst enables a relative dating of those texts. Operating with the categories "more", "same", and "fewer", a subsequent comparison yields the following relative chronology with tentative dates of production: *Ca.* 1402–1404 for *Hg*, 1405–1406 for *Sa*, 1407–1409 for *Tc³*, and 1410–1412 for *El* (Samuels [1983b] 1988b: 46).

Recently, Horobin and Mooney (2004) have palaeographically attributed a copy of William Langland's *Piers Plowman, Cambridge, Trinity College, MS B.15.17* [*Tc¹*], to Pinkhurst, following tentative suggestions made previously by Kane and Donaldson, Hanna, and other scholars that the copy might be his work. An initial qualitative comparison of linguistic profiles shows a close match between *Tc¹*, *Hg*, and *El*. However, infrequent forms of common lemmata – minor forms – that appear in corresponding locations across several scribal copies of the same work, and forms that cluster in particular textual segments, most likely derive from the source materials, rather than from the scribe's orthography. The presence of numerous forms can be accounted for in this manner and these forms discounted. This step results in a closer match still between the profiles, thus strengthening the claim that the manuscripts are the responsibility of a single scribe.

To cement the attribution, Horobin and Mooney fit *Tc¹* in the relative chronology arrived at by Samuels. They apply a set of orthographic criteria that is inspired by that used by Samuels but which is non-identical to it. Vowel doubling, for example, is traced in a few specific lexical items only, where Samuels imposed no such restriction, and the presence or absence of an "otiose" stroke on the *d* or *h* graphs is left out of consideration. The forms are considered for their association with the incipiently standardized varieties of written Middle English known as "Types II and III" after Samuels (1963), their occurrence is more fully quantified, and the complete text of the manuscripts is taken into account. *Tc¹* comes first in the chronology.

The addition of *Tc¹* to the Pinkhurst corpus weakens the basis for positing Type III as a variety generally available to scribes in the London-Westminster area during the period *ca.* 1380–1430, since it makes Pinkhurst responsible for the majority of the texts defining that variety. Laura Wright (1996) draws the opposite conclusion from an examination of a range of macaronic business documents of similar date and location, arguing for a broad basis for Type III's successor, Type IV or Chancery Standard, that extends beyond courtly circles. This would mean that the process of orthographic standardization was more gradual and metropolitan English more tolerant of diversity than is often portrayed.

However, evidence indicates that Pinkhurst's selection between functionally equivalent forms were at least in part dictated by other concerns, and the discussion now turns to these concerns. Classifying the forms according to their length, several of the criteria Samuels relies on translate into "short" forms – w[i]t[h], (-)[er]-, and *boke* – as a characteristic of *Hg* against "long" forms – *with*, (-)*er*-, and *booke* – as a characteristic of *El*. A cross-stroke on a word-final *h* graph or a tail on a word-final *d* graph counts as a "long" form if it is otiose, because of the extra stroke required for its execution as compared with a plain *h* or *d* graph. It counts as a "short" form if it represents a final -*e*, because of the fewer penlifts required to produce it as compared with an *e* graph. In *Hg* and *El* the added stroke is otiose. Variation of this type has been addressed intermittently by various scholars. It is enlightening to summarize their findings.

The *Canterbury Tales* is written in a variety of poetic styles: Rhyming couplets, rime royal, prose, octaves, *etc.* No shift of style falls in mid-tale, although sometimes such shifts take place between a prologue to a tale and its narrative part, as in the case, for example, of the "Clerk's Tale". Two tales are written in prose: The "Tale of Melibee" and the "Parson's Tale". Short forms such as þ[a]t 'that' and w[i]t[h] 'with' are especially common in these two tales in *Hg*, and there Pinkhurst probably employed them as a space-saving device (Doyle and Parkes 1979: xxxvii). In addition to this appeal to spatial constraints, it has been noted that Pinkhurst's use of þ[a]t seems to be syntactially governed, since he prefers this abbreviated form when 'that' occurs pleonastically after subordinators (*whil* þ[a]t, *sith* þ[a]t, *etc.*) (Samuels [1983b]: 45]). And the orthographic differences between *Hg* and *El* have been attributed to the contrast between them with regard to their intended audience and function – the sumptuous, more accomplished *El* having a more consistent orthography with fewer short forms and more decorative strokes on graphs than does the rough-and-ready *Hg* (Horobin 2003: 144).[1]

These views are clearly at variance with one another. If Pinkhurst invoked short forms primarily to satisfy spatial constraints, their lower occurrence in *El* can hardly be due primarily to a chronological shift in his orthographic habits, or *vice versa*. And if he terminated a word-final *d* graph with a tail and equipped an *h* graph with a cross-stroke primarily to decorate *El*, their relative prominence in that manuscript can hardly indicate any chronological shift either. A need therefore exists to review Pinkhurst's use of short and long forms in the light of fuller evidence and with due attention paid to the codicological and palaeographic context for their occurrence within the individual manuscripts. Below, after a brief overview of the extralinguistic evidence for the dating of *Hg* and *El*, I address this need, concentrating exclusively on these two manuscripts.

---

1   Horobin (2003: 118–137) argues from the presence/absence of a handful of orthographic forms that some later *Canterbury Tales* scribes may have engaged in the deliberate archaisation of their language to add a Chaucerian flavour to their manuscripts. Smith (1988b) argues along the same lines for the contemporary scribal tradition of the *Confessio Amantis*. If this line of argumentation is accepted, it constitutes an example of another way in which a scribe may adjust his orthography according to the intended audience.

Manly and Rickert, whose work culminated in their eight-volume edition of the poem from 1940, originate the view that no manuscript of the *Canterbury Tales* was produced until after Chaucer's demise late in 1400. According to them, *Hg* dates significantly before *El* but both date within the range 1400–1410, thus closely corresponding with the dates proposed four decades later by Samuels. Their view has influenced much subsequent scholarship on the poem, but there is growing recognition today that both manuscripts may date earlier, as might other manuscripts of the poem, such as *Oxford, Corpus Christi College, MS 198* and *London, British Library, MS Harley 7334*.

The evidence to support such an antedating is varied and marks a return to the study of the manuscripts themselves. It includes that palaeographers consider the Pinkhurst scribal hand oldfashioned for the early fifteenth century (Doyle and Parkes 1979: xx; Hanna 1989a: 9) and that art historians have put forward a date of near 1400 for the *El* decorative borders (Margaret Rickert, in Manly and Rickert 1940, 1: 565–567; Scott 1995). *Hg* has a complex codicological makeup that almost certainly reflects repeat hiatus in the availability of source materials and hesitation about the intended order. Many of the anomalies in its codicological systems are paralleled in *El* and in other early manuscripts of the *Canterbury Tales*, not in terms of the nature of the anomalies themselves but in terms of the locations at which they are found. This suggests that the manuscripts are all based on very similar, fragmentary source materials. The anomalies tend to occur at locations in the text where the various manuscripts differ in their ordering and inclusion/exclusion of material, most of which is usually considered to be material of Chaucerian origin. Examples include whether the "Squire's Tale" is positioned after the "Man of Law's Tale" or after the "Merchant's Tale", and whether the "Man of Law's Endlink" is present. To certain scholars, this congruence suggests an authorial presence at least initially in the production of these manuscripts and also that the manuscripts were produced in parallel (Stubbs 2000, 2007; Blake 1997).[2] A further piece of evidence comes from the records of Pinkhurst's life. He was active in the metropolitan area from the late 1370s and throughout much of his career as a copyist seems to have had a close working relationship with Chaucer himself (Mooney 2006), promoting the likelihood that he worked on tranches of the *Canterbury Tales* while the poet was still alive. There are, therefore, extralinguistic grounds for reconsidering the dates and particularly the relative chronology of *Hg* and *El*.

---

2   Earlier recognition of the conceivable pre-1400 starting date for *Hg* is found in Hanna (1989a: 10, 1989b). Similarly, Doyle and Parkes (1979: xx) recognize the possibility of the production of *Hg* and *El* having overlapped.

3. Corpus

The present orthographic data were collected from the electronic transcripts of *Hg* and *El* published on the *Hengwrt Chaucer Digital Facsimile* (Stubbs 2000), and for *London, British Library, MS Additional 35286* [Ad^3] from an electronic transcript of it prepared by the *Canterbury Tales Project* and kindly made available to me.

I retain the division of the poem into links and tales, but omit all links from consideration because of their brevity, except for the "Wife of Bath's Prologue", and include all tales, except for the "Cook's Tale", for the same reason. Links and tales constitute the major unit of transposition and inclusion/exclusion between the various manuscripts of the poem, and can individually be regarded as being comparatively homogeneous in terms of poetic style. The division therefore allows for a ready comparison between the manuscripts as well as between their tales.

The transcripts were prepared using the transcription principles developed by Peter Robinson and Solopova (1993) for the purposes of the *Canterbury Tales Project*. All graphemes are retained along with all marks that may potentially serve as a mark of abbreviation. For example, tailed *d*, the *per* brevigraph, and the macron are all retained, but the various shapes of the *r* and *s* graphs are not kept separate.

4. Data

The appended Tables 1 and 2 give the occurrence, by tale, of a range of short and long forms in *Hg* and *El* respectively. For each tale, the occurrence is given relative to the length of that tale (the number of characters it contains) so as to enable a direct comparison. The following sets can be identified:

For both manuscripts, one set characterizes the two prose tales – the "Tale of Melibee" and the "Parson's Tale" – its distinguishing feature being that the abbreviated forms [*and*], -[*er*](-), (-)*p*[*er*]-, (-)*p*[*ro*]-, *p*[*a*]*t*, *w*[*i*]*t*[*h*], and the macron are especially prominent. Another characteristic of the set is that doubled vowel graphs are rare, especially *ee*. These tendencies are stronger in *Hg* than they are in *El*, and they are particularly strong in the "Tale of Melibee".

A second set characterizes the *Hg* "Nun's Priest's" and "Manciple's Tales". This set exhibits many of the same tendencies that characterize the two prose tales, albeit less strongly. The reason for keeping it separate from the first set will become apparent below.

A third set characterizes *El*, its distinguishing feature being that otiose strokes on the *d* and *h* graphs are especially common.

For all the short forms in the three sets, the corresponding long forms are complementarily distributed and *vice versa* (not shown), including forms with the postvocalic nasal written out in full as an inverse correlate to the macron.

The *Hg* and *El* orthographies are very similar in terms of the forms that occur, including minor forms. The above forms distinguish the two orthographies in terms of relative occurrence only and the differences are sufficiently slight as to fall within the expected range of variation in the output of a single scribe. Nonetheless, some of the data defining the three sets are statistically significant at the 95 percent level or higher (> $\mu \pm 1.96\sigma$), indicating that the sets are individually present for a specific reason.

Since the forms in all three sets show a comparatively weak correspondence between the two manuscripts in terms of their locations in the text, they are less likely to be inherited from any possibly shared source materials, although those materials seem from other scholarship to have been very similar, as was mentioned above. It is known that neither manuscript served as the immediate exemplar for the other. Accordingly, the forms more likely reflect Pinkhurst's own orthography.

5. Discussion

Prose offers a degree of freedom from the constraints of rhyme, metre, and alliteration typical of verse, which may lead a scribe more readily to depart from replicating the orthography of his source materials. In addition, prose requires a different ruling from verse and makes it more difficult for a scribe to calculate the amount of text that will fit on a page because the text is less clearly segmented. Where a verse line typically takes up less than the available space for it, a prose line fills that space and the graphs may have to be squashed. In situations where space is tight, it would be unsurprising if, like the early compositors that succeeded him, the mediaeval scribe would select the shortest of the functionally equivalent forms available to him. Short forms clearly take up less space than their longer equivalents.

That spatial constraints affected Pinkhurst's selection of form is suggested by the particular prominence of short forms in the prose found in *Hg*, since space is ampler in *El*. For example, Doyle and Parkes note the tight page width in the *Hg* prose tales (1979: xxxvii) and the variable size of the writing area in its quires 27–29 (1979: xxii). Those quires contain the "Tale of Melibee", in which short forms are especially frequent. It seems that the quires provided Pinkhurst with a pre-set space to fit this tale into, for the last of them is irregular with ten folios rather than the regular eight, having been enlarged to take the last lines of the tale (Doyle and Parkes 1979: xxii, xxxii; Blake 1985: 60; Stubbs 2000). This irregular quire, which has no catchword, also terminates one of the five structurally freestanding groups of quires that make up the manuscript. The writing area is smaller by 25–40 mm in the horizontal dimension as compared with *El*, and the tale shorter by more than 1,000 mm in the aggregate.[3]

---

3   The *Hg* "Tale of Melibee" occupies fols. 216r–234v or thirty-eight pages. At forty lines to the page and with a variable frame width of 115–130 mm, the length of, or amount of space occupied by, the "Tale" totals something in the range of 17.5 to 19.8 m. The corresponding

An increase in the unevenness and size of the handwriting after careful opening stretches suggests that Pinkhurst worked under some time pressure when preparing *Hg* (Doyle and Parkes 1979: xxii, xxvi), and certain features of the codicological systems suggest particular haste in finishing it (Stubbs 2000: n.p.). The manuscript is executed in four or five inks, of which a yellow one appears to have been brought into service late in the production process. Apart from two short links and the opening title that are excluded from the present corpus on account of their brevity, two tales are written in this ink: The "Nun's Priest's" and "Manciple's Tales", which follow one another.

The forms that make up the second orthographic set are short forms. Such forms are clearly quicker for a scribe to execute than their longer equivalents, as they require fewer penstrokes. Their comparative prominence in the two *Hg* tales Pinkhurst completed late therefore tallies well with the impression of the codicologists and palaeographers of a scribe finishing his work at some speed. A rule of thumb says that the extent to which a scribe replicates the orthography of his source materials when he is copying them is inversely related to the speed at which he works (Benskin and Laing 1981 [McIntosh *et al.* 1986, 1: 29–30]). It is therefore especially likely that the short forms here represent Pinkhurst's own orthography.

El is the more carefully executed and better planned manuscript in comparison with *Hg*, as has been mentioned. Where *Hg* has a plain appearance, *El* comes with lavish decoration in the shape of frequent paraphs, twenty-three pilgrim miniatures, and seventy-one demivinet borders, all of the highest artistic quality. Also of the highest grade is the material employed as the writing support – abortive vellum. The page size is among the largest of any *Canterbury Tales* manuscript, the margins unusually wide, and all signatures and catchwords cropped, affording a seamless finish.

Pinkhurst has correspondingly increased his attention to palaeographic detail. The top lines on the pages, the running heads, and the rubrics come with elaborate ascenders on supralinear graphs, and graphs occurring in final position in the verse line tend to be embellished with flourishes (Hanna 1989a; Doyle and Parkes 1978: 187, 1979; Stubbs 2000). The otiose stroke on the *h* and *d* graphs – the third orthographic set – adds a calligraphic quality to *El* and so constitutes an integral part of its decorative programme, although the strokes in fact exhibit no restricted occurrence to line-final position in the verse at all, but are a global feature of the

---

El "Tale" occupies fols. 153v–168r or twenty-nine pages. At forty-four lines to the page and with a fixed frame width of 155 mm, the "Tale" is *ca.* 19.8 m long. Furthermore, the quiring and location of the textual boundaries suggest that Pinkhurst could have prepared the *El* "Tale of Melibee" separately too, originally having left blanks first and last to facilitate its joining to other tales at a subsequent stage in the assembly of the manuscript. The tale thus starts on the first verso of quire 20 (fol. 153v) and ends on the last recto of quire 21 (fol. 168r). Certain other tranches of the *El* text are laid out in a similar manner.

El lines.[4] The set has the reverse characteristics of the other two sets: Time and space were plentiful, and the level of formality high. Pinkhurst produced long forms as a result.

Forms demonstrably belonging to Pinkhurst's own orthography provide adequate material for a study of his habits. The forms discussed in the preceding pages almost certainly fulfill the criterion of not being inherited from the source materials used for the two manuscripts, as has been mentioned. The above discussion strongly suggests that Pinkhurst chiefly produced them in response to spatial, temporal, and functional constraints. These constraints exerted an influence on him in the direction of short forms in his work on *Hg* but in the direction of long forms when he prepared *El*, leading to the skews in their relative occurrence that other scholars have accepted as indicative of a chronological shift in his orthographic habits.

Hg, therefore, cannot be placed before *El* chronologically primarily based on the relative occurrence of short and long forms in them. Moreover, since the variation between short and long forms is dictated by the physicality of the copy the scribe is making rather than by the orthography of the materials he is copying from, Horobin and Mooney have taken a study of one aspect of Pinkhurst's orthography as the starting point for their analysis of a different aspect of that orthography. Having arrived at this conclusion, which has negative consequences for the relative dating of Tc^1, the attribution itself of this Langland manuscript to Pinkhurst may now be addressed. To attribute it to him, an undisputed set of his idiolectal forms must be shown to characterize his manuscripts uniquely. The availability of a profile of Chaucer's orthography will aid in the isolation of such a set.

No certain Chaucerian holograph survives, although scholars have proposed that the unique copy of the *Equatorie of the Planetis* preserved in *Cambridge, Peterhouse College, MS 75.I* is one. The direct association of this copy with the poet is the occurrence of his surname on the margin beside one of the astronomical tables appended to it (fol. 5v). His surname, or signature, likewise appears on various fourteenth-century documents. Chaucer may be responsible for one or more of these, but palaeographers disagree about whether any of the signing hands is identical with that found in the *Peterhouse* manuscript.[5]

---

4   291 of the total of 643 examples of tailed *d* in *El* are found in a lemma that occurs in line-final position in a verse line, thus showing some overrepresentation in that position. However, the examples of crossed *h* show no such overrepresentation: Just 281 examples out of the total of 2,695 are found in that position. In addition, it could perhaps be ventured that the function of the otiose stroke on the *d* graph was punctuative, since a tailed *d* can be indistinguishable from a regular *d* followed by a virgule in some scribal hands. However, the data provided by *El* fail to substantiate this hypothesis, since 172 of the total of 643 examples of tailed *d* immediately precede a virgule.

5   For a palaeographic assessment of the evidence surrounding the *Equatorie*, see Pamela Robinson (1991). For reproductions of the occurrences of the poet's surname in the *Peterhouse* manuscript and contemporary documents, see Petti (1997: 45, plates 1–2), Pamela Robinson (1991), or Rand Schmidt (1993: plates A–H).

An external control for the study of Chaucer's orthography may be provided by the *Oxford, Bodleian Library, MS Fairfax 3* and *San Marino, California, Huntington Library, MS El 26.A.17* copies of *Confessio Amantis*, as some scholars regard these manuscripts as accurate witnesses to the orthography of Gower (Samuels and Smith 1981). Samuels ([Smith 1988a: 34]) subtracts a set of archetypal Gowerian forms from the linguistic profile for Pinkhurst's stint of Tc^3 and advances the remnant as Pinkhurst's contribution, although without explicitly validating this step by clarifying the stemmatic position of the *Trinity* copy.

Subsequent subtraction of this contribution from the conflated profile for *Hg* and *El* yields a set of purportedly archetypal *Canterbury Tales* forms, which might also be Chaucerian: *agayn(s), ageyn(s)* 'again(st)', *biforn, bifore* 'before', *nat* 'not', *say* and *saw* 'see' past tense, *swich(e)* 'such', *wirke* 'work', and *yit* 'yet'; rhyming evidence supports the authorial status of /i/ in 'yet'.[6]

The classes of variant represented by these forms recur in the *Equatorie* as well as in a textually important scribal copy of Chaucer's *A Treatise on the Astrolabe* and another of his *Boece*, except that *saw* 'see' past tense and *wirke* 'work' are unattested in the *Astrolabe* copy and 'again(st)' is spelled with *ay-* in the copy of *Boece*. No other contemporary London-Westminster text in the reference corpus attests every member of the set, strengthening the case for the *Equatorie* being a Chaucerian holograph (Samuels 1983a [Smith 1988a: 34]).

Certain minor forms of those same lemmata appear in correlating locations of the text in *Hg, El*, and a third copy of the *Canterbury Tales, Cambridge, University Library, MS Gg.4.27*, among them *ay-* in 'again(st)' and *werche(n)* 'work'. This correlation suggests that these forms are archetypal of the *Canterbury Tales* tradition and so possibly authorial. The forms are also found in *Cambridge, Corpus Christi College, MS 61* of *Troilus and Criseyde* – the "best" manuscript of that Chaucer text – as well as in other contemporary metropolitan manuscripts and documents, but not in *Equatorie*. This lack of congruity with the set of forms isolated by Samuels weakens the case for *Equatorie* being a Chaucerian holograph (Benson 1992).

However, details of the data from *Gg.4.27* are here in error. A reassessment of the evidence by Simon Horobin (1998, 2000, 2003) relies on several more manuscripts of the poem and employs the same methodology of positing as archetypal those minor forms that occur in correlating locations of the text across the manuscripts and whose occurrence there cannot be attributed to a local constraint. Singled out as archetypal by this means are *ay-* in 'again(st)', *theigh* 'though', and *werche, wirche* 'work', but the locations in which these forms are attested number so few as to indicate that they were minor forms already in the

---

6 Samuels's data for the authorial status of /i/ in 'yet' must be regarded with suspicion, as they are taken from three nineteenth-century Chaucer Society rhyme indices to the poet's works (Samuels 1983a [Smith 1988a: 36 n. 20]).

archetype. Each may, therefore, represent one, but not the exclusive, form available to Chaucer for the given lemma, to the extent that the archetype was itself not a scribal copy.

Scholars are, in other words, far from in accord about the profile of Chaucer's orthography. A particular difficulty with the proposed set of archetypal *Canterbury Tales* forms cited in support of elevating the *Equatorie* copy to the status of a Chaucerian holograph is the regular occurrence of the same set in other contemporary London-Westminster texts. Its wider currency means that the set almost certainly represents the dialect of the poet but is inadequate as a diagnostic of his idiolect (Rand Schmidt 1993: 40–46). This difficulty also applies to the set of forms advanced as supporting the attribution of Tc^1 to Pinkhurst, as will now be further elaborated on.

Horobin and Mooney (2004) present linguistic profiles for Tc^1, *Hg*, and *El* as their Table 1. A range of the forms from these profiles may be assigned to the source materials used for the three manuscripts, yielding a set of forms that establishes Pinkhurst as their shared scribe. This set is the following: *swich(e)* 'such', *muche* 'much', *wheither* 'whether', *if* 'if', *yet* 'yet', *bifore(n)* 'before', *noght, noȝt, nouȝt, nat* 'not', *thogh, though, þouȝ* 'though', *werch-, wirch-, werk-, wirk-* 'work', *thurgh, þoruȝ, thoruȝ, thorugh, thorgh* 'through', and *saugh, sauȝ, seigh(e), seiȝ(e), say, saw(e)* 'see' past tense. Of these forms, *thogh, thurgh, say,* and *saw(e)* are unattested in Tc^1, and *nouȝt, þoruȝ, thoruȝ, thorugh,* and *thorgh* unattested in both *Hg* and *El* and should therefore be discounted. Also among them are several of the forms whose possible Chaucerian status was discussed above, for example *swich(e)* and the four forms of 'work'; if these forms are accepted as Chaucerian, they cannot diagnose Pinkhurst.

So, questions may be asked about the strength of this set of forms as support for Pinkhurst being the scribe of Tc^1. Further questions arise when the evidence of yet another copy of the *Canterbury Tales*, Ad^3, is taken into account. This copy dates to a generation or later after Chaucer's demise. Its exact stemmatic position is unclear, but it has been shown that neither *Hg* or *El*, nor an archetypal copy of the poem, constituted its immediate source materials. It has also been shown that the Ad^3 orthography results from the thorough, progressive "translation" of the source materials into the scribe's own orthography, which latter may be described as Type III (Thaisen 2008).

The appended Table 3 is adapted from Horobin and Mooney (2004) Table 1 to include an extra column with data for Ad^3. It can be seen that every member of the set of forms put forward as diagnostic of Pinkhurst's orthography is attested in Ad^3, with the sole exception of *wheither*. It can also be seen that of the thirty-three forms and types of forms included in Table 3, Tc^1 shares eighteen with *Hg* and eighteen with *El*, but nineteen with Ad^3. The table includes only exact matches so as to ensure absolute comparability. Relaxation of this criterion to accept Ad^3's *ayeyne* 'again(st)', *naught, nought* 'not', and *wyrch-, wyrk-* 'work' as matches, raises the number of forms shared by Tc^1 and Ad^3 to twenty-four. So, the profile for Ad^3 matches the profile for Tc^1 more closely than does the profile for either *Hg* or *El*.

In other words, while it remains a possibility that Pinkhurst is responsible for the scribal work on Tc^1, all that Horobin and Mooney (2004) have shown is that its text is written in a variety of London-Westminster English that is close to Chaucer's own dialect. This variety is the one commonly referred to as Type III, and its presence in Ad^3 indicates that it was still available to scribes a generation or more after the production of *Hg* and *El* – surely the mark of an incipient standard.

6. Conclusion

There exists a contrast between *Hg* and *El* in the relative occurrence of form pairs such as [*and*] vs. *and* 'and', -[*er*] vs. -*er*, þ[*a*]*t* vs. *that* 'that', single vowel graph vs. double vowel graph, plain *d* graph vs. tailed *d* graph, and w[*i*]*t*[*h*] vs. *with* 'with'. These forms may be classified according to their length. For codicological and palaeographic evidence supports the existence of a cline with a "short" pole characterized by a scarcity of space, a speedy execution of graphic shapes, and a low level of formality, and a "long" pole having the opposite characteristics. Pinkhurst's forms vary in their position on this cline in response to spatial, temporal, and functional constraints influencing him, with him having been in sufficient command of his orthography to be able consciously to exploit its inherent variability to his own benefit in carrying out the copying task. The contrast between *Hg* and *El* in these form pairs therefore reflects no chronological shift in Pinkhurst's orthographic habits.

Middle English scribal orthographies are notoriously variable. They result from the interplay of the scribe's orthography with that or those found in the source materials, and scholarly discussions tend to focus on the separation of scribally-induced from exemplar-induced forms in the given text under investigation. An established means by which to achieve this separation is to subdivide a profile of the forms found in the text along dialectal lines. The *modus operandi* of the "short"-"long" cline is different, as it seems to respond directly to the copy rather than to the exemplar. It can be studied by appreciation of the codicological and palaeographic context for the manifestation of the given forms and is closely related to the hierarchy of scripts available to late mediaeval English scribes. This is because orthography, palaeography, and codicology are overlapping realms of the archaeology of the book.

Table 1. Occurrence, by tale, of selected forms in *Hg* (per ten-thousand characters)

Form	GP	KN	MI	RE	WBP	WBT	FR	SU	ML	SQ	ME	FK	NU
[and]	0.9	0.4	0.4	0.6	0.6	–	1.3	–	0.7	–	–	1.3	3.5
-[er]	7.4	4.5	4.1	1.2	12.2	16.1	10.7	9.3	12.7	14.9	11.0	13.9	9.7
tilde	9.7	20.0	10.8	8.9	17.2	19.1	19.5	14.4	15.0	11.6	15.6	20.4	15.0
(-)p[er]-	3.7	2.0	1.5	4.2	3.3	3.6	2.0	3.0	4.8	3.3	3.8	3.5	1.8
(-)p[ro]-	1.1	0.5	1.5	1.2	2.7	0.6	1.3	0.8	0.9	2.2	1.3	1.6	0.9
þ[a]t	13.1	23.0	19.7	21.4	13.4	14.3	10.7	3.8	20.2	24.7	23.2	16.9	6.6
w[i]t[h]	1.1	2.0	2.6	1.8	1.5	–	2.0	1.3	1.4	0.4	1.3	3.8	0.9
tailed *d*	5.7	0.1	1.5	1.2	–	–	–	–	1.4	–	0.2	1.3	–
crossed *h*	3.1	1.4	3.3	17.2	2.1	0.6	4.7	2.5	0.5	3.3	2.1	0.3	2.2
-eeCe(-)	2.4	1.2	0.7	0.5	0.5	0.9	0.7	0.9	0.8	1.0	0.7	0.7	1.0
-ooCe(-)	10.5	9.0	11.9	7.1	8.3	6.0	6.0	12.7	10.0	10.9	8.8	11.0	6.6

Table 1 (continued). Occurrence, by tale, of selected forms in *Hg* (per ten-thousand characters)

CL	PH	PD	SH	PR	TT	TM	MO	NP	MA	PA	n	μ	σ
1.2	–	5.3	2.3	1.0	11.6	51.3	1.6	0.4	0.9	39.1	901	5.2	12.7
14.1	17.7	15.8	9.0	10.1	1.7	18.7	7.3	3.5	5.6	15.1	915	10.3	5.1
19.4	16.0	13.9	8.4	10.1	6.6	18.9	21.8	28.5	25.1	31.0	1,487	16.5	6.2
2.9	3.4	4.1	2.3	3.0	13.3	9.6	3.8	2.7	1.9	6.7	357	3.9	2.6
1.8	0.8	1.5	0.6	1.0	–	4.9	1.3	0.4	0.9	3.6	153	1.4	1.1
22.3	22.8	23.7	20.3	12.1	5.0	54.9	19.6	30.8	21.3	49.5	2,148	20.6	11.8
1.8	0.8	1.1	1.1	1.0	1.7	6.1	3.5	5.0	8.4	6.6	237	2.4	2.1
1.0	–	1.1	0.6	–	–	0.1	–	0.8	–	0.2	53	0.6	1.2
0.6	–	4.5	15.2	6.1	1.7	–	0.9	–	0.9	2.1	181	3.1	4.3
1.0	1.6	0.5	1.2	1.3	2.2	0.1	0.7	0.5	0.6	0.2	640	0.9	0.5
9.2	12.6	11.7	8.4	6.1	8.3	11.7	8.5	12.3	6.5	15.0	838	9.6	2.5

Table 2. Occurrence, by tale, of selected forms in *El* (per ten-thousand characters)

Form	Tale GP	KN	MI	RE	ML	WBP	WBT	FR	SU	CL	ME	SQ	FK
[*and*]	4.5	1.7	–	0.6	1.1	1.4	0.6	0.6	0.8	0.6	0.6	1.7	1.3
-[*er*]	6.8	5.9	3.3	4.1	9.3	15.7	16.7	11.7	10.9	17.0	12.6	19.5	21.8
tilde	20.7	25.9	18.9	31.5	34.3	28.7	25.3	29.2	32.6	43.9	36.9	44.8	39.8
(-)*p*[*er*]-	2.0	1.9	1.9	4.1	4.2	4.8	4.0	3.2	4.0	2.6	3.2	2.4	3.3
(-)*p*[*ro*]-	1.1	0.3	0.7	0.6	0.4	1.7	0.6	1.3	0.8	0.4	–	1.0	0.8
þ[*a*]*t*	9.6	14.7	5.9	7.0	6.7	12.4	14.4	16.9	9.7	10.5	21.7	18.8	14.2
w[*i*]*t*[*h*]	5.7	7.7	5.2	2.3	1.8	1.7	2.9	3.9	2.8	3.6	4.2	3.1	3.5
tailed *d*	7.9	4.0	1.5	8.7	4.9	3.1	2.9	5.8	6.0	3.0	4.8	10.9	7.9
crossed *h*	23.8	29.2	18.9	45.5	22.5	20.0	36.8	14.9	27.7	26.9	41.1	35.9	34.5
-*eeCe*(-)	7.1	10.7	13.4	8.2	13.8	7.6	17.3	14.3	11.7	16.2	10.2	9.2	10.1
-*ooCe*(-)	8.5	9.4	14.5	9.9	13.3	9.8	6.3	6.5	14.5	11.7	9.8	11.6	11.4

Table 2 (continued). Occurrence, by tale, of selected forms in *El* (per ten-thousand characters)

Tale PH	PD	SH	PR	TT	TM	MO	NP	NU	CY	MA	PA	n	μ	σ
2.4	3.3	3.2	1.0	6.3	7.0	1.5	1.1	0.8	1.5	6.2	6.8	302	2.4	2.2
20.3	15.5	13.3	14.4	3.2	21.5	11.7	11.3	13.0	17.3	15.1	17.7	1,380	13.2	5.5
34.9	26.0	30.8	27.8	31.6	42.1	27.7	26.7	23.4	28.2	37.4	38.5	3,234	31.5	7.0
4.1	6.9	3.2	3.8	14.2	10.0	4.8	4.1	2.1	3.9	2.7	7.6	477	4.4	2.8
–	0.7	0.5	1.0	–	4.9	0.9	0.4	0.4	1.2	0.9	2.5	139	1.1	1.0
17.8	18.8	19.6	13.4	7.9	13.2	12.4	12.8	9.6	19.1	16.0	7.7	1,202	13.2	4.6
4.9	4.0	5.8	1.9	4.7	1.6	6.3	3.0	5.4	3.9	5.2	0.8	332	3.8	0.5
18.6	10.1	12.2	10.5	15.8	7.6	10.8	14.3	4.6	13.1	13.3	4.0	643	8.3	4.6
36.5	43.0	40.3	33.5	26.9	23.4	41.3	24.4	43.9	24.3	32.9	18.9	2,695	30.7	8.9
21.9	6.5	13.3	24.0	33.2	4.3	9.0	9.8	18.8	14.0	14.2	3.2	945	12.9	6.6
13.8	14.1	11.7	22.0	12.7	13.3	10.8	13.9	9.2	9.7	6.2	12.7	1,121	11.5	3.3

Table 3. Linguistic profiles for Tc^1, Hg, El, and Ad^3 [a]

Lemma	Form	Tc^1	Hg	El	Ad^3
'such'	*swich(e)*	111	348	410	236
'much'	*muche(l)*	69	70	81	20
'whether'	*wheither*	10	24	30	0
'if'	*if*	253	471	575	131
'again(st)'	*agayn(s)*	2	172	230	68
	ageyn(e,s)	7	16	20	61

	again(s,st)	0	1	3	0
	ayein(s)	55	9	0	2
	ayeyn(s)	1	0	11	5
'yet'	yet	40	246	288	43
	yit, ȝit	13	8	7	192
'before'	bifore(n)	52	112	131	85
	afore	5	0	0	0
	tofore	2	0	0	0
	toforn	2	0	1	0
'not'	noght, noȝt	335	235	190	153
	nouȝt	17	0	0	0
	nauȝt	7	0	0	0
	nat	4	819	1,058	552
'though'	thogh	0	175	64	117
	though, þouȝ	67	24	173	57
	theigh	14	7	0	9
'work'	werch-, wirch-	56	12	17	7
	werk-, wirk-	1	39	42	53
'through'	thurgh	0	99	148	87
	þoruȝ/thoruȝ	165	0	0	0
	thorugh	1	0	0	0
	thorgh	1	0	0	5
'see' past tense	saugh, sauȝ	6	31	124	46
	seigh(e), seiȝ(e)	45	13	3	3
	sy	0	0	1	0
	say	0	48	12	33
	saw(e)	0	43	5	0

[a] The figures for Tc^1, Hg, and El are after Horobin and Mooney (2004: 81, Table 1).

References

Beal, Peter (ed.)
    1989   *English manuscript studies 1100–1700: Volume 1*. Oxford: Blackwell.
Beal, Peter – Jeremy Griffiths (eds.)
    1992   *English manuscript studies 1100–1700: Volume 3*. London: The British Library – University of Toronto Press.
Benskin, Michael – Michael L. Samuels (eds.)
    1981   *So meny people longages and tonges: Philological essays in Scots and mediaeval English presented to Angus McIntosh*. Edinburgh: Middle English Dialect Project.

Benskin, Michael – Margaret Laing
  1981   "Translations and *Mischsprachen* in Middle English manuscripts", in: Michael Benskin – Michael L. Samuels (eds.), 55–106.
Benson, Larry D.
  1992   "Chaucer's spelling reconsidered", in: Peter Beal – Jeremy Griffiths (eds.), 1–28.
Blake, Norman F.
  1997   "Geoffrey Chaucer and the manuscripts of the *Canterbury Tales*", *Journal of the Early Book Society for the Study of Manuscripts and Printing History* 1: 95–122.
Blake, Norman F. – Peter M. W. Robinson (eds.)
  1993   *The Canterbury Tales Project occasional papers volume I*. (Office for Humanities Communication Publications 5.) Oxford: Office for Humanities Communication.
Doyle, Andrew Ian
  1995   "The copyist of the *Ellesmere Canterbury Tales*", in: Martin Stevens – Daniel H. Woodward (eds.), 49–67.
Doyle, Andrew Ian – Malcolm B. Parkes
  1978   "The production of copies of the *Canterbury Tales* and the *Confessio Amantis* in the early fifteenth century", in: Malcolm B. Parkes – Andrew G. Watson (eds.), 163–210.
  1979   "Paleographical introduction", in: Paul G. Ruggiers (ed.), xix–xlix.
Gray, Douglas – Eric G. Stanley (eds.)
  1983   *Middle English studies presented to Norman Davis in honour of his seventieth birthday*. Oxford: Oxford University Press.
Hanna, Ralph
  1989a "Introduction", in: Ralph Hanna (ed.), 1–17.
  1989b "The *Hengwrt* manuscript and the canon of the *Canterbury Tales*", in: Peter Beal (ed.), 64–84.
Hanna, Ralph (ed.)
  1989c *The Ellesmere manuscript of Chaucer's "Canterbury Tales": A working facsimile*. Cambridge: D. S. Brewer.
Horobin, Simon C. P.
  1998   "A new approach to Chaucer's spelling", *English Studies* 79: 415–424.
  2000   "Chaucer's spelling and the manuscripts of the *Canterbury Tales*", in: Irma Taavitsainen – Terttu Nevalainen – Päivi Pahta – Matti Rissanen (eds.), 199–208.
  2003   *The language of the Chaucer tradition*. (Chaucer Studies 32.) Cambridge: D. S. Brewer.
Horobin, Simon C. P. – Linne R. Mooney
  2004   "A *Piers Plowman* manuscript by the *Hengwrt/Ellesmere* scribe and its implications for London standard English", *Studies in the Age of Chaucer* 26: 65–112.

Manly, John M. – Edith Rickert (eds.)
    1940   *The text of the "Canterbury Tales": Studied on the basis of all known manuscripts.* 8 vols. Chicago: Chicago University Press.
McIntosh, Angus – Michael L. Samuels – Michael Benskin, with the assistance of Margaret Laing and Keith Williamson (eds.)
    1986   *A linguistic atlas of late mediaeval English.* 4 vols. Aberdeen: Aberdeen University Press.
McIntosh, Angus – Michael L. Samuels – Margaret Laing (eds.)
    1989   *Middle English dialectology: Essays on some principles and problems.* Aberdeen: Aberdeen University Press.
Mooney, Linne R.
    2006   "Chaucer's scribe", *Speculum: A Journal of Medieval Studies* 81: 97–138.
Parkes, Malcolm B. – Andrew G. Watson (eds.)
    1978   *Medieval scribes, manuscripts, and libraries: Essays presented to N. R. Ker.* London: Scolar Press.
Petti, Anthony G.
    1977   *English literary hands from Chaucer to Dryden.* Cambridge: Harvard University Press.
Ramsey, Roy Vance
    1982   "The *Hengwrt* and *Ellesmere* manuscripts of the *Canterbury Tales*: Different scribes", *Studies in Bibliography* 35: 133–154.
    1986   "Paleography and scribes of shared training", *Studies in the Age of Chaucer* 8: 107–144.
Rand Schmidt, Kari Anne
    1993   *The authorship of the "Equatorie of the Planetis".* (Chaucer Studies 19.) Cambridge: D. S. Brewer.
Robinson, Pamela
    1991   "Geoffrey Chaucer and the *Equatorie of the Planetis*: The state of the problem", *Chaucer Review* 26: 17–30.
Robinson, Peter M. W. – Elizabeth Solopova
    1993   "Guidelines for transcription of the manuscripts of the *Wife of Bath's Prologue*", in: Norman F. Blake – Peter M. W. Robinson (eds.), 19–52.
Ruggiers, Paul G. (ed.)
    1979   *The "Canterbury Tales": A facsimile and transcription of the "Hengwrt" manuscript, with variants from the "Ellesmere" manuscript.* (Variorum Edition of the Works of Geoffrey Chaucer 1.) Norman, Okla.: University of Oklahoma Press.
Samuels, Michael L.
    [1963]
    1989   "Some applications of Middle English dialectology", in: Angus McIntosh – Michael L. Samuels – Margaret Laing (eds.), 64–80. [Reprinted from *English Studies* 44: 81–94.]
    [1983a]
    1988a   "Chaucer's spelling", in: Jeremy J. Smith (ed.), 23–37. [Reprinted from Douglas Gray – Eric G. Stanley (eds.), 17–37.]

[1983b]
1988b   "The scribe of the *Hengwrt* and *Ellesmere* manuscripts of the *Canterbury Tales*", in: Jeremy J. Smith (ed.), 38–50. [Reprinted from *Studies in the Age of Chaucer* 5: 49–65.]

Samuels, Michael L. – Jeremy J. Smith
1981   "The language of Gower", *Neuphilologische Mitteilungen* 82, 294–304.

Scott, Kathleen L.
1995   "An hours and psalter by two *Ellesmere* illuminators", in: Martin Stevens – Daniel H. Woodward (eds.), 87–119.

Smith, Jeremy J.
1988   "Spelling and tradition in fifteenth-century copies of Gower's *Confessio Amantis*", in: Jeremy J. Smith (ed.), 96–113.

Smith, Jeremy J. (ed.)
1988   *The English of Chaucer and his contemporaries: Essays by M. L. Samuels and J. J. Smith*. Aberdeen: Aberdeen University Press.

Stevens, Martin – Daniel H. Woodward (eds.)
1995   *The "Ellesmere" Chaucer: Essays in interpretation*. San Marino, California: Huntington Library.

Stubbs, Estelle
2007   "'Here's one I prepared earlier': The work of scribe D on *Oxford, Corpus Christi College, MS 198*", *Review of English Studies* 58: 133–153.

Stubbs, Estelle (ed.)
2000   *The "Hengwrt" Chaucer digital facsimile*. Leicester: Scholarly Digital Editions.

Tatlock, John S. P.
1935   "The *Canterbury Tales* in 1400", *Publications of the Modern Language Association of America* 50: 100–139.

Thaisen, Jacob
2008   "Overlooked variants in the orthography of *British Library, Additional MS 35,286*", *Journal of the Early Book Society for the Study of Manuscripts and Printing History* 11: 121–143.

Taavitsainen, Irma – Terttu Nevalainen – Päivi Pahta – Matti Rissanen (eds.)
2000   *Placing Middle English in context*. Berlin: De Gruyter.

Wright, Laura
1996   *Sources of London English: Medieval Thames vocabulary*. Oxford: Clarendon Press.

A V or not a V? Transcribing abbreviations in seventeen manuscripts of the "Man of Law's Tale" for a digital edition[1]

Joanna Kopaczyk, Adam Mickiewicz University

1. Introduction

In his 1956 paper, Angus McIntosh argued for the study of *written* Middle English, which then could shed light on Middle English dialectology. Even with the monumental *Linguistic atlas of late medieval English* (*LALME*) based on original manuscripts, a great part of our understanding of Middle English comes from nineteenth century editions, now computerized and searchable. It is therefore advisable to confront this knowledge with manuscripts again, trying to represent faithfully the linguistic information embedded in scribal conventions. Whether this task is achieved will depend on consistent and unbiased digitalization procedures.[2]

The current paper stems from observations made when working for the *Canterbury Tales Project*, preparing the "Man of Law's Tale" for a digital, searchable and comparative edition. One of the decisions which need to be taken during the transcription process is how to represent abbreviations in the edition. As the policy of the project is to keep as close to the manuscript as possible on the graphemic level, with some attention paid also to the graphetic choices (Robinson and Solopova 1993: 1.3–1.5), transcribers have to decide how to render a particular abbreviation shape in their electronic version of the text. The idea is not to expand the abbreviation but rather to represent a particular shape by a consistent transcription convention.[3] However, the manuscript reality may prove difficult to be captured in a neat set of conventions (as admitted *e.g.* by Vander Meulen and Tanselle 1999: 201), and abbreviations score high on the list of problematic cases. The pun in the title of the paper aims at drawing attention to vowel shapes used as abbreviations, or the shapes we may arbitrarily or, indeed, mistakenly, interpret as vowel graphemes.

---

1 The present paper stems from my work and research carried out within the Polish Ministry of Science and Higher Education project no. N 104 045 32/ 4256.
2 Such considerations are prompted by the 'how' question in the context of digital editions. In his contribution to *Literary and Linguistic Computing*, Robinson (2009) insists that the 'what' and 'why' questions, pertaining to the object and the potential audience of the digital edition, should underlie all decisions as the basic editorial principle.
3 Other digitizing projects may have different solutions when it comes to abbreviations. For instance, the *Piers Plowman Electronic Archive* transcription guidelines insist on expanding them. See the critique of this approach in further sections of the paper.

2. Scribal practice and editorial decisions

Typically, medieval scribes were copying from exemplars written in a variety of the language other than their own. In his analysis of medieval writing systems, McIntosh (1989 [1973]: 92) introduces a classic typology of scribal options when it comes to their adherence to an exemplar: transcribing, translating, or a mixture of the two – the latter not being the most clear-cut category but very often needed. As Blake and Thaisen aptly observe (2004: 94), "a scribe's spelling is affected by two factors: his own spelling system and the system(s) of the exemplar(s) he is copying". One should remember that a scribal system is not uniform or homogenous, being subject to various external factors. I would divide these factors into two strands: the one connected with the reality of the copying procedure, such as time limits, space limits, and the amount of time which had passed since working on a given manuscript, as well as the one concerning individual socio-geographic traits: education, familiarity with the copied text and/or its spelling system, place of origin, history of migration, *etc.* Both types of factors will make an impact on the abbreviating procedures.

Drawing attention to the spelling awareness of medieval scribes, Laing and Lass (2003: 258) insist that "[t]he scribes were capable of sophisticated and subtle linguistic analysis. This can be demonstrated without anachronistically attributing to them any uniquely modern theoretical concepts. Nothing we claim [...] is incompatible with the medieval doctrine of *littera*, or what intelligent scribes may be presumed to have understood by it". This influential theoretical model for the understanding of a graphic sign, a letter, *littera*, was put forward by the Roman grammarian Aelius Donatus (late fourth century AD). Familiar with this model, both a medieval scribe and his reader would know that every *littera* had a name (*nomen*) and possible actual representations on parchment (*figurae*). There was, of course, the question of *potestates*, the sound hidden behind the letter, which falls outside the main focus of this paper.[4] Usually, the concept of a *littera* is applied in studies of letter shapes, their intended graphemic value and phonological implications (Laing 1999: 255–259; Laing and Lass 2003). Digital transcribers, having designed a pool of symbols and conventions, appear to construct their own meta-version of the manuscript, providing a single symbol, *littera*, for a range of shapes on the page. It is also possible to look at abbreviations through the same lens. The application of Donatus's model to abbreviations can be illustrated on the basis of a frequent abbreviation symbol, here referred to as 'superscript *a*' (Fig. 1).

---

[4] One should, however, appreciate the repercussions of inconsistent or misleading transcription procedures in the interpretation of the underlying phonetic value of abbreviations.

Figure 1. Potential *litterae* for superscript *a*[5]

> [*ra*] as in p*y 'pray'
> [*au*] as in pen*nce 'penance'
> [*ua*] as in countyn*ns 'countinuance'
> [*a*] as in mysch*unce 'mischance'[6]

What one can see on the page is the *figura*. The *litterae* have to be substituted in the decoding process by the reader (or another scribe, the copyist, for instance; see the discussion of inferential unpacking below). However, for a digital transcriber the most important thing is to design a symbol which will be consistently applied to represent a given *figura*, or a range of *figurae* with the same underlying *litterae*.

Medieval scribes and their audience were familiar with the classic abbreviation system of Latin manuscripts, as evidenced by the bulk of abbreviated Latin words, compiled by Martin ([1910] 2007). One can surely notice the continuation of Latin patterns into vernacular writings (Roberts 2005: xx). The scribes must have been selecting their variants in a fully conscious manner and, consequently, a contemporary reader was able to reconstruct the textual fabric without much difficulty.

Figure 2 illustrates the interpretation process: a graphic shape (*figura*) (an abbreviation, in our case) is interpreted to have an underlying letter value (one or more *litterae*) as well as a sound value. In the case of abbreviations, the decoder must be aware of the potential underlying value (or values) of a given graphemic shape, and unveil it along similar lines to those presented in the figure: consult his or her mental lexicon and reach a decision as to what is possible in a given context.[7]

---

5 The position of the abbreviation is indicated with an asterisk.
6 This example shows that a character associated with abbreviation may, in fact, stand for an unsuppressed letter. It is unclear why a scribe would put it in a raised position, just like a genuine abbreviation.
7 Rogos (2009) draws attention to the fact that abbreviating shapes may look very similar, if not identical, but still be intended to stand for different underlying *litterae*.

Figure 2. Inferential unpacking in Litteral Substitution Sets (after Laing and Lass 2003: 261)

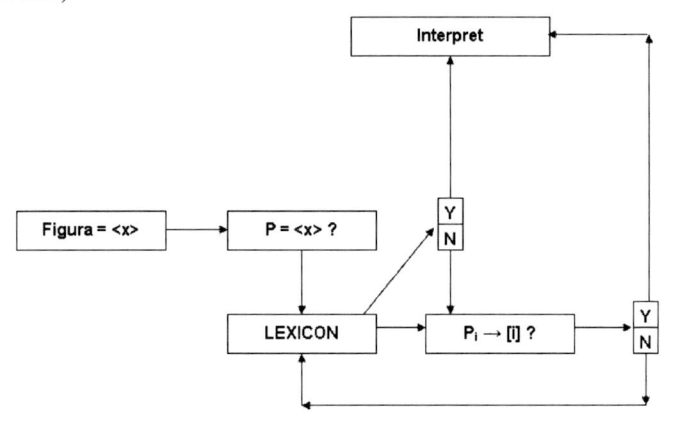

Digital editors are faced with a similar demand. The problem is that very often medieval scribes are not as neat in their execution of graphemes, abbreviation characters notwithstanding, as we would like them to be. Often the shapes used are far from handbook versions of manuscript conventions (*e.g.* Martin [1910] 2007:[8] vii–ix; Petti 1977: 22–24) and the transcription decision becomes a matter of interpretation, regardless of whether one wants to expand the abbreviation or simply represent it by means of a consistent symbol. This is a reminder that any transcription is, in essence, a translation, a substitution of one semiotic system with another, and as such "must be seen as fundamentally incomplete and fundamentally interpretative" (Robinson and Solopova 1993: 21).

3. Writing systems and dialects

Middle English writing systems are not just idiosyncratic. They may indicate the provenance of the manuscript and enable us to place a specific scribal tradition on a geographical map. Laing and Lass (2003) admit to such localizability in early Middle English, positing that the map of writing systems, even if marred with surface nubbliness, as they call it, may reveal the intended phonetic variants and thus lead to a fuller understanding of the Middle English dialectal continuum.

---

[8] He admits that his "marks of contraction" represent what is typically found on the page and "necessarily appear more formal and uniform than those which may vary with the caprice or carelessness of a scribe" ([1910] 2007: vii). The early-twentieth century patronizing tone aside, Martin makes an observation valid for all editing: that our symbols are a result of an agreement about what is typical and common. Problem cases are solved in an even more arbitrary fashion, very often at a discretion of a single transcriber.

Abbreviations also hide a specific sound intention, or *potestas* as Donatus would have it. The decision how to treat abbreviations, whether to expand them or not, and if so, how, is perhaps one of the most tantalizing tasks. In the end, abbreviated spellings may also serve as indicators of the scribe's dialect. For dialect comparison, *LALME* is *the* candidate for a reference tool. The atlas provides expanded abbreviations in italics and does interpret them dialectally. There are two things one should bear in mind, though. *LALME*'s selection does not cover all the lexical variants and,[9] what is more, there are some misinterpretations in the atlas as to the underlying meaning of an abbreviation. For instance, earlier research has revealed cases where a derivational suffix is taken for a plurality marker (Bugaj 2004a, 2004b).[10] Therefore, comparative studies with the help of such vast resources as *LALME* should be done with caution.

Moreover, expanding abbreviations may introduce arbitrary detail into the scribal repertoire. The *Piers Plowman Electronic Archive* guidelines advocate the use of expansion tags "to indicate the resolution of standard abbreviations", which is tricky because one quite often comes across non-standard abbreviations, not to be found in reference books, or indeed standard ones, which are put into an unexpected use. How can one be sure what the scribe's intention was when he used a superscript *a*, as in Fig. 1? Was his intention just a superscript letter or an abbreviated *au*? Expanded abbreviations, especially in the word-final position, provide an imaginary indication of a scribe's dialect. It often happens, though, that a scribe is inconsistent and may, for instance, use spelled out *-es* as well as an abbreviation typically expanded as *-us* for inflectional endings. I would personally be careful not to expand even a well-established abbreviation into what *we think* is the underlying letter value, not to mention the sound value.[11]

4. Abbreviation typology

Abbreviation serves a variety of functions. Apart from the self-suggestive time and space restrictions, Roberts (2005: 9–12) notices that more abbreviations were used in less important texts or less valued copies. This is quite enlightening when one compares the ratio of abbreviations used in various manuscripts of the *Canterbury Tales*. A more detailed enquiry of this kind falls, however, outside our scope here. Roberts (2005: 11) divides abbreviations into two major types on the

---

9   *LALME* includes a selection of diagnostic lexical items, *e.g.* 'daughter', but not 'winter'.
10 My study based on the *Wigtown Burgh Court Book*, which served as research material for the atlas as well, has shown that the expanded abbreviation *-us* was not a plurality marker, as the atlas has it, but an adjectival ending for a single but very common adjective 'wrangus'.
11 Further reasons for not expanding abbreviation are presented in Robinson and Solopova (1993), together with the basic principles of the *Canterbury Tales Project* transcription guidelines.

basis of the underlying *litterae*: letter abbreviations, and syllable abbreviations. This division is rather misleading as it introduces the notion of a syllable for what really should be treated just as a sequence of letters, as in Roberts's examples *co[ur]t* or *p[er]sone*. Another approach to categorizing abbreviations, stemming ultimately from Chassant's *Dictionnaire des abreviations latines et francaises*, is presented in Petti (1977). He distinguishes four major types: contraction, suspension (also known as curtailment), brevigraphs, and superscript letters. The type of abbreviation relevant for this paper somehow oscillates between a brevigraph and a superscript letter. A brevigraph, according to Petti (1977: 23–24), is a symbol representing at least two letters or a syllable, which may be similar in shape to one of these letters or look like an arbitrary shape (Figs. 3–4).

Figure 3. A selection of brevigraphs representing [*er*] (after Petti 1977: 23)

Figure 4. A hook in the word *eu[er]y* (*Ii*, fol. 64^r, ML 54)

A superscript (or superior) letter is a raised letter indicating that some of the immediately preceeding letters have been omitted (Fig. 5).

Figure 5. A superscript *t* in *þ[a]t* (*Lc*, fol. 70^v, ML 27)

With *r*+V / V+*r* combinations, the distinction is far from clear. In cases like *sp^{i}nge* or *g^{a}ce* (Fig. 6) the Vs may be interpreted either as a brevigraph, standing for the sequence of two letters, or a superscript letter indicating the omitted *r*.

Figure 6. Abbreviated [*ri*] and [*ra*]

For the sake of clarity, in this chapter such abbreviations will be referred to as superscript letters, to underline their supralinear position and their similarity to the non-abbreviated *figurae*.

5. Editorial practice in digital editing

Essentially, digital editing consists in transporting a text into the electronic medium. As Robinson and Solopova rightly point out (1993: 21), "text written by hand is not the same as the text on the computer screen. [The two semiotic systems] are formally distinct, in that a manuscript may contain an unlimited variety of letter forms but a computer fount ordinarily will not". In the ideal world, making an editorial decision should be based on an insight into all the possible variations to be encountered in a manuscript. It happens, though, that digital editors are faced with spellings and other features of manuscripts for which there are no procedures. Even though the *Canterbury Tales* is possibly one of the most well-described and well-known collections of manuscripts, there are still features of scribal behaviour which may destroy a preconceived transcription method. Work on the project has shown that rendering abbreviations is, indeed, one of such problematic issues.

In the project guidelines, the following has been established as to rendering abbreviations. There are symbols included in the transcription founts which represent the hook standing for [*re*]/[*er*] abbreviating hooks (Fig. 7).

Figure 7. Canterbury Tales Project transcription symbol for a 'hook' brevigraph in the word 'every'

The flourish representing the *es*, *is*, *ys* endings, as well as the macron standing for an omitted nasal are also included as separate graphic symbols. Other superscript characters are rendered by means of a tag "[sup][/sup]" which includes the particular letter used as a superscript. Problems arise when one cannot really discern the value of the encountered superscript shape, and such a dilemma is also present in the case of *r*+V / V+*r* abbreviating shapes.

6. Consistency of transcription *vs.* abbreviating conventions ("The Man of Law's Tale")

The manuscript material for the present study consists of seventeen manuscripts of the "Man of Law's Tale" (ML), digitalised in Poznań within the *Canterbury Tales Project*. The selection is not particularly biased towards any of the tale orders (Manly and Rickert 1940; Owen 1991; see the list in Table 1 below). This is important because ML is a tale which does not belong to any particular order of tales in the collection (Seymour 1997: 7), but is included in all manuscripts nonetheless.

Table 1. Genetic relationship of consulted manuscripts (Manly and Rickert 1940; Owen 1991)[12]

group a	$En^2, En^3, Ha^5, Ph^2, Ps$
group b	He, Ii, Mc
group d	$Bw, En^2, Fi, Ha^2, Ii, Lc, Ld^1, Ld^2, Ph^2, Ph^3, Ry^2$
additional	Hk, Ld^1, Mc

The manuscripts consulted for the purpose of this paper come from practically all groups distinguished on the basis of tale ordering by Manly and Rickert (1940), but for group c. What interested me, having for once access to such a range of hands and scripts, was whether the transcription procedures of the project team are uniform across this varied corpus, and whether the shapes and their underlying *litterae* can indeed be unified under a limited inventory of digital transcription symbols.

In the transcripts of the "Man of Law's Tale" all abbreviations possibly implying *r*+V / V+*r* were checked and compared against their actual shapes in the facsimiles. The resulting observations have been arranged by superscript shapes and presented below.

6.1. Superscript *e*

As expected, this superscript letter is not used for the *r*+*e* / *e*+*r* sequence, as the sequence in question would normally be rendered by a hook. By all means, the *e* *is* used in the manuscripts but for a different function, practically only for the definite article $þ^e$, where the superscript is clearly unconnected with an *r* value.

---

[12] Sigils are expanded in the list of primary sources.

6.2. Superscript *i*

The following manuscripts utilize this abbreviation: *Bw*, *En²*, *Fi*, *Hk*, *Ii*, *Lc*, *Ld²*, *Mc*, *Ph²*, *Ph³*, and *Ry²*. The abbreviation implying *r+i* / *i+r* is unproblematic because in all manuscripts the shape used in the superscript looks alike and, indeed, resembles the letter *i*. In practically all cases, the abbreviation stands for [*ri*], as in *cⁱst*, *pⁱue*, *sacⁱfises*, *etc.* whereas in only one word, 'circumstance', is the sequence [*ir*] abbreviated by means of the same shape (Fig. 8).

Figure 8. Superscript *i* used for [*ir*] *(Ry²,* fol. 71ᵛ, ML 219)

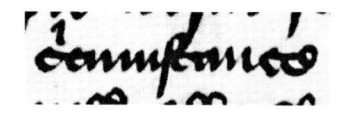

6.3. Superscript *a*

The situation looks more complex in the case of the superscript *a*. The execution of the superscript letter very often diverges substantially from a regular-sized *a*. The lemmatic context, however, makes it possible to decipher the underlying sequence of letters (see Fig. 2 and the discussion of grapheme interpretation in context). Manuscripts fall into several categories with regard to how this symbol is used:

1) for [*ar*]/[*ra*]: *Hk* [*ra*], *Ph³* [*ra*], *Ry²* [*ra*]

Figure 9. Superscript *a* used for [*ar*]/[*ra*]: *g*ce* (*Ry²*, fol. 70ʳ, ML 109)

2) for both [*au*]/[*ua*] and [*ar*]/[*ra*]: *Fi*, *Ha⁵*, *Lc*, *Mc*, *Ph²*, *Ps* (with [*ra*] preference)

Figure 10. Superscript *a* used for [*au*]/[*ua*], *ordyn*nce* (*Fi*, fol. 87ʳ, ML 665)

3) for *a* (superscript proper): *Ld^l a*

Figure 11. Superscript *a* used for *a, gr*unted* (*Ld^l*, fol. 141^v, ML 995)

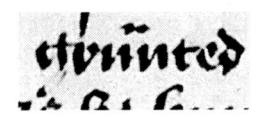

4) for *a* and [*au*]: *He*
5) for *a* and [*ra*]: *Ld^2*

Handbooks such as Petti (1977), which lists this abbreviation as a brevigraph for [*ra*] only, tell only half of the story. However, such sources make it justifiable to transcribe this shape as a superscript *a*. The logics also suggests this option as the *a* element is always implied, be it paired up with *r*, *u*, or standing on its own.

6.4. Superscript *u*

The following manuscripts utilize this abbreviation: *Fi, Ha^2, He, Ld^2, Mc, Ph^2, Ph^3, Ps, Ry^2*.

Figure 12. Superscript *u* for [*ur*]/[*ru*]: *c*ell* (*Fi*, fol. 81^r, ML 203), *hono*e* (*He*, fol. 48^v, ML 906)

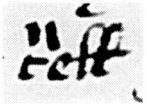

The shape in 'honour' (Fig. 12), the only such abbreviation in the whole ML *He*, has been transcribed by the project team as "[sup]u[/sup]". On closer inspection, however, doubts arise whether it should not have been represented with a different superscript symbol.

In the manuscripts, there is one more superscript abbreviating shape which requires attention at this stage. It is a shape composed of two strokes, with the possibility of the final one being an otiose stroke. Compare three images from three different manuscripts included in the material.

Figure 13. Superscript shape for *r*+V / V+*r* : *hono** (*En²*, fol. 61ʳ, ML 1025); *eu*y* (*Mc*, fol. 15ᵛ, ML 219); *vnd** (*Ph³*, fol. 50ᵛ, ML 691)

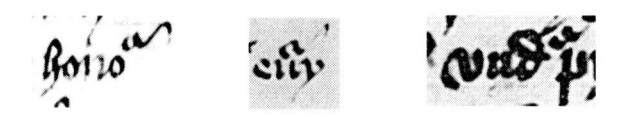

First of all, even though some scribes used it in words such as 'honour' (Figs. 12–13), this shape cannot be transcribed as a superscript *u* because it appears in other contexts where *ur/ru* would not be possible (Fig. 13). For the time being, let us consider this shape to be a superscript *r*.

6.5. Superscript *r*

The following manuscripts use this abbreviation: *Bw*, *En²*, *Ha²*, *Hk*, *Ii*, *Ld¹*, *Ld²*, *Mc*, *Ph³*, *Ps*, *Ry²*, some only in *ur* / *ru* contexts, some in other more ambiguous ones. MS *Mc* is particularly interesting at this stage, as it utilizes all the superscript characters discussed here, with clearly defined underlying sequences, and it also uses the *r* symbol.

Figure 14. The "Man of Law's Tale" (*Mc*, fol. 14ᵛ, ML 141–145), with abbreviations

```
How þ[sup]t[/sup] þ[sup]e[/sup] soudan & his baronage
And alle his leges sholde c[sup]i[/sup]sten be
And shall haue custance in mariage
And certeyn gold I not what q[sup]a[/sup]ntite
And þ²to founden þei sufficiant seu[sup]r[/sup]te
```

In *Mc*, however, this shape represents *r*+any vowel, not just *r*+*u* (Fig. 14).

The superscript shape which functions as a representation of a *r*+V sequence should be properly described as a brevigraph, using Petti's terms introduced above. The shape is arbitrary and, at times, confusing – as the case with superscript *u* illustrates. From the dialect reconstruction point of view, the *r* brevigraph is ambiguous when used in inflectional endings, like the comparative of adjectives, or in words treated as diagnostic variants, e.g. *water*. The superscript letters proper, with an unambiguous shape and an easily decoded underlying value, do not raise questions.

There are several doubts which arise on closer inspection of the symbol's employment. Considering the examples in Fig. 15, one faces a puzzling situation. In these words, the same abbreviating shape may stand just for *r* or for a V+*r* sequence, like in *eu** (*Mc*, fol. 17ᵛ, ML 323) and *eu*y* (*Mc*, fol. 15ᵛ, ML 219); alternatively, it could be just an *r*, as in *comaunde** (*Ld²*, fol. 88ᵛ, ML 397).

Figure 15. Possible underlying *litterae* for superscript *r*: *r*, V+*r* or *r*+V

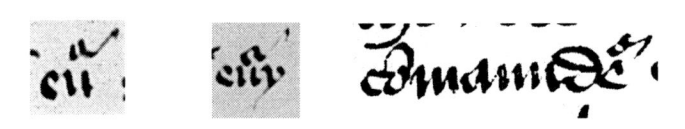

Especially in these hands (Fig. 16), a practically identical superscript shape is used. The first one has been transcribed by the project as superscript *u* in *neighbo*s*, with the underlying *u*+*r* / *r*+*u* interpretation, and as superscript *r* in *lux*ie*; if the shape is practically the same, a unanimous decision should be taken whether to transcribe it in the digital version as a *u* or *r*.

Figure 16. Brevigraph *r* transcribed as superscript *r* (*He*, fol. 65ʳ, ML 827) and as superscript *u* (*Ha²*, fol. 56ᵛ, ML 17)

This brevigraph is not just used in *u*+*r* contexts. Especially *Mc* utilizes this abbreviation for what seems to be a much wider range of underlying vowels:

a) in words like *aft**, *bitt*(nesse)*, *neu**, *neiþ**, *und**, *lett**, *douht**, *mod**, *fad**, *oþ*(e)*, *wheþ**, *wond**, *wynt**, *wat**; here the underlying sequence may vary depending on the dialect. The intended letter sequence in the word *water* may have been *watir* (but then perhaps the *i*-abbreviation would be used), *water*, or *watar*. Admittedly, for the Worcestershire area, where *Mc* has been located, albeit tentatively, by Manly and Rickert (1940, 1: 357–358), *LALME* has an unabbreviated or expanded -*ur* in the final syllable of *after*, *neither*, and *whether*. So, at least in these three lexical items, the intended letter sequence may have been *ur* and it could be represented in a digital edition by superscript *u*. However, in the other words *ur* would not be very likely, cf. for instance *under*, *never*, and *water*.

b) in some words where this shape seems to stand mostly for *er*, as an alternative to a hook, e.g. *mayst** in *Mc*, fol. 18ᵛ, ML 376. This is a good example of a word which could be *maystir* or *mayster* but no other options seem to be possible; similarly *leu**, *leng**, *grett**, *seu*te* 'surete/surite'. A rather straightforward *er* sequence seems to be intended in *ou**, *ou*come*, and *gou*naunce*. So this *figura* could also have *er/re* as a possible underlying sequence of *litterae*.

c) in words where this shape may either stand for *ur* or just *r*, as in *hono**, *labo**. Other such words include *myro**, *treso**, *trayto**, *Empo**, *senato**, *p*ueaunce*, *p*chase*, *p*poos*, *t*ne(d)*, *colo**, *tormento**, and *yo**.

d) in *t*ment*, where the shape could stand for *our* or *or* rather than any other V+*r* sequence.

This abbreviating symbol is, indeed, more ambiguous and versatile than any other abbreviation. One thing that connects all its uses is the underlying *r*, either on its own, or with any possible vowel. This is why the shape presented in Fig. 13, 15, and 16 should be transcribed at all times as superscript *r*, without assuming its constant relationship with the *u* vowel.

7. Conclusions

Scribal behaviour is very often difficult to capture within a preconceived set of transcription patterns. Digital editors, however, should pay the utmost attention to ensure that the procedures adopted are used consistently at all times. The survey of *r*+V / V+*r* abbreviation conventions has shown that some shapes are used very dependably and it is unproblematic to produce a transcription convention for them (as in the case of superscript *i*). Other shapes vary in *figurae*, but the context allows for them to be deciphered (the abbreviation for *au*, for instance). There are also cases where under one transcription symbol, as in superscript *a*, different selection of *litterae* may be hidden (*ra*, *au*, etc.). Finally, there are such abbreviations whose shape is rather arbitrary, and whose underlying *litterae* may actually vary from one manuscript to another. The superscript *r* is such an abbreviation. Its relationship to the hook and underlying *litterae* has been summarized in Fig. 17 below.

104   J. Kopaczyk

Figure 17. Relationship between abbreviations implying *r* and transcription conventions

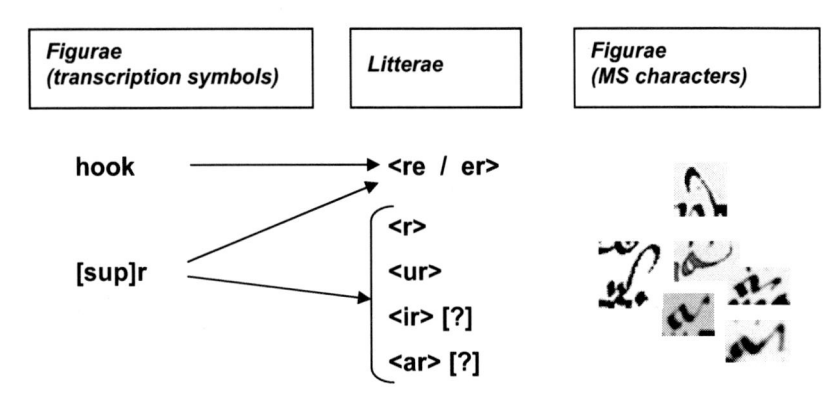

Figurae (transcription symbols)	**Litterae**	**Figurae** (MS characters)
hook	<re / er>	
[sup]r	<r> <ur> <ir> [?] <ar> [?]	

What matters is consistency of transcription procedures. As soon as we notice a problematic usage of a given transcription symbol, we should reach a decision and revise our practice. So it is advisable to transcribe this particular shape in Fig. 13–16 as a superscript *r* consistently, regardless of what kind of vowel grapheme it could also be represented with. Medieval scribes were by no means consistent and it is not our task to impose this consistency upon them. But if we want a trustworthy diplomatic digital edition, then consistency in representing the manuscript reality is crucial.

Primary sources (the "Man of Law's Tale"):

Bw   Oxford, Bodleian Library, MS Barlow 20
En²   London, British Library, Egerton MS 2863
En³   London, British Library, Egerton MS 2864
Fi   Cambridge, Fitzwilliam Museum, McClean MS 181
Ha² London, British Library, Harley MS 1758
Ha⁵ London, British Library, Harley MS 7335
He   Princeton, Firestone Library, MS 100 ("Helmingham")
Hk   Holkham, Earl of Leicester MS 667
Ii   Cambridge, University Library, MS Ii.3.26
Lc   Lichfield, Cathedral Library, MS 29
Ld¹   Oxford, Bodleian Library, Laud Misc. MS 600
Ld²   Oxford, Bodleian Library, Laud Misc. MS 739
Mc   Chicago, University Library, MS 564 ("McCormick")
Ph²   Cologny, Geneva, Bibliotheca Bodmeriana, MS 48
Ph³   Cheltenham, Phillipps Library, MS 8137
Ps   Paris, Bibliotheque Nationale, Fonds anglais MS 39
Ry² London, British Library, Royal MS 18 C.II

References

Blake, Norman F. – Jacob Thaisen
    2004   "Spelling's significance for textual studies", in: Cay Dollerup (ed.), 93–107.
Blake, Norman F. – Peter M. W. Robinson (eds.)
    1993   *The Canterbury Tales Project occasional papers*. Vol. 1. (Office for Humanities Communication Publications 5.) Oxford: Office for Humanities Communication.
Bugaj [Kopaczyk], Joanna
    2004a   *Middle Scots inflectional system in the south-west of Scotland.* (Studies in English medieval language and literature 8.) Frankfurt am Main: Peter Lang.
    2004b   "'for ye vrangus haldyn of thre bollis of beire fra hyre': Nominal plurals in south-western Middle Scots", *Linguistica e Filologia* 19: 53–74.
Dollerup, Cay (ed.)
    2004   *Worlds of words: A tribute to Arne Zettersten.* (Nordic Journal of English Studies 3, 1.) Oslo: University of Oslo.
Krygier, Marcin – Liliana Sikorska (eds.)
    2009   *Comoun peplis language.* (Medieval English Mirror 6). Frankfurt am Main: Peter Lang.
Laing, Margaret
    1999   "Confusion 'wrs' confounded: Litteral substitution sets in Early Middle English writing systems", *Neuphilologische Mitteilungen* 100, 3: 251–270.
Laing, Margaret – Roger Lass
    2003   "Tales of the 1001 nists: The phonological implications of litteral substitution sets in some thirteen-century South-West Midland texts", *English Language and Linguistics* 7, 2: 257–278.
McIntosh, Angus
    1956   "The analysis of written Middle English", *Transactions of the Philological Society* 1956: 22–25.
McIntosh, Angus
    [1973]
    1989   "Word geography in the lexicography of mediæval English", in: Angus McIntosh – Michael L. Samuels – Margaret Laing (eds.), 86–97. [Reprinted from *Annals of the New York Academy of Sciences* 211: 55–66.]
McIntosh, Angus – Michael L. Samuels – Michael Benskin, with the assistance of Margaret Laing and Keith Williamson (eds.)
    1986   *A linguistic atlas of late mediaeval English* [*LALME*]. 4 vols. Aberdeen: Aberdeen University Press.
McIntosh, Angus – Michael L. Samuels – Margaret Laing (eds.)
    1989   *Middle English dialectology: Essays on some principles and problems.* Aberdeen: Aberdeen University Press.

Manly, John M. – Edith Rickert
 1940 *The text of the "Canterbury Tales"*. Vol. 1: *Descriptions of the manuscripts*. Chicago: The University of Chicago Press.
Martin, Charles Trice
 [1910]
 2007 *The record interpreter. A collection of abbreviations, Latin words and names used in English historical manuscripts and records*. London: Clearfield.
Owen, Charles A.
 1991 *The manuscripts of the "Canterbury Tales"*. Cambridge: D. S. Brewer.
Petti, Anthony G.
 1977 *English literary hands from Chaucer to Dryden*. Cambridge, Mass.: Harvard University Press.
[*Piers Plowman*]
 Piers Plowman Electronic Archive and SEENET: Transcription protocols. (http://www.iath.virginia.edu/seenet/piers/protocoltran.html) (date of access: Feb. 2009.)
Roberts, Jane
 2005 *Guide to scripts used in English writing up to 1500*. London: British Library.
Robinson, Peter M. W.
 2009 "What text is really not, and why editors have to learn to swim", *Literary and Linguistic Computing* 24, 1: 41–52.
Robinson, Peter M. W. – Elizabeth Solopova
 1993 "Guidelines for the transcription of the *Wife of Bath's Prologue*", in: Norman F. Blake and Peter M. W. Robinson (eds.), 19–52.
Rogos, Justyna
 2009 Transcribing and editing graphetic detail in the manuscripts of Chaucer's "*Man of Law's Tale*", in: Marcin Krygier – Liliana Sikorska (eds.), 70–86.
Seymour, Michael C.
 1997 *A catalogue of Chaucer manuscripts*. Vol. 2: The *Canterbury Tales*. Aldershot: Scolar Press.
Vander Meulen, David L. – G. Thomas Tanselle
 1999 "A system of manuscript transcription", *Studies in Bibliography* 52: 201–213.

Copying space, length of entries, and textual transmission in Middle English tables of lessons[1]

Matti Peikola, University of Turku

1. Introduction: Medieval scribes and copying space

The output of a medieval scribe was in many ways constrained by the limitations imposed by the quantity and physical size of the writing support. In addition to the economic limitations arising from the cost and availability of the material chosen as support – especially in the case of good-quality parchment – spatial constraints were also caused by various other factors.[2] Even in manuscript projects where the available budget or channels of supply did not restrict the acquisition of material, scribal treatment of the written space was conditioned by the intended use of the book under preparation. If the book was intended to be portable, for example, its outer dimensions and weight would have to stay within reasonable limits. As illustrated by the thirteenth-century Latin "pocket" Bibles, this practical requirement could make scribes reduce the size of their handwriting to accommodate the intended amount of text in the codex – sometimes to a degree which probably hindered reading. As a case in point, De Hamel (2001: 119) mentions *Free Library of Philadelphia MS 39* – a tiny Bible of 55 lines per page with "hardly more than a millimetre a line".

Professional scribal practice also involved a number of layout conventions which would have an impact on the scribal treatment of space. Among other things, later medieval professional scribes were expected to furnish their texts with adequate margins and leave enough room for initials, rubrics, running heads and other elements signalling the *ordinatio*.[3] Scribes also had to take into account the requirements imposed on written space by genre expectations, such as placing each verse of a poem in a separate line.[4]

---

1 I am grateful to the following institutions and libraries for allowing me to inspect their manuscripts and/or obtain reproductions of them for the research reported in this article: The Beinecke Rare Book and Manuscript Library, New Haven; Cambridge University Library; Corpus Christi College, Cambridge; Emmanuel College, Cambridge; Gonville & Caius College, Cambridge; The John Rylands University Library, Manchester; Magdalene College, Cambridge; The Morgan Library, New York; The New York Public Library; Queen's College, Oxford; and The Scheide Library, Princeton. The research reported here has been funded by the Academy of Finland, decision numbers 136404, 141022.
2 For the economic factors involved in the acquisition of parchment, see *e.g.* Bischoff (1990: 10), De Hamel (1992: 12–13), Clanchy (1993: 121–122), and De Hamel (1994: 86). The significance of the writing support for the study of medieval texts more generally has recently been discussed by Caie (2008: 12–17).
3 For elements of the *ordinatio* in gothic manuscripts see especially Parkes (1976).
4 Medieval layout conventions for verse are discussed for example by Clemens – Graham (2007: 87–88).

In addition to their impact on extra-linguistic or extra-textual elements, spatial constraints on manuscript production would also affect the language and content of scribal texts and thereby play a role as a source of variation in textual transmission. In a situation where the space available in the copy under preparation was for one reason or another more restricted than in the exemplar, the scribe might attempt to abridge the text(s) being copied in various ways, including summary, omission and/or abbreviation. A scribe's use of conventional abbreviations need not as such reflect a concern with copying space, but when an increased use of abbreviations correlates with increasingly compressed handwriting – for example at the end of a quire or a booklet – there is obviously more reason to suspect the influence of spatial constraints.

Some scribes were prompted to omit textual material to save copying space (and time) when one and the same stretch of text occurred more than once in the exemplar. This motivation is very concretely expressed in a rubric at the end of the *Psalter* in a copy of a complete *Wycliffite Bible* in *Oxford, Bodleian Library, MS Fairfax 2*: "Here endith the Sauter, but mo salmes suwen, than ben writen in the Sauter, whiche ben writen in dyuerse chapitles of the bible before and after, whiche it is no nede to writen hem twies; therfor we enden here, and here bigynneth a prologe vpon Prouerbis of Salomon" (Forshall – Madden 1850, II: 888). The exemplar presumably contained the *Canticles* after the *Psalter*, in the manner characteristic of many manuscripts of the *Wycliffite Bible*. As the text of the *Canticles* was derived from other biblical books contained in the same volume, the scribe chose not to duplicate them in his work. Instead, he simply provided a list of them with book and chapter references (see Forshall – Madden 1850, I: xlviii; Dove 2007: 257).

Scribes may also have judged that some elements of the text in the exemplar were less central than others to the *matere* of the manuscript being prepared and therefore chose to omit them from the copy to save space. Extensive marginal glosses, for example, seem to have been in danger of being excised or shortened for this reason. An example is provided by *Warminster, MS Longleat House 29* – a fifteenth-century anthology which contains a copy of the "Parson's Tale" (for the manuscript, see Ogilvie-Thomson 1988: xvii–xxxi). According to Partridge (2007: 340), small margins seem to have been one of "the determining factors" in the tendency of the scribe of the manuscript "to select among and abbreviate indexing glosses". Although indexing glosses, which reproduce in the margin the names of *auctores* mentioned in the body of the text, are an established element in the transmission of the *Canterbury Tales* (see *ibid.* 352 n. 26), the scribe of the *Longleat* manuscript evidently felt that their full preservation was not necessary for the purposes of the anthology he was compiling.

An effective method of saving space was to provide *incipits* (opening words) for passages instead of writing them out in their entirety. Passages often subjected to such treatment in Middle English texts include citations from *auctoritates* – for example various biblical and patristic quotations used by writers to back up their argumentation – and common prayers. This practice especially seems to have been applied to passages in Latin incorporated into sermons and other vernacular theological writings. In a passion meditation ascribed to Richard Rolle in *Oxford, Bodleian Library, MS e Mus. 232*, for example, the text consists of a long series of supplications, many of which conclude with Latin prayers for which only the *incipit* followed by *etcetera* is provided; for example *Domine Ihesu Criste, fili dei viui, pone passionem, etcetera*, in the opening words of a prayer in *The Hours of the Cross* (Ogilvie-Thomson 1988: 70).

Providing *incipits* for citations of *auctoritates* and common prayers may have signalled the scribe's assumption of the audience's familiarity with the passages quoted, so that only cues needed to be provided for them. In addition to the familiarity factor, the scribe could also opt for citation by *incipit* if one and the same passage was repeated several times within the same text or manuscript (cf. the case of *Fairfax 2*). This practice is found for example in *Yale University, Beinecke Library, MS 360*, which is an early fifteenth-century *Psalter-Hours* in English, i.e. a book in which the *Hours of the Virgin* follow the *Psalms*. Since the text of all the psalms was given in full in the *Psalter* part of the manuscript, the scribe provided only *incipits* for the psalms occurring in the *Hours of the Virgin* (and in the *Penitential Psalms* and *Office of the Dead* copied after the *Hours*).[5]

2. Tables of lessons

Texts formatted as tables could present scribes with particular spatial challenges. In the tabular genre discussed in this chapter, *incipits* form the major content of the texts. Tables of lessons (*capitularia*) were developed as liturgical reference tools, allowing the user to easily find in the *Bible* the passages (pericopes) read at Mass on the various fixed and moveable occasions occurring during the ecclesiastical year.[6] Since they are referential tools linked to the text of the *Bible*, the tables provide only a short text sequence from the beginning of each pericope, enabling the user to locate it unambiguously in the full text.

Since the Mass pericopes were read (or recited) in Latin, it is only natural that the great majority of medieval representatives of the *capitularia* genre were likewise written in this language. In England, however, a large number of these texts survives in English.[7] They are almost invariably affixed to fifteenth-century cop-

---

5   A description of the manuscript is available in Shailor (1987: 204–206).
6   For the historical development and context of these texts, see the discussion in Peikola (2005–2006). The study by Klauser (1935) remains a foundational work on the genre.
7   The question concerning the contexts in which the Middle English *capitularia* were used remains partly unresolved (for further discussion see Peikola 2005–2006: 365–367; Dove 2007: 62–67).

ies of the Wycliffite translation of the *Bible*, especially in manuscripts containing books of the *New Testament*.[8] Although the tables are a regular companion of the *Wycliffite Bible* – present in circa forty per cent of the approximately 250 extant manuscripts – their research potential for the study of its transmission has so far been largely neglected.

Unlike many earlier Latin tables, the Middle English tables of lessons also contain the *explicits* (closing words) of the pericopes. In general, the tables have an air of professionalism as regards their scribal presentation. Adjacent columns tend to be written in differently coloured ink (text ink *vs.* red ink) and the cell boundaries have usually been meticulously ruled to create a regular and compartmentalized layout. The script generally preferred in the tables is *textualis*. In later medieval England similar conventions of presentation occur for example in some medical and astronomical tables.[9]

My preliminary survey of the layout, rubrics, and range of contents in a large sample of the tables indicates that they often seem to have been prepared together with the rest of the manuscript to which they are appended (Peikola 2005–2006). It is probable that the metropolitan stationers, who evidently arranged the copying of these manuscripts on a large scale in the first half of the fifteenth century, also sought to furnish them with the tables of lessons (see Dove 2007: 61). The preliminary survey also shows that the tables represent two major redactions.[10] The tables belonging to the larger (and presumably later) redaction can be further divided into a number of subgroups on the basis of three macro/paratextual features: (1) their organization of the liturgical material; (2) the contents and ordering of their rubrics; (3) certain elements of the *mise-en-page*, such as the order and layout of the text columns (see further Peikola 2005–2006). Variation in the three features tends to correlate, strengthening the probability that the subgroups are associated with specific contexts or stages in the transmission of the *Wycliffite Bible*.

---

8   The Wycliffite tables have recently been discussed by Peikola (2005–2006) and Dove (2007: 58–67). Peikola (2005–2006, Appendix A) provides a provisional inventory of the tables.
9   See Voigts (1989: 356–380) for the use of tables and other visual material in medieval English scientific and medical books. Eisner (1980) and Mooney (1998) have edited two influential later fourteenth-century English calendrical texts which largely rely on tabular presentation of the material.
10 The tables can be divided into two major redactions on the basis of the letters of the alphabet used in them to identify the subdivisions of biblical chapters. One (presumably earlier) redaction survives in a few tables only; its readings generally conform to the Earlier Version of the *Wycliffe Bible*. The other is represented by a great majority of the extant tables, and its readings variably tend towards the Later Version. The different alphabetical schemes of the redactions and the high degree of textual variation between them suggest that they may be derived from different archetypes and have largely separate textual traditions (see further Peikola 2005–2006).

The preliminary survey makes it possible to construct a broad typology of the tables based on the macro/paratextual subgroups, but it does not address the precise textual relationships between (or within) different subgroups or adequately explain how the tables are associated with the evolution and transmission of the manuscripts in which they occur. Obtaining such information calls for an analysis of textual variation in the *incipits* and *explicits* of the table – an area that was decidedly overlooked in my earlier survey.

3. *Problematique*, data, and research setup

Even a cursory survey of the tables indicates that the amount of text in an individual entry (*incipit* or *explicit*) varies considerably from one manuscript to another. In the table of *Hereford Cathedral Library MS O.VII.1*, for example, the *incipit* for the first Sunday epistle in Advent is "We knowe[n] þis tyme þ[a]t þe our is" (fol. 6ʳ), while *New York Public Library MS MA 66* reads simply "we knowe[n]" (fol. 2ʳ; abbreviations expanded in square brackets). At the same time it may be observed that in some tables the entries fill the cells drawn for them quite fully, whereas in other tables many entries are conspicuously shorter than the size of the cells would allow.[11] Variation of this kind suggests that the size of the cells and the copying space available in them may have affected the length of entries in the tables and thereby played a role in their textual transmission. The purpose of the present paper is to explore this variation and its textual implications more systematically.

To study the impact of the copying space on the transmission of the tables, I chose to collate forty readings in a sample of seventeen tables of the later redaction, for which photographic images were available to me.[12] The tables represent five subgroups as follows:

Subgroup 1 (three tables)

Cambridge, Corpus Christi College, MS Parker 147 (1a)
Princeton, William H. Scheide, MS 12 (1b)
Dallas, Southern Methodist University, Bridwell Library, MS 7 (1c)[13]

---

11 Examples of tables of the first kind are those of *Cambridge, University Library, MS Ll.1.13; Manchester, John Rylands University Library, MS English 80*; and *New York Public Library, MS MA 64*. Short entries in comparison to the size of the cells are found for example in the tables of *London, British Library, MS Lansdowne 455* and *MS Royal 1.B.vi*, and *Cambridge, Corpus Christi College, MS Parker 147*.

12 Since the relationship between the redactions is not a concern of the present enquiry, no tables representing the first redaction were included in the analysis.

13 The Bridwell manuscript is available in a digital facsimile edition, published by the Octavo Corporation on a CD-ROM in 1999.

Subgroup 2 (three)

Cambridge, University Library, MS Ll.1.13 (2a)
Cambridge, Emmanuel College, MS 34 (2b)
Cambridge, Gonville & Caius College, MS 343/539 (2c)

Subgroup 3 (four)

New York, Public Library MS MA 65 (3a)
Princeton, William H. Scheide, MS 13 (3b)
Oxford, Queen's College, MS 388 (3c)
Oxford, Christ Church College, MS 146 (3d)

Subgroup 4 (five)

Cambridge, Emmanuel College, MS 108 (4a)
Cambridge, Magdalene College, MS Pepys 2073 (4b)
New York, Morgan Library, MS M.400 (4c)
Oxford, Christ Church College, MS 145 (4d)
Manchester, John Rylands University Library, MS English 80 (4e)

Subgroup 5 (two)

Cambridge, Magdalene College, MS Pepys 15 (5a)
New York, Public Library, MS MA 64 (5b)

The forty readings collated in these tables comprise the *incipits* and *explicits* of the first twenty epistle, gospel and *Old Testament* pericopes from the beginning of the *Temporale* – the section found at the beginning of the tables. The pericopes are identified in Table 1 by their liturgical occasion and biblical reference. Henceforth the readings will be referred to by the number of the pericope (1–20), followed by an "*in*" (for *incipit*) or "*ex*" (for *explicit*).

Table 1. The pericopes analysed

No.	Liturgical occasion	Biblical reference
1	First Sunday in Advent: Epistle	Romans 13:11–14
2	First Sunday in Advent: Gospel	Matthew 21:1–9
3	First Wednesday in Advent: Epistle	James 5:7–10
4	First Wednesday in Advent: Gospel	Mark 1:1–8
5	First Friday in Advent: Epistle	Isaiah 51:1–8
6	First Friday in Advent: Gospel	Matthew 3:1–6

7	Second Sunday in Advent: Epistle	Romans 15:4–13
8	Second Sunday in Advent: Gospel	Luke 21:25–33
9	Second Wednesday in Advent: Epistle	Zachariah 8:3–8
10	Second Wednesday in Advent: Gospel	Matthew 11:11–15
11	Second Friday in Advent: Epistle	Isaiah 62:6–12
12	Second Friday in Advent: Gospel	John 1:15–18
13	Third Sunday in Advent: Epistle	1 Corinthians 4:1–5
14	Third Sunday in Advent: Gospel	Matthew 11:2–10
15	Ember Wednesday in Advent: Lesson	Isaiah 2:2–5
16	Ember Wednesday in Advent: Epistle	Isaiah 7:10–15
17	Ember Wednesday in Advent: Gospel	Luke 1:26–38
18	Ember Friday in Advent: Epistle	Isaiah 11:1–5
19	Ember Friday in Advent: Gospel	Luke 1:39–47
20	Ember Saturday in Advent: First lesson	Isaiah 19:20–22

In addition to the collation of the readings, the length of each entry was calculated by counting the number of characters (letters and numbers) it contains; to avoid ambiguity in the procedure, all punctuation marks, line fillers, and superscripted graphs (used to signal abbreviation or possibly simply otiose in function) were excluded from the count. On the basis of the character counts for each pericope, the average (mean) and standard deviation for the length of the *incipits* and *explicits* was calculated for each table. To interpret the character counts of the entries in the context of how writing space is generally used in each table, two other variables were also included in the analysis: The number of written lines per manuscript page in the table, and the number of characters per line in the table. The latter variable was calculated as the mean length of the first five consecutive lines in the opening rubric of the table.[14]

4. Analysing copying space in the tables

4.1. A working hypothesis

The maxim *lectio brevior potior* advises textual critics to opt for the shorter variant as the more original reading when all other criteria fail to indicate the direction of variation in a lemma – *i.e.* whether observed variation is to be interpreted as an instance of scribal expansion or abridgement.[15] The maxim is evidently based on

---

14 In a few tables with short opening rubrics, the average had to be based on fewer than five lines.
15 According to Miller (2006), *lectio brevior potior* is often attributed to the German biblical editor Johann J. Griesbach (d. 1812). Although the principle has been repeated in recent authoritative handbooks of textual criticism, Miller regards its perception as a maxim as inher-

the scribes' presumed tendency to elaborate readings in their exemplars by making their sense more complete and explicit.[16] It can be argued, however, that in the tables of lessons at hand there are in general no such scribally motivated grounds to regard the shorter variants as the more original ones. If anything, the opposite position seems more warranted: In other words, the general direction of variation was for the entries to become shorter in the course of transmission.

The nature of the tables as texts suggests that if the entries were already short in the exemplar, scribes as a rule would not have taken the trouble of trying to extend them. To extend the entries beyond expanding their conventional abbreviations would have required the scribe to extract the longer *incipits* and *explicits* one by one out of the biblical text – a laborious and time-consuming procedure – unless another table of lessons or a full-text lectionary in English was readily available, or the scribe was capable of supplementing the entries from memory. Moreover, unlike many other medieval genres, where there was usually room for at least some scribal creativity when a "deficient" exemplar had to be emended (cf. Kane 1960: 128–146), we can surmise that scribes copying tables of lessons would generally have been reluctant to extend short entries unless they were relatively certain of the accuracy of the readings. Since the tables were intended to function as referential aides for locating precise textual passages, a cavalier attitude in the extension of entries would easily have led to catastrophic consequences with regard to the referential integrity between a table and the corresponding full text. On the other hand, shortening the entries found in the exemplar, for example to make them fit into the cells in the copy under preparation, would obviously not have required any extra compilatory efforts from the part of the scribe. On these grounds, then, the position that longer readings generally represent an earlier stage in the transmission of the tables will be adopted as a working hypothesis for the following analysis.

4.2. General observations

The analysis shows, to start with, that the length of the entries does not vary randomly between the five subgroups, but that there seems to be a correlation between length and subgroup membership. As illustrated in Table 2, the entries in any single subgroup deviate less from the average length in that subgroup than is the case in the data as a whole. In other words, there is more variation in entry length across the subgroups than within them. This finding indicates that the length of the entries is con-

---

ently problematic: "While the shorter reading is often, perhaps usually, preferable, this is only a symptom and not a cause" (ibid. 16).

16 Kane (1960: 136), discussing *Piers Plowman*, formulates this tendency as follows: "In general they [scribes] were anxious to make the text more intelligible. To this end they very often made its utterance more explicit, changing its wording so that relationships of meaning were more fully expressed". See also Miller (2006: 13).

nected with the transmission of the tables, and that the subgroups seem to offer a meaningful basis for exploring the influence of copying space.

Table 2. Standard deviation in lengths of entries in subgroups 1–5

Subgroup	1	2	3	4	5	1–5
Incipits	1.54	2.14	2.16	2.07	1.20	3.23
	(60)	(60)	(80)	(100)	(40)	(340)
Explicits	2.93	2.95	2.19	2.08	1.57	3.68
	(60)	(60)	(80)	(100)	(40)	(340)

Note: Numbers in brackets indicate the number of entries on which the calculation is based.

Another general observation regarding the data as a whole is that the *explicits* are on average slightly longer than the *incipits*. As illustrated in Table 3, in addition to characterizing the whole data, this finding applies specifically to four of the five subgroups. The layout of the entries in the tables may offer a clue to interpreting the finding. Since the explicits are always placed in the final column of the tables – the one located furthest towards the right-hand margin – scribes were able to extend them across the cell boundary into the margin if they wished to copy the exemplar readings in their full length (see *e.g.* tables 2a and 5a). The same treatment could not be applied to the *incipits*, however, as the column containing them is located in the middle of the table.

Table 3. Average length of entries in subgroups 1–5

Groups	1	2	3	4	5	1–5
Incipits	13.40	17.30	11.10	11.00	9.00	12.31
	(60)	(60)	(80)	(100)	(40)	(340)
Explicits	13.68	17.93	12.73	10.18	9.88	12.73
	(60)	(60)	(80)	(100)	(40)	(340)

Note: Numbers in the brackets indicate the number of entries on which the calculation is based.

A third general observation concerns the relationship between the length of the lines and the length of the entries in one and the same table. Table 4 shows that there is no one-to-one correlation between these two variables: The tables with the longest lines do not automatically have the longest entries or *vice versa*. Table 4d is a case in point: With 70 characters per line it has the third longest lines among the tables, but there are no fewer than twelve tables with a higher mean entry length (1abc, 2abc, 3abcd, 4bc).

Table 4. The tables of lessons arranged in decreasing order by number of characters per line

Table	Scope	Characters	Lines	Entries
2b	NT	76	42	18.55
3c	ONT	72	60	12.60
4d	ONT	70	42	10.43
1a	ONT	69	60	13.55
1b	ONT	68	60	13.30
1c	NT	66	37	13.83
2c	NT	60	39	18.53
3b	NT	58	38	13.38
4c	NT	55	39	13.13
3d	NT	55	42	10.60
4b	NT	45	30	10.88
4e	NT	43	31	9.73
2a	NT	43	29	15.70
5b	NT	42	34	10.13
3a	NT	41	35	11.08
5a	NT	39	27	8.75
4a	NT	36	30	8.70

Note: "Table" = shorthand identifier for each table; "Scope" = scope of the manuscript containing the table ("NT"= *New Testament*, "ONT" = complete *Bible*); "Characters" = number of characters per line; "Lines" = number of lines per page in the table; "Entries" = mean length of entries (*incipits* and *explicits*) in the table.

As shown in Table 4, table 4d is affixed to a manuscript of the complete *Bible* (ONT). Among manuscripts of the *Wycliffite Bible*, complete *Bibles* tend to have a larger writing area than *New Testaments* (see Peikola 2008: 35–36). This characteristic is also reflected in the length of their lines. It is therefore probably not coincidental that the four tables affixed to a complete *Bible* in the present material (1a, 1b, 3c, 4d) are all among those tables with the highest number of characters per line. In tables 1a, 1b and 3c the physical size of the manuscript is also visible in the number of lines written per page (N=60), which is noticeably higher than in the other tables inspected. The smaller number of lines per page (N=42) in table 4d is possibly explained by the status of the table as a later addition to the manuscript (*Oxford, Christ Church College, MS 145*).[17] Although the original biblical

---

17 In addition to its paleographical features, the status of the table as a later addition in the manuscript is suggested by its use of the later redaction of the Wycliffite tables. The biblical translation contained in the manuscript is the Earlier Version of the *Wycliffe Bible* (see *e.g.* Dove 2007: 143).

part of the manuscript has fifty-eight lines per page (Dove 2007: 259), the scribe who copied the table did not choose to retain the same layout in his work.

Table 4 indicates that despite the conspicuous length of their lines, the tables in the complete *Bibles* do not systematically have the longest entries. This finding may mean – in support of our working hypothesis – that despite the available copying space in these manuscripts, the scribes of the tables reproduced the readings from their exemplars without seeking to fill the cells ruled for the entries in their entirety by supplementing the readings from another source.

There is some concrete evidence for such a scribal attitude in individual tables. In table 3c, for example, the use of short wavy line fillers at the end of many *incipits* and *explicits* implies that the scribe was concerned about not leaving empty space in the table cells (out of aesthetically motivated *horror vacui*?). At the same time, the presence of the line fillers bespeaks the scribe's reluctance to extend the text of the entries from that evidently contained in the exemplar.[18]

In table 4d the scribe similarly seems to have been concerned about the shortness of the entries in his exemplar *vis-à-vis* the larger spaces available for them in the copy under preparation. His partial remedy for the problem was to use unusually broad capital letters at the beginning of the entries and to expand some conventional abbreviations, including markedly even an instance of *nomina sacra* (*ihesu*), not normally expanded by medieval scribes (example 1).[19]

Example 1

a. *lord ihū c̄st* (4a)
b. *lord ihū crist* (4b)
c. *þe lord ihū crist* (4c)
d. *Lord ihesu crist* (4d)
e. *lord ihū crist* (4e)
(entry 1*ex*)

---

18 It is worth noting that three of the four tables in subgroup 3 (3bcd) contain line fillers at the end of the entries, so a scribe's adoption of them may also have been influenced by the exemplar. In the *Temporale* sections of the tables of the other subgroups, line fillers are only used in 2b.

19 For the *nomina sacra* and their abbreviations, see e.g. Clemens – Graham (2007: 89). The data also contain a few other expanded *nomina sacra*, possibly reflecting similar spatial concerns as in example (1). These include *Jesus* (Table 4b for pericope 2in), *Jerusalem* (5a for 11in), and *Jerusaleem* (5b for 11in).

4.3. Copying space and length of entries in subgroups 1–5

4.3.1. Length of entry as a textual variable

In terms of their character count for entry 1*ex* (see example 1), the five tables in subgroup 4 have the following order: tables 4c and 4d (fourteen characters); tables 4b and 4e (twelve); table 4a (ten). Despite their shared length of fourteen characters, however, the readings of tables 4c and 4d differ substantially as regards the presence of the definite article *þe* at the beginning of the entry. Moreover, although table 4a has the lowest character count, its entry for pericope 1*ex* is substantially the same as that of 4b, 4d, and 4e; the lower character count of 4a is explained by the presence of two abbreviated words in the entry (*ihū*, *c̄st*) against the single abbreviation (*ihū*) of 4be. These observations provide an obvious caveat to the discussion of entry length from a textual perspective: When individual entries in any given subgroup are compared in terms of length, arguments concerning the general shortening of the entries during transmission should not rely on character counts alone. We also need to look at the number of words included in the entry.

4.3.2. Observations on individual subgroups

4.3.2.1. Subgroup 4

Is it tenable, then, to argue that table 4c (in *New York, Morgan Library, MS M.400*), with its highest word count in entry 1*ex*, might represent the earliest textual stage among the five representatives in the subgroup (cf. the working hypothesis outlined in 4.1.)? As shown in Table 4, the average length of the entries in 4c (in number of characters) is clearly the highest in the group (13.13). This result is based on forty entries, so there is no doubt that it provides a better starting point for advancing the argument than a single entry such as pericope 1*ex*. Importantly, the result is also supported by the analysis of entry length in terms of number of words: When the entries differ in this variable, table 4c always has the longest reading (as in example 1). Moreover, if we compare the longer entries in table 4c with the readings in the other tables for those entries, we find – consistently with the working hypothesis – that such entries in table 4c are not idiosyncratic variants but are clearly part of the larger textual tradition of the tables. This is illustrated in example 2, giving all seventeen readings for entry 3*ex*, arranged by the decreasing number of words in the entry and with the number of characters as the secondary ordering principle (example 2a, for instance, contains seven words and nineteen characters).

Example 2

a. *Ʒou in þe name of þe lord* (1a) [7/19]
b. *Ʒou in þe name of þe lord* (1b) [7/19]
c. *Ʒou in þe name of þe lord.* (2b) [7/19]
d. *Ʒou ī þe name of þe lord* (1c) [7/18]
e. *Ʒou ī þe name of þe lord* (2c) [7/18]
f. *in þe name of þe lord* (2a) [6/16]
g. *ī þe name of þe lord* (3d) [6/15]
h. *name of þe lord* (3a) [4/12]
i. *name of þe lord* (3b) [4/12]
j. *name of þe lord* (3c) [4/12]
k. *name of þe lord* (4c) [4/12]
l. *Of the lord* (4d) [3/9]
m. *of þe lord* (4a) [3/8]
n. *of þe lord* (4b) [3/8]
o. *of þe lord.* (4e) [3/8]
p. *of þe lord* (5a) [3/8]
q. *of þe lord* (5b) [3/8]
(entry 3*ex*)

4.3.2.2. Subgroup 3

Example (2) indicates that in entry 3*ex* the reading of table 4c – which is the longest in subgroup 4 in terms of both word count and character count – agrees with the three shortest entries in subgroup 3 (tables 3abc). The longest entry of subgroup 3 (table 3d) for its part agrees substantially with the shortest entry of subgroup 2 (table 2a). Unlike 4c, however, table 3d (*Oxford, Christ Church College, MS 146*) may not represent the earliest textual stage in its subgroup. As shown in Table 4, the average length of the entries in 3d in terms of number of characters is only 10.60, which is the lowest in the whole subgroup. In terms of character count, the longest average entries in the subgroup (13.38) are those of table 3b (*Princeton, MS Scheide 13*).

A comparison of the lengths of the entries in subgroup 3 in terms of the number of words correlates with the results of the character count. The comparison indicates that among the thirty entries (of the forty analysed) which differ in the number of words, table 3b either has the single longest entry or shares it with one or two other tables in no fewer than twenty-seven instances. The only exceptions comprise three *explicits* (2*ex*, 3*ex*, 14*ex*) where table 3d has the longest entry compared to the three other tables of the subgroup (see example 2). In the light of our working hypothesis, it would therefore seem that table 3b represents the earliest textual stage of the tables analysed in subgroup 3.

The layout of table 3b shows that the scribe has copied some *explicits* across the cell boundary into the right-hand margin, which may reflect his general endeavour to reproduce the entries of the exemplar as fully as allowed by the tabular structure. The rather spacious layout of table 3d for its part indicates that the general brevity of the entries in the table was not due to a lack of copying space, but must have been derived from the exemplar. More textual data than those used in this study are required to explain the presence of the three long *explicits* in table 3d.

4.3.2.3. Subgroup 5

A similar investigation of entry length (in both characters and words) for the other three subgroups indicates that on the basis of the present data only subgroup 5 seems to offer a relatively unambiguous case. Of the two tables in this subgroup, 5b (*New York Public Library, MS MA 64*) has a higher average character count than 5a (*Cambridge, Magdalene College, MS Pepys 15*) – 10.13 *vs.* 8.75 – and it also always contains the longer reading in terms of the number of words when the tables differ in this variable (in nine entries).

As Table 3 shows, the *incipits* and *explicits* of this subgroup are on average the shortest among the five subgroups. The layout of the entries in both tables shows concrete evidence of the scribes' wrestling with copying space and of the shortening of the entries in the textual transmission. In the tables, many *explicits* have been extended into the right-hand margin across the cell-boundary and the *incipit* cells have systematically been completely filled up. Moreover, there are several *incipit* entries where the last word has been truncated unconventionally in the middle without a sign of abbreviation, probably because there was no more space in the cell (example 3).

Example 3

a. *So a mā ge[sse]* (5a, 13*in*)
b. *Þe aūgel ga[briel]* (5b, 17*in*)

4.3.2.4. Subgroup 1

Subgroup 1 shows remarkably little variation in the average character counts of the entries of its three tables (1a–13.55, 1b–13.30, 1c–13.83). A similar homogeneity characterizes the entries with regard to the number of words they contain, as only two of the forty entries show variation in this feature. One of the instances involves a possibly later correction in table 1a for entry 11*in*; the other consists of what appears to be an idiosyncratic scribal omission of a word in table 1b.

The similarities observed in the tables of group 1 may at least partly be explained by the production history of the manuscripts. Paleographically it seems not unlikely that tables 1a and 1b were in fact copied by one and the same scribe.

Moreover, both tables are found in complete *Bibles* (*Cambridge, Corpus Christi College, MS Parker 147*; *Princeton, MS Scheide 12*) which share some conspicuous codicological and textual features, such as being unusually collated in 12s and containing the rare "General Prologue" (see Dove 2007: 234–237 and 264–266).

Both tables 1a and 1b testify to the apparent scribal reluctance to expand their entries from those contained in the exemplar, along the lines envisaged in the working hypothesis. As tables attached to complete *Bibles*, the layout in both tables is relatively spacious. The tables, however, contain some instances where *incipits* end abruptly in the middle of a word (sometimes without any sign of abbreviation), even though there would have been plenty of space in the cell to write out the word in its entirety. The *incipit* of the *Old Testament* lesson for the second Mass of Christmas, for example, has the reading *þe spirit of þe lo* where the scribe has not expanded the last word into *lord* (quoted from 1b). It is probable that at some stage of the textual tradition preceding the copying of tables 1a and 1d, the size of the cell had constrained the copying of the *incipit* and had led to the truncation of the final word to *lo* (cf. the discussion of subgroup 5 in 4.3.2.3). In table 1c the same entry also ends abruptly in *lo*, but here the space in the cell would not have allowed the scribe to write out the word in full. While it is not impossible that the scribe of 1c copied the reading from his exemplar, the apparent lack of space in the cell may also mean that the scribe truncated the word himself. If so, 1a and 1b could be viewed as derivatives of 1c (subject to a fuller textual analysis of the tables).

4.3.2.5. Subgroup 2

The three tables of subgroup 2 have the longest entries in terms of both character count (2a–15.70, 2b–18.55, 2c–18.53) and word count in the individual entries. The length of the entries may mean that the subgroup belongs to an early stage of transmission of the Wycliffite tables belonging to the later redaction. In this case there is tentative evidence to suggest that the exemplar of the booklet which contains tables 2b and 2c in *Cambridge, Emmanuel College, MS 34* and *Gonville & Caius College, MS 343/539* respectively, may have been written in 1397 – an early date for a table of the later redaction.[20]

---

20   Both *Emmanuel 34* and *Gonville & Caius College 343/539* have the following note in their table which lists the *Sanctorale* pericopes: *þis was write[n] i[n] þe ʒer of g. su[n]dai next aftir lepe ʒeer of. b. In þe ʒeer of þe lord .M'. CCC°. lxxxxvij.* (quoted from *Emmanuel 34*, fol. 7v). On the grounds of the presence of independent errors in both tables, neither of them is likely to be a direct copy of the other, so the note evidently descends from a common ancestor dated to 1397 (see Rand Schmidt 2001: 73; Peikola 2005–2006: 348–349; Dove 2007: 59, n. 114). Because the note is not located in the table which lists the *Temporale* pericopes (*i.e.* 2b and 2c), the evidence does not directly imply that the hypartype of these tables must be dated to the year 1397. Nonetheless, since the *Sanctorale* and *Temporale* tables found in the *Emmanuel* and *Gonville & Caius* manuscripts were apparently designed to form a coherent

The forty entries analysed in tables 2b and 2c differ in their number of words on three occasions only. One of them involves a correction in 2c (entry 2*in*), while another is the result of an idiosyncratic scribal omission error in 2b (entry 13*ex*) – both in the middle of the entry. Neither of these readings is readily identifiable with an earlier textual status. In the third instance (entry 10*in*), the reading of 2c contains one word more at the end of the *incipit* than 2b. This suggests that 2c may be textually the earlier of the two, but a single attestation hardly warrants a firm conclusion.

The third table 2a (of *Cambridge, University Library, MS Ll.1.13*) has clearly the shortest entries in the group in both character and word count, so it is possibly textually later than 2b and 2c. As Table 4 indicates, the lines of 2a are noticeably short in comparison to the average length of its entries in terms of the number of characters. Similarly to tables 5a and 5b, the layout of 2a indicates that its exemplar probably had longer entries (such as those of 2b and 2c). This may be seen in the extension of many *explicits* into the right-hand margin, the fullness of the *incipit* cells, and the abrupt truncation of several *incipits* at the cell boundary (cf. example 3).

5. Conclusion

This chapter has explored the effects of copying space on textual transmission in a selection of Middle English tables of lessons attached to manuscripts of the *Wycliffite Bible*. I have argued that the nature of the tables as referential texts and their strictly compartmentalized layout in the manuscripts are conducive to a working hypothesis according to which the entries (*incipits* and *explicits* of pericopes) in general gradually became shorter in the course of their transmission in the tables. According to the working hypothesis, a major factor contributing to this development was the shortage of copying space in tables attached to small-sized manuscripts, which led scribes to truncate entries to fit them into the cells.

To investigate the issue empirically, I explored forty entries in seventeen tables representing five subgroups of the later redaction of the tables. The exploration indicated that several tables showed signs of the scribes' work having been constrained by copying space, and that the evidence of individual manuscripts generally supports the working hypothesis. Although the sample of entries investigated was relatively small, the results suggest that the method of exploring the length of entries by subgroup is readily applicable to a larger-scale textual criticism of the tables, for example with an editorial purpose in mind.

---

section which even circulated as a separate booklet (see Peikola 2005–2006: 348–349), it is likely that they are at least roughly contemporaneous.

The approach taken in the present study generally underlines the importance of taking into account the genre properties and manuscript layout (*mise-en-page*) of texts in the consideration of their textual matters – in this case specifically the use of space. For example, in the textual tradition investigated here, the presence of many abbreviated or truncated words in table entries – especially at the end of *incipits* – undoubtedly reflects scribal concerns with space. The reappearance of similarly truncated words in one and the same entry in several tables indicates, nonetheless, that what started as an individual scribe's "accidental" response to a spatial problem in his copy turned into a textually substantial feature in the transmission of the tables.

References

Alexander, Jonathan J. G. – Margaret T. Gibson (eds.)
    1976   *Medieval learning and literature: Essays presented to Richard William Hunt*. Oxford: Clarendon Press.
Bischoff, Bernhard
    1990   *Latin palaeography: Antiquity and the middle ages*. Cambridge: Cambridge University Press.
Caie, Graham D.
    2008   "The manuscript experience: What medieval vernacular manuscripts tell us about authors and texts", in: Graham D. Caie – Denis Renevey (eds.), 10–27.
Caie, Graham D. – Denis Renevey (eds.)
    2008   *Medieval texts in context*. London: Routledge.
Clanchy, Michael T.
    1993   *From memory to written record: England 1066–1307*. (2nd edition.) Oxford: Blackwell.
Clemens, Raymond – Timothy Graham
    2007   *Introduction to manuscript studies*. Ithaca, New York: Cornell University Press.
De Hamel, Christopher
    1992   *Medieval craftsmen: Scribes and illuminators*. London: British Museum Press.
    1994   *A history of illuminated manuscripts*. (2nd edition.) London: Phaidon Press.
    2001   *The book: A history of the Bible*. London: Phaidon Press.
Dove, Mary
    2007   *The first English Bible: The text and context of the Wycliffite versions*. Cambridge: Cambridge University Press.
Eisner, Sigmund (ed.)
    1980   *The Kalendarium of Nicholas of Lynn*. London: Scolar Press.

Forshall, Josiah – Frederic Madden (eds.)
    1850   *The holy Bible containing the Old and the New Testaments with the apocryphal books, in the earliest English versions made from the Latin Vulgate by John Wycliffe and his followers.* 4 vols. Oxford: Clarendon Press.

Griffiths, Jeremy – Derek Pearsall (eds.)
    1989   *Book production and publishing in Britain 1375–1475.* Cambridge: Cambridge University Press.

Kane, George (ed.)
    1960   *Piers Plowman: The A version.* London: University of London, The Athlone Press.

Klauser, Theodor
    1935   *Das römische Capitulare Evangeliorum.* Vol. 1. Münster in Westfalen: Verlag der aschendorffschen Verlagsbuchhandlung.

Miller, J. David
    2006   "The long and short of 'lectio brevior potior'", *The Bible Translator* 57: 11–16.

Mooney, Linne R. (ed.)
    1998   *The Kalendarium of John Somer.* Athens: The University of Georgia Press.

Ogilvie-Thomson, Sarah J. (ed.)
    1988   *Richard Rolle: Prose and verse.* (Early English Text Society OS 293.) Oxford: Oxford University Press.

Parkes, Malcolm B.
    1976   "The influence of the concepts of 'ordinatio' and 'compilatio' on the development of the book", in: Jonathan J. G. Alexander – Margaret T. Gibson (eds.), 115–141.

Partridge, Stephen
    2007   "Wynkyn de Worde's manuscript source for the *Canterbury Tales*: Evidence from the glosses", *The Chaucer Review* 41: 325–359.

Peikola, Matti
    2005–2006   "'First is writen a clause of the bigynnynge therof': The table of lections in manuscripts of the *Wycliffite Bible*", *Boletín Millares Carlo* 24–25: 343–378.
    2008   "Aspects of 'mise-en-page' in manuscripts of the *Wycliffite Bible*", in: Graham D. Caie – Denis Renevey (eds.), 28–67.

Rand Schmidt, Kari Anne
    2001   *The index of Middle English prose. Handlist XVII: Manuscripts in the library of Gonville and Caius College, Cambridge.* Cambridge: D. S. Brewer.

Shailor, Barbara A.
    1987   *Catalogue of medieval and renaissance manuscripts in the Beinecke Rare Book and Manuscript Library, Yale University.* Vol. 2. Binghamton, New York: Medieval & Renaissance Texts & Studies.

Voigts, Linda Ehrsam
    1989   "Scientific and medical books", in: Jeremy Griffiths – Derek Pearsall (eds.), 345–402.

The "Prologue" to the *Wycliffe Bible* with an English royal book stamp in the National Library of Russia

Olga Frolova, National Library of Russia

Henry VIII Tudor died in January 1547. He was succeeded by his son Edward, whose reign witnessed the final victory of the protestant Reformation in England (Elton 1991: 210, 212), in contrast with the continual vacillations between catholicism and a new protestant doctrine which were characteristic of the last years of his father's reign.

The very first parliament of the new reign, assembled in November 1547, repealed all the previous laws concerning heresies. Thus, "the writing, printing, distribution and retention of dissident religious matter was an open matter, to be resolved anew" (Youngs 1975: 171). Since new acts concerning this question did not appear till 1551, England for some time became a country where all types of religious literature could be published freely (Siebert 1952: 51). Various protestant movements (from moderate to extremely radical) became active, along with the representatives of older English heresies, first of all, the Lollards.

Lollards formed religious communities which appeared in England in the later fourteenth century, the name being first applied to the adherents of the famous reformer and theologian, John Wycliffe, in 1382 (Herbermann *et al.* 1917). English Lollards, who demanded the reformation of the English catholic church, were cruelly suppressed in the early fifteenth century. However, Lollards and their ideas survived in England until the Reformation in spite of persecution and a prohibition on disseminating their learning (Youngs 1975: 169, Trevelyan 1899: 346–348, Trapp 1999: 37). It is necessary to point out that one of the most important aspects of Lollard activity was edification, since they believed that the authority of the scriptures was prior to that of the priesthood. John Wycliffe and his pupils produced the first full translation of the *Bible* into English, a translation closely connected to the subject of this article. They also distributed the *Bible* in English among the middle and lower social classes.

Once Lollardy had become entangled with politics as a result of the Peasants' Revolt (1381), despite Wycliffe's personal opposition, it could hardly have escaped repression. A declaration of heresy came in 1382, and some of Wycliffe's followers were persecuted. A somewhat later, but ferocious official response was the law *De haeretico comburendo* of 1401, which required burning at the stake for owning or translating a *Bible*. Archbishop Arundel's *Constitutions* of 1409 (see Rymer 1727, 8: 627) imposed further penalties on heresy, where constitution "seven" explicitly forbade translation, and Sir John Oldcastle's attempted rebellion in 1413 only reinforced the royal distaste for Lollardy.

Some parts of the *Bible* had been translated into English well before Wycliffe by scholars such as Bede, who translated the gospel of St John (Fowler 1976). So-called glosses were composed in the Old English period (seventh–tenth centuries), some of which are interlinear translations of gospels and psalms, those parts of the *Bible* which occupied a central place in the church service.

These glosses were compiled by monks for their own use. Beside these, so-called paraphrases, the poetical accounts of the *Bible* were circulated. A considerable part of the *Old Testament* was also translated into Anglo-Saxon by the scholar and Benedictine monk Ælfric at the end of the tenth century. However, "the first and only complete Bible in English made during the Middle Ages…" is the *Wycliffe Bible* (Fowler 1976: 148). William Tyndale's later but incomplete version was first published in Cologne, possibly by Fuchs or Quentell in 1525, and in Worms by Peter Schoeffer the following year.

Up to now there has been no unanimity among researchers about the degree of Wycliffe's participation in this translation. The views could be summarized as follows. The existing manuscripts of the *Wycliffe Bible* are divided into two groups, early and late versions of the translation. The translations were made from the *Vulgate* – the Latin translation of the *Bible* made by St Jerome at the end of the fourth and the beginning of the fifth centuries. The early version was created during Wycliffe's lifetime (about 1370–80), Wycliffe himself contributing to this translation along with his pupils, such as Nicolas Hereford, John Trevisa and perhaps some others. The later version, which is considerably improved and was more widely disseminated and better known, was probably by John Purvey, a popular Lollard preacher.

2. The "Prologue" to the *Wycliffe Bible*

Considerable doubt still surrounds the authorship of the "Prologue" to the *Wycliffe Bible*. It was long believed that Wycliffe himself was the author of the original of *The true copye of a prolog*, but Margaret Deansley argued in 1920 for John Purvey, a pupil of Wycliffe. The work was published by Gough in 1540 under the title of *The dore of holy scripture* (*STC* 25587.5), and a second time by Robert Crowley, a London printer, publisher and protestant apologist author, in 1550. Crowley did not depend directly on Gough, however, since his text shows considerable fidelity to one of the manuscripts, *Cambridge University Library Mm.2.15* (Hudson 1985: 232–233). The most likely date of composition of the original seems to be around 1400, since there was a debate in Oxford on the question of translating the *Bible* about that time (Hudson 1985: 67–83; cf. Fowler 1976: 160; Stephen – Lee, eds. 1896: 51–52 [cited hereafter as *DNB*]).

This text is also the last of a series of Lollard publications which appeared between 1530 (*A proper dyaloge* Antwerp, [?1530] and *A compendious olde treatyse*

Antwerp Johannes Hoochstraten, 1530) and 1550. Hudson argues that the latter, a treatise arguing for the *Bible* in English, is largely the work of Richard Ullerston (Hudson 1985: 75–83; see also Hudson 1975). There were other contributors to what was a lively theological debate as well, perhaps stimulated by the appearance of the first parts of the *Tyndale Bible* in the 1520s. It seems significant that a text forming part of what appears to be a concerted effort to print Wycliffite works in the face of official disapproval also faithfully preserves the linguistic features of the original late Middle English text, rather than modernizing it, as one would expect, as if to valorize this form of the language as quintessentially and authoritatively Wycliffite.

As already mentioned, Wycliffe's works and those of his adherents were severely persecuted in England for about a century and a half, many manuscripts being destroyed. The Lollard legacy died hard, however, with both Thomas More and Thomas Cranmer associating protestantism with Lollardy. As for the Wycliffite translation of the *Bible*, it was very popular and was widely disseminated, often being read aloud to large audiences and rewritten many times (Hellinga – Trapp 1999: 16), especially in the first half of the fifteenth century,[1] which explains why many manuscripts have been preserved despite the repression. However, it was finally published only in the middle of the nineteenth century.[2] In the fifteenth and sixteenth centuries (before the appearance of Crowley's edition) only the "Prologue" had been published, in 1540 by Gough (British Library 1979: XXXI, 44, Ames 1749: 188). These editions were suppressed during Henry VIII's reign (Ames 1749: 188).

3. Crowley's edition: The copy in the National Library of Russia

There is a copy of Crowley's edition in the foreign stock of the National Library of Russia [NLR], which unfortunately lacks a title-page. We have identified the book by reference to the printer's name, the date of printing and the running title (*the path waye to perfect knowledge*) (Sayle 1907: IV, 373, Pollard – Redgrave 1976: II, *s.v.* Wycliffe). Finally, we have had an opportunity to compare the beginning of our book with the first leaf of one of the manuscripts of the *Prologue*, preserved in the Bodleian Library (*MS Bodley 277*) and published by the well-known Conrad Lindberg in 1999 (Lindberg 1999).

Furthermore, Crowley himself writes in his address to the reader: "I had perused this prolog (gentle reader) and was fully determined to set it in print to the edifiyinge of all suche as be desyrouse to reade and understand the holi Bible [...] It hath bene preserued wonderfully, euen in al the stormis of persecution [...]"

---

1 See the article about John Wycliffe in *DNB*, 63: 211.
2 In Forshall – Madden 1850.

("Prologue", fol. A4 recto et verso),[3] a comment which also made it clear that the NLR copy was indeed the "Prologue" to the *Wycliffe Bible*.

It is necessary to say something here about Crowley (?1518–1558), the printer and the publisher of our edition.[4] He was a poet, translator, theologian, preacher, and ardent partisan of the Reformation ideas. He is known to have taken part in the project of "producing a small library of protestant polemics and medieval literature with reputed Wycliffite associations" (Fowler 1976), and to have opened a shop for selling these editions in the 1540s and 1550s (King 1999: 167). Crowley was part of a larger movement which was producing these texts, often, as in this case, with the original late Middle English preserved – the motivation for which deserves further research. He was the first to publish *Piers Plowman* (the B-text only), a masterpiece of English medieval literature which was influenced by Lollard ideas, in 1550. Crowley explained Langland's English in the preface to the reader as "The Englishe is according to the time it was written in, and the sence somewhat darcke, but not so harde, but that it may be vnderstande of suche as will not sticke to breake the shell of the nutte for the kernelles sake" (fol. *ii^v), making no mention of the dialect. By contrast, the difficulty of the language is not mentioned at all in the preface to the "Prologue". Crowley also strongly associates *Piers Plowman* with the Wycliffite movement "in whose tyme it pleased God to open the eyes of many to se hys truth […] and crye oute agaynste the workes of darckenes as did John Wicklefe […] There is no maner of vice […] whiche this wryter [Langland] hath not godly, learnedlye, and wittilye rebuked" (fol. *ii^r).

Crowley also published three works for William Salesbury, the noted Welsh lexicographer, scholar, and *New Testament* translator, in the same year, one being a defence of the protestant doctrine of clerical marriage.[5]

We are not going to analyze the contents of this *Prologue* here, several works having been devoted to this subject, including *The Bible in early English literature* by D. C. Fowler.[6] However, it is essential to point out that the "Prologue" "[…] is not a translation, but an English introduction to the Old Testament […]" ("Prologue", fol. B4 recto). First of all, it is a Lollard polemical pamphlet, in which the author says that the *Bible* should be read by people of all estates (including *simple men*) ("Prologue", fol. R1 recto et verso). Secondly, the "Prologue" gives a survey of the *Old Testament* books as well as an explanation of their contents.

In the last chapter (the fifteenth) the author tells us how he translated the *Bible*. First, he speaks about his methods of translating in a particularly well-known passage:

---

3 In all quotations the orthography of the original is preserved.
4 See *DNB*, 13: 241–243 for details about his life.
5 *Ban wedy i dynny air yngai…* (*STC* 21612).
6 Cf. Fristedt (1953: 8).

...thys symple creature [as the author calls himself – O. F.], had mych trauaile wyth diuers felowis...to gather mani eld Bibles and...comune glosis...to make oo latine Bible somedell trwe,and than to studie it of the newe, the text with the glose, &other doctours as he might get: and specially Lire [Nicholas of Lyra] on the elde testamente, that helpyd full miche in hys werke[.] The thyrde tyme to Counsell wyth elde gramariens and elde diuinis, of harde wordis and harde sentensis, how hy [sic] myght beste be vnderstanden & translated. The fourth tyme, to translate as cleerly as he could...and to haue many good felowis...at the correctinge of the translation ("Prologue", fol. R1 recto et verso).

The author then gives some practical advice to translators. For example, he recommends first studying a sentence as a whole and understanding its meaning, but not translating word by word. He writes, "First it is to know that þe beste translatyng out of Latyne into Englysh is, to translate after the sentence, and, not onely after the wordis" ("Prologue", fol. R7 verso). He continues: "therfore a translatoure hath greate nede to studye well the sentence both before and after [the translating – O. F.]" (Davenport 1909: 234). The author also gives his recommendation on how to translate various Latin constructions, such as the ablative absolute.

As to the appearance of our copy, it is a very modest octavo, bound in brown leather without any particular decoration. However, there is a book stamp which is of special interest. The so-called Tudor rose under the royal crown is stamped in the center of both covers.[7] It is not clear whether this stamping was gold (if it was it has vanished in the course of time). There are two frames stamped along the perimeter of both book covers (one inside another), and stamped vignettes in the corners.

The so-called Tudor rose is specifically depicted (it looks double, since it encloses the white rose of York within the red rose of Lancaster) under the royal crown ('crowned') or without it. This rose appeared among the heraldic insignia of English kings during the reign of the first Tudor king, Henry VII. Descended from the Lancaster family himself, he married a daughter of Edward IV of York and united the dynasties of Lancaster and York, whose symbols were red and white roses (Davenport 1909: 216–217, Fletcher 1895: Plate V). The Tudor rose was used as a book stamp by Tudor monarchs: Henry VIII (Davenport 1909: 160–161, Fletcher 1895: Plate XXXI) and Elizabeth I (Davenport 1909: 245, Fletcher 1895: Plate XXXI), and then by James I, the first Stewart (Brassington 1894: 215–217).

4. Royal owners and translators

We can thus suppose that our copy belonged either to Elizabeth Tudor, or to James I (Henry VIII having died before its appearance in print).[8] Monarchs own-

---

7   Davenport (1909: 234). It is neither slipped nor dimidiated.
8   It cannot be Edward, since neither Davenport nor Fletcher mention the Tudor rose among his badges.

ing the *Wycliffe Bible* itself was apparently not unusual. Crowley claims that the version of the "Prologue" he used was to be found between the *Old* and the *New Testaments* in a copy "now in þe Kyng his maiesties Chamber" (prolog: t.p.). Henry VI also owned a *Wycliffe Bible* (Hudson 1985: 182).

As for Elizabeth, it is known that she possessed a considerable library, which contained books in beautiful silk and velvet bindings, decorated with embroidery (sometimes made by the queen herself, who was very skilled in embroidering) (cited in Warton 1840: III, 11), gold and jewels. A German traveller, Paul Hentzner, left memoirs of his visit to this library, kept in Whitehall at that time, in 1598. According to Hentzner, Queen Elizabeth's library "was well furnished with Greek, Latin, Italian and French books, all bound in velvet of different colours, yet chiefly red, with clasps of gold and silver, and [...] the covers of some were adorned with pearls and precious stones" (Brassington 1894: 228). But apart from books in richly decorated bindings, Elizabeth owned modest-looking books as well, often bound in leather and decorated with one of the royal heraldic insignia. A well-known English expert on book bindings, W. S. Brassington, writes that "upon a number of small volumes dated 1569 in the library of Lichfield cathedral we find a simple Tudor rose ensigned by a royal crown tooled upon the center of the sides (these books probably belonged to Elizabeth)".[9] The illustrations in the works of such outstanding English book-binding researchers as Davenport and Fletcher, also show pictures of a Tudor rose (similar to ours) on the books which belonged to Elizabeth (John Rylands Library 1907: 35).

Moreover, it is known that the *Bibles* were often presented to the Queen, the so-called *Wycliffe Bible* being among them. An exhibition of the English versions of the *Bible* was held in the John Rylands library in 1907, where the manuscript of the four gospels englished by Wycliffe was exhibited (John Rylands Library 1907: 35). This manuscript, historical evidence suggests, was presented to Elizabeth during her "progress through the City of London in January, 1558–1559" (Pemberton 1997 [1899]: viii, Jenkins 1958: 20–21, Black 1959: 4). Thus, our copy may well also have been presented to the Queen by Crowley, who was a popular preacher in London in the years of her rule.

However, this book could have found its way into the Queen's library in another way. She could have acquired it herself for her translating studies, which could have happened before her accession to the throne. In this case, a royal bookstamp could have appeared on it later. When this book was published, Princess Elizabeth was seventeen. She had acquired a brilliant education by this time from well-known and experienced teachers, among them the famous English humanist and teacher, Roger Ascham, under whose guidance the Princess translated from Latin into English and vice versa. She had a very good command of French, Italian, and Latin and a good command of Greek (Pemberton 1997 [1899]: vii, Wal-

---

9 See section 3 above.

pole 1758: I, 27–28). It is known that she did translations from French, Greek and Latin (from Boethius and Sallust) into English (Walpole 1758: I, 24). She also translated from Greek into Latin and from English into other languages (Williams 1972: 20–21). In 1545, she translated prayers and meditations of her stepmother, Catherine Parr, into Latin, French and Italian.[10] Perhaps she used Purvey's recommendations in the "Prologue" for her translation work.

As has already been mentioned above, our copy could also have belonged to Elizabeth's successor, King James I, since the Tudor rose appears among his book-stamps as well (Willson 1956: 19–20). It is known that he was descended from the Tudors, his grandmother being Margaret Tudor, Henry VII's daughter and Henry VIII's sister.

James was one of the best educated men of his time. He had a lonely, unhappy, difficult childhood, which resulted in the young king (James VI of Scotland) becoming addicted to reading very early on. One of his teachers was the famous Scottish humanist, the poet and historian George Buchanan (Willson 1956: 22).[11] The young king's library contained about 600 volumes and was likely to have been the biggest library in Scotland at that time (Willson 1956: 214). James maintained his love of books during his later life, *Bibles* and theological books occupying pride of place in his collection. James was fond of theological disputes and besides he needed these books for writing his own polemical works.

James I occupies an important place in English history as an inspirer and organizer of the creation of the so-called *King James Bible* (the English translation of the *Bible*, published in 1611). By the beginning of the seventh century, an urgent necessity for creating a new translation of the *Bible* for common use in England had arisen. Two different translations of the *Bible* (the so-called *Bishop's Bible* and the *Geneva Bible*) had been in use before this time.

The best linguists of the country were invited to prepare the new translation. The king himself supervised the process of their choosing and drew up instructions for them. These instructions contained many purely linguistic notes. The main purpose, according to the king, was to create a *Bible* which was easy for general understanding (Willson 1956: 214). It is interesting to note here that James's view coincided with the opinion of John Purvey, who had been persecuted and oppressed two centuries before. By the way, James could borrow some ideas from the author of the "Prologue". It has been believed that James himself translated some abstracts for the new *Bible*, but this has not been confirmed (Willson 1956: 214). However, he is known to have translated psalms from Latin into English (Willson 1956: 215), which he began in his childhood. In 1601, while still King of Scotland, he proposed to create a new metrical version of the psalms for

---

10 See section 3 above.
11 The National Library of Russia foreign stock contains a number of editions of Buchanan's works.

church and private service. He translated about thirty psalms and may have been interested in Purvey's advice.

It has not been possible to discover how and when our copy of the "Prologue" left the English Royal library. However, it is known that it came to the Imperial Public library (the National Library of Russia) as a part of the so-called Załuski library (collected by the famous Polish bibliophile Załuski brothers in the eighteenth century and brought to Russia after the partition of Poland at the end of the eighteenth century). The Russian National Library copy of the "Prologue" to the *Wyclif Bible* has a twofold interest for researchers. On the one hand, it is one of the first printed editions of a seminal tract in Middle English. On the other hand, its ownership, so far as it can be established, allows us to trace the perception of ideas contained in this work by later generations of readers. It also represents, ironically, the conscious preservation of a form of English rapidly becoming less comprehensible as part of the effort to make the *Bible* and Lollard tracts easily accessible to the common man. Finally, it is of the greatest interest that the monarch should own a copy of such a document, given the contentious history with which it was associated.

References

Ames, Joseph
    1749   *Typographical antiquities*. London: W. Faden.
Black, John Bennett
    1959   *The reign of Elizabeth, 1558–1603*. Oxford: Oxford University Press.
Brassington, William Salt
    1894   *A history of the art of bookbinding*. London: Elliot Stock.
[British Library]
    1979   *The British Library general catalogue of printed books to 1975*. Vol. 31. London: Clive Bingley.
Cole, C. Robert – Michael E. Moody (eds.)
    1975   *Essays for Leland H. Carlson: The dissenting tradition*. Athens: Ohio University Press.
Davenport, Cyril
    1909   "The bindings made for Henry, Prince of Wales", *The book-lover's magazine* 8: 234–235
Elton, Geoffrey R.
    1991   *England under the Tudors*. London: Routledge
Fletcher, William
    1895   *English bookbindings in the British museum*. London: K. Paul, Trench, Trubner and company.

Forshall, Josiah – Frederic Madden (eds.)
    1850   *The Holy Bible containing the Old and New Testaments with the Apocryphal Books, in the Earliest English Versions made from the Latin Vulgate by John Wicliffe and his Followers.* 4 vols. Oxford: Oxforf University Press.

Fowler, David C.
    1976   *The Bible in early English literature.* Seattle: University of Washington Press.

Fristedt, Sven L.
    1953   *The Wycliffe Bible, Part I: The principal problems connected with Forshall and Madden's edition. Stockholm studies in English* 4. Stockholm: Almqvist and Wiksell.

Herbermann, Charles George – Edward Aloysius Pace – Condé Bénoist Pallen – Thomas Joseph Shahan – John Joseph Wynne – Andrew Alphonsus MacErlean (eds.)
    1917   "Lollards", in: *The Catholic Encyclopedia.* New York: Encyclopedia Press, Inc., an online version available at http://www.newadvent.org/cathen/09333a.htm. Date of access: 11 February 2008.

Hellinga, Lotte – J. B. Trapp
    1999   "Introduction", in: Lotte Hellinga – J. B. Trapp (eds.), 1–30.

Hellinga, Lotte – J. B. Trapp (eds.)
    1999   *The Cambridge history of the book in Britain. Vol.3: 1400–1557.* Cambridge: Cambridge University Press.

Hudson, Anne
    1975   "The debate on Bible translation", *English Historical Review* 90: 1–18.
    1985   *Lollards and Their Books.* London: Hambledon.

Jenkins, Elizabeth
    1958   *Elizabeth the Great.* London: V. Gollancz

John Rylands Library
    1907   *Catalogue of an exhibition of Bibles illustrating the history of the English versions from Wiclif to the present time, including the personal copies of Queen Elizabeth, Elizabeth Fry and others.* Manchester: Manchester University Press.

King, John M.
    1999   "The book-trade under Edward VI and Mary I", in: Lotte Hellinga and J. B. Trapp (eds.), 164–178.

Lindberg, Conrad
    1999   *King Henry's Bible Ms Bodley 277. The Revised Version of the Wyclif Bible*, vol. 1. Stockholm Studies in English 89. Stockholm: Almqvist & Wiksell International.

Pemberton Caroline (ed.)
    [1899]
    1997   *Queen Elizabeth Englishings of Boethius, Plutarch and Horace.* OS 113. London: Early English Text Society.

Pollard, Alfred W. – Gilbert Richard Redgrave
    1975   *Short-title Catalogue*, 2nd ed., vol. 2. London: Bibliographical Society.

Rymer, Thomas
    1704-35   *Foedera, conventiones, litterae, et cujuscunque generis acta publica inter reges Angliae et alios quosvis imperatores, reges, pontifices, principes, vel communitates (1101–1654)*, vol. 8. 2nd ed. London: Jacob Tonson.

Sayle, Charles E.
    1907   *Early English printed books in the University Library Cambridge (1475 to 1640). Vol. 4 (Indexes)*. Cambridge: Cambridge University Press.

Siebert, Frederick S.
    1952   *Freedom of the press in England, 1476–1776*. Urbana: Illinois University Press.

Stephen, Leslie – Sidney Lee (eds.)
    1896   *Dictionary of national biography*, vol. 47. London: Smith, Elder, and Co.

Trapp, J. B.
    1999   "Literacy, books and readers", in: Lotte Hellinga – J. B. Trapp (eds.), 31–43.

Trevelyan, George Macaulay
    1899   *England in the age of Wicliffe*. London: Longmans.

Walpole, Horace
    1758   *A catalogue of the royal and noble authors of England, with lists of their works*. Vol. 1. Strawberry-Hill.

Warton, Thomas
    [1774-81]
    1840   *The history of English poetry*. [Reprinted by Thomas Tegg, London]

Williams, Neville
    1972   *The life and time of Elizabeth I*. London: Weidenfeld and Nicolson

Willson, David Harris
    1956   *King James VI and I*. New York: Henry Holt.

Youngs, Fr. J.
    1975   "The Tudor government and dissident religious books", in: C. Robert Cole – Michael E. Moody (eds.), 167–190.

Improvements, corrections, and changes in the *Gutenberg Bible*

Mari Agata, Keio University

1. Introduction

1.1. Variants at press

Variants within the same setting of a work are commonly found in books of the hand-press period; if any defect was found in an earlier printed sheet while the actual print run was still in progress, the press crew could and did briefly stop printing in order to correct it without reference to copy (Gaskell [1974]: 336–360). The resultant variants are thus called "stop-press" corrections or "stop-press" variants.

A collation undertaken by the present author has revealed stop-press variants in copies of the *Gutenberg Bible* (or the *42-line Bible*: hereafter referred to as the *B42*),[1] which proves that the first printing house in Europe already employed the practice of stop-press correction on a regular basis. As is often the case, the stop-press variants so far found in the *B42* are generally so subtle that they do not seem to be textually significant, especially since all of them, with only one exception, are what is known as "accidentals" – that is, minor changes to "spelling, punctuation, word-division, and the like, affecting mainly its formal presentation" (Greg 1950–1951: 21) made to a copy-text by scribes or compositors.

All stop-press variants, however, deserve attention. Even if they do not affect the meaning of a text, they can provide equally important clues as to what happened to the text at the printer's shop, and it is always worth examining what kinds of mistakes were considered so important that it was worth stopping an operating press to correct them. To some degree, those variants that are parallel to the accidentals that occurred at the composition stage are the richest source of information about the printing process; because they were made independently of a copy-text or a corrector's instruction, they may more clearly betray the hands of the press crew.

The purpose of this article, then, is to show that all stop-press variants deserve attention, in any examination of how the hands of the press-crew combined to transmit a text at the printing stage, even though the variants are not necessarily the result of corrections made in order to improve a text (in other words, intentional corrections) but could well have been the result of simple accident.

---

1   GW 4201.

1.2. Background of the research

The *B42* is regarded as the first substantial book printed in Europe using movable metal type. It is now commonly accepted that Johann Gutenberg of Mainz produced this two-volume Latin *Vulgate* around 1455. Despite its revolutionary impact, however, there are still gaps in our knowledge, both about the invention of printing itself and about the first ever printing shop, even though extensive studies have been conducted by a number of scholars to help improve the state of our knowledge. Despite their work, we still lack concrete details about the exact number of presses and workers, the extent to which they were allowed to make decisions for themselves, the number of copies in the edition, and the kinds of emendation sheets received during the printing stage – to mention but a few areas of uncertainty. With this in mind, it is clear that a detailed examination of the *B42* will produce a much clearer picture of the first printing shop than the one that we have currently. How can this material be generated? One approach is to make a systematic collation of the extant copies, but difficulty of access and the limitations of the method for collating early printed book materials have hitherto prevented researchers from taking this route. However, recent developments in digital technology have provided a possible solution to these problems.

In 1997, the *Humanities Media Interface Project* at Keio University (hereafter *HUMI*) created the first digitized copy of the *B42*, using a volume in the possession of Keio University. *HUMI* is an inter-faculty initiative supporting research in the field of digital bibliography, and supporting the construction of a research environment for that purpose.[2] One of the main activities of *HUMI* is to digitize extant copies of the *B42* around the world and thus promote a comprehensive collation of the text. Since creating the first digitized copy of the *B42*, *HUMI* has digitized ten other copies in the United Kingdom, Germany, Poland, and in the United States of America; the author was allowed to participate in most of *HUMI's* digitizing projects that took place from 1998 to 2005. The images of the six copies produced by *HUMI* were kindly supplied to this study in the original resolution. Five other copies have been also digitized as the result of independent projects.[3] Thus sixteen copies have been digitized.

The resultant digital images have been made available on the web, via CD-ROMs, and on campuses, and their existence supports work in bibliographical studies such as the science of collation.

---

2   For further details about *HUMI*, please visit the official website: <http://www.humi.keio.ac.jp/en/>.
3   *P29*, *P30*, *V6*, *V8* and *V11* in Appendix 1.

2. Stop-press variants in the *Gutenberg Bible*

2.1. Collation procedure

The existence of stop-press variants in extant copies of the *B42* was revealed as a result of systematic collation performed by the author, by means of the superimposition of digital images (Agata 2003: 147–165, Agata 2006: 124–263). A short summary of the collation procedure follows a short guide to interpreting Appendix 1, which lists the collated copies.[4]

In Appendix 1, the "Data" column indicates the form in which each copy was collated: digital images used in the primary collation ("digital"), digital images used in the secondary collation ("digital facsimile"), paper facsimiles ("paper facsimile"), and originals (*i.e.*, original copies; those which were examined by the author are marked "#"). In the "Copy No." column, each copy is numbered according to Needham's census of 1985 (Needham, 1985a: 355–374), and this copy number is used hereafter; the copies preceded by "P" are printed on paper, and the copies preceded by "V" are printed on vellum. The "Library" column lists the institutions holding the copies. The "Level" column shows whether the collation of each copy was comprehensive or partial.

The process of collation consists of two steps. For the first step – described as "primary collation" – nine digitized copies were used, to allow for a comprehensive cross-copy collation. A total of 1,282 pages of text in forty-two-line double columns (comprizing 324 leaves [648 pages] of the first volume and 317 leaves [634 pages] of the second volume) were precisely collated between the same setting (the first, the second, and the common settings). In this article, only the results of the first setting are discussed, since both the numbers of copies and pages collated, and the detected variants, are small in the second setting.

For the secondary collation, digital images of three copies, three paper facsimiles, and fifteen originals were examined in those places where a stop-press variant was found in the primary collation ("spot-check"). The results of partial on-site investigations of eleven original copies were kindly supplied to the author during the course of this study, and these results are placed under the heading "supplied data" in Appendix 1;[5] with the exception of *P36* and *V2*, these results were later confirmed by the author, either through recourse to a digital facsimile or to original copies.

In sum, a total of thirty-two copies (twenty-two paper and ten vellum) were collated. All the detected stop-press variants found in twenty-two separate copies (including sixteen paper and six vellum copies) were confirmed. Ten other copies

---

4   Technical accounts are omitted here. Please refer to Agata (2003: 141–144) and Agata (2006: Chapter 3).
5   I owe the results of *V1* and *P44* to Dr. Antoine Coron; those of *V2* to Dr. Stephen Tabor; those of *V8, V9, P26, P28, P36,* and *P38* to Dr. Paul Needham; those of *P13* to Dr. Bettina Wagner; and those of *P23* to Dr. Peter McNiven.

(comprizing six paper and four vellum copies: *P22, P26, P28, P36, P38, P44, V1, V2, V9,* and *V12*) had been examined at an early stage of this research, and the variants which only later came to light were not confirmed.

2.2. Summary of results

As a result of the primary collation of the first volume, forty-six stop-press variants were detected across thirty-five separate pages, of which only one had been previously recorded (Needham 1986: 59–60). In the second volume, seventy-one variants appeared across fifty-three different pages, of which only three had hitherto been discovered (Needham 1986: 59–60; Powitz 1990: 78–79).

In addition, changes in the spacing between words and letters were observed on ninety-nine pages in the first volume and on twenty-nine pages in the second volume. Such anomalies can prove troublesome. It is often difficult to determine whether there is a real difference in spacing, or whether the page surface or the filming conditions simply make it look different. In such cases, an examination of multiple copies sometimes allows for greater accuracy, and facilitates the recognition of the fact that there are not only intentional changes (which were presumably made by stopping the press for improvement in justification and alignment), but also many seemingly incidental changes, such as lines shifted to the right or left, letters formed crookedly (shifting either clockwise or anti-clockwise – see 3.3, example 4), and letters drifting within a line (see 3.3, example 3). These incidental changes may suggest that the pages of the *B42* tended to be rather loosely set; there is also a possibility that the changes sometimes occurred at a continuously operating press rather than at a stopped press. Ideally, then, these "accidental" changes would be analyzed separately, and they also provide evidence relevant to the issue under discussion (see section 3.3).

All of these variants may be tentatively classified into the nine categories listed in Appendix 2, which shows the number of variants apportioned to each category; please note that some of the category A variants are unlike the other variants, as many of them are probably not "stop-press" variants.

These categories are not mutually exclusive or absolute. For example, a correction of a misspelling (category G) may cause a change in the use of a contraction (category F). Moreover, the distinction between them is not always clear. A correction of an inverted type *i* can be definitely classified as category B, but the correction of types *n* and *u* might be better classified into category G, at least in some cases. Thus these categories are not meant to be overly prescriptive. They are proposed only to make it easier to see what kind of changes the text received at press in the *B42* printing house.

There is only one example of a "substantive" (in Greg's sense) change in the *B42*: the addition of words (category I). On I 195ra 2 (20/7r) (1 *Chronicles* 3: 22), all the copies except *P33* read [*et*] *naaria et sa=* / *phat* [*et*] *sesa sex numero*. *P33* does not have the two words [*et*] *sesa*; instead, they have been added, clearly by hand, in the left margin.[6] On the strength of these manually added words, this stop-press variant was identified by Needham (1986: 59–60).

The results of the collation provide conclusive evidence that stop-press corrections were already being carried out in the first printing shop in Europe. Although there are many mistakes left uncorrected, the number of variants is large enough to suppose they were predominantly, although not very systematically, intended: 117 variants have been identified on 88 separate pages (out of the total of 1,282 pages), excluding category A variants.

Even for the pages showing more than one variant, only two versions of a page exist, and in general there are fewer copies of the first, uncorrected, version than the later, corrected, version. The results strongly support the hypothesis that the stop-press variants were made at an early stage in the print run of each page, and only once; and that the vellum pages were printed after the corresponding paper pages.

2.3. Distribution of variants

The data collected from a study of the variants should not be treated in isolation, but studied in conjunction with analysis of the textual units revealed by previous scholars, based on detailed investigations of paper (Dziatzko 1890: 41–47; Schwenke 1900: 51–60), the results of which were later confirmed with several amendments by a cyclotronic analysis of ink (Schwab *et al.* 1987) and by a minute study of paper stock (Needham 1985a: 328–334). Their results suggest that the composition of the *B42* comprises four major text units. This fourfold division is a consequence of the fact that the work was apportioned to different compositors, which allowed the text to be compiled in separate sections, all running concurrently, thus speeding up the process. Printing started from quire I 1, soon to be followed by I 14, then II 1, and finally II 17. These printing sections are labelled A, B, C, and D, respectively, and subdivided into twelve subdivisions (*i.e.*, A1, A2, *etc.*) to represent later additional divisions of copy (Needham 1983: 319–320).

Figure 1 illustrates a rough chronological overview of this process, based on the chart first proposed by Schwenke (1923: 29) and then modified by Schwab *et al.* (1987: 406). Each cell represents a quire, and the table runs chronologically from left to right. However, this chart differs in one way from preceding charts in that it does not try to allocate each quire to a specific press (or presses). Further-

---

[6] This addition required a partial resetting of the text from a2 to a9, but after the tenth line, the text is again synchronized.

more, it does not establish each quire very precisely on the time-line, because further investigations are required in order to establish dates so precisely.[7]

Figure 1. Chronological overview

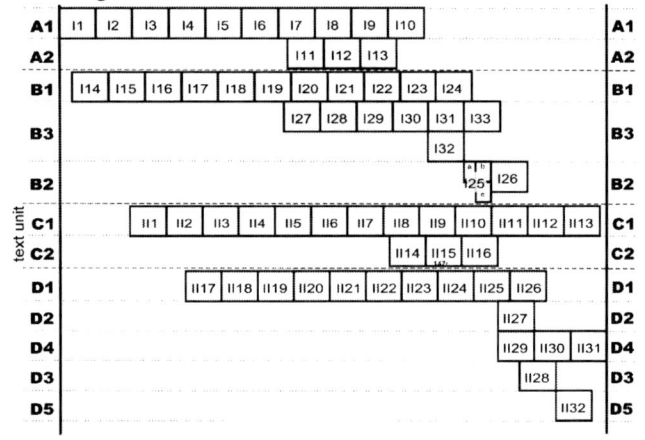

A1	I1	I2	I3	I4	I5	I6	I7	I8	I9	I10					**A1**
A2							I11	I12	I13						**A2**
B1	I14	I15	I16	I17	I18	I19	I20	I21	I22	I23	I24				**B1**
B3					I27	I28	I29	I30	I31	I33					**B3**
							I32								
B2									I25 I26						**B2**
C1	II1	II2	II3	II4	II5	II6	II7	II8	II9	II10	II11	II12	II13		**C1**
C2									II14	II15	II16				**C2**
D1			II17	II18	II19	II20	II21	II22	II23	II24	II25	II26			**D1**
D2										II27					**D2**
D4										II29	II30	II31			**D4**
D3										II28					**D3**
D5											II32				**D5**

(text unit)

The categories B to I variants are not evenly distributed among the text units. Rather, the tendencies of the categories and the frequency differ from unit to unit. There is a greater variety of categories of variants, and they occur with greater frequency in units B1, C1, and D1 than in other units, for example, and variants appear only sporadically in unit A. Each text unit was presumably allocated to a different compositor and then to a different press-crew team, and so the results strongly suggest that these variants were made by a press-crew, rather than by a specially appointed corrector or one who worked under the direction of such a corrector. Therefore, an analysis of the stop-press variants will lead to new findings about the work of the *B42* press-crews.

2.4. Composition rules

Before going further, an account of the known composition rules of the *B42* will be necessary. These rules were minutely investigated by Schwenke (1900: 18–22; see also Needham 1985b: 414–415). To begin with, the *B42* fount seems to have been designed to equalize the gaps between perpendicular strokes as much as possible. For that purpose, secondary forms, known as "abutting types", of almost every letter of the alphabet were made; the left (or hind) side of an abutting type is

---

[7] In a familiar quotation, Schwenke proposed, in 1900, that there were six presses, but he later stated (in his 1923 *Ergänzungsband*) that his chart was not intended to imply such a strict relationship between the six units and presses.

flat, without the diamond shaped spur which is characteristic of the Gothic script, so that it can be placed close to the preceding type when necessary. For example, whichever letter follows the long *s* (ſ) appears in its primary form, except when it is also a tall letter, such as the letter *b*, in which case the abutting form is used. After *c*, *e*, *f*, *g*, *r*, *t*, *x*, and *y*, the abutting form is used; this rule was strictly followed, with only a few exceptions.

Another rule concerns the position of the punctuation mark at the end of a line. The period (.), the double hyphen (//) (which indicates that a word has been separated over two lines), and the final *s* (shaped like the figure *5* and standing above the line) all protrude outside the column, whereas the colon (:) does not do so. Initially, no rule appears to have been in place for the raised mid-point (·), but in the later parts of the *B42* it always appears flush with the line ending.

The relationship between punctuation marks and upper/lower case letters is standardized, so that periods and question marks are always followed by upper-case letters, the only occasions where capital letters are used. Colons and raised mid-points are always followed by a lower-case letter.

2.5. Intentions behind the variants

At first glance, it may seem obvious that variants occurred when mistakes were spotted and corrected. The reality, however, is more complicated than this. There were in fact clear intentions underlying the variants, which can readily be divided into three groups: typographical improvements, corrections, and other changes.

1) The first group is a simple typographical improvement in the justification (*i.e.*, categories A and F) and direction of a type (*i.e.*, category B), which were presumably made intentionally.

2) The second group contains the correction of grammatical errors (*i.e.*, categories F, G, and H) and one example of a correction of a textual error (*i.e.*, category I). The variants in this group must have been intentionally made by a person who was fairly literate in Latin.

3) The last group comprises "other changes". In some cases, variants were made according to the composition rules (*i.e.*, categories C, D, and E); even an illiterate person, who only knew the rules by rote, would have been able to make these sorts of changes. Other variants, however, cannot be explained by the known composition rules, or by typographical or textual errors. Such changes are also not necessarily consistent with each other. Another interesting fact is that not all the changes render the text more legible; in some cases, they make the text worse.

This suggests that this final group consists of both intentional changes (*i.e.*, categories C, D, E, F, and G), and accidental changes (*i.e.*, categories A, B, F, and G). The former includes false corrections as a sub-group (some of categories F and G).

These changes as a whole demand special attention for the present purpose, since these changes are more likely to reflect the habits, tastes, level of care, meticulousness, and degree of literacy of the person who was responsible for them than do the other improvements and corrections. It is to these changes that this essay now turns.

3. Intentional changes and accidental changes

3.1. Intentional changes

Although a study of all of the changes would be useful for expanding our understanding of the variants of the *B42*, the focus of this section is on specific variants, from categories C and F, because these variants have interesting qualities.

3.1.1. Conventions

Before these variants are considered in detail, it is worth outlining the conventions for referring to them. In describing each example, the Roman numeral (I/II) stands for "first/second volume", the succeeding Arabic numeral refers to the folio number, the letter after this numeral ("r" or "v") stands for "recto/verso", "a" or "b" refer to the left or right column, the next Arabic numeral refers to the line number, and the final numeral in parentheses refers to the quire number. Thus the sequence "I 250vb 33 (26/1v)" means "first volume, folio 250 verso, right-hand column, line 33 (the verso of the first leaf of quire 26)". Further numerals and letters in parentheses at the end of the sequence denote the book and chapter in the *B42*, to which is added a number that refers to the appropriate verse in modern editions of the *Vulgate*, to aid in locating the text, because some copies of the *B42* lack hand foliations.[8]

In transcribing, a contracted word is expanded and put in square brackets "[ ]", and a ligatured letter is enclosed in round parentheses "( )". A word broken across two lines is indicated by "/", and the preceding or following part of the word is shown in parentheses.

---

8   I have consulted *Biblia Sacra Iuxta Vulgatam Versionem*. For reference, book and chapter are shown in accordance with the *Newly Revised Standard Version* with *Apocrypha*, if the division of the books is different from the modern English text.

3.1.2. Category C variants

Category C variants arose from a compositional rule of the *B42* that was certainly modelled on the manuscript tradition: the use of primary and abutting forms of letters. Twenty-eight examples fall into this category, and the distribution pattern for them is noteworthy. Of the twenty-eight variants, five are found on II 35v (4/5v) (*Ecclesiasticus* 27) and two on II 257r (26/6r) (1 *Corinthians*); the quires I 29, II 10, II 22, and II 29 each contain two variants. This concentration can be explained in one of two ways. Either (1) the compositor(s) to whom these pages and quires were allocated made more mistakes than they did with the others; or (2) the press crew(s) in charge of these sections were more careful than other press crew(s), and they spotted (or, thought they spotted) deviations from the rule and then amended them.

Five variants on II 35v (4/5v) (*Ecclesiasticus* 27) deserve further attention. Here, *P15*, *P16*, *P17*, *P23*, *P25*, *P29*, *P30*, *P33*, *P35*, and *P46* represent the earlier version, and the rest represent the later version. All five are examples of the variant in which an abutting form is exchanged for a primary standard form. Four of them, however, break the basic composition rule for the placement of abutting forms, which are used correctly in the original form: *locupletari* appears with an abutting *i* on line a10, *denu=* with an abutting *n* on line b5, *caprea* with an abutting *a* on line b13, and *co[n]tine[n]s* with an abutting *ō* on line b38. They are needlessly replaced with standard forms, and so it is possible that the person responsible for these changes might have misunderstood the rule.

Figure 2. Change from a standard "r" to an abutting shorter "r" on I 282vb 25

querit:ro

a. P25 (High Priests' Seminary Library, Pelplin): a standard "r" of the primary form

querit:ro

b. P39 (Keio University Library): an abutting and shorter "r"

There are four variants that involve the use of two different kinds of an abutting form of the letter *r*. One form is of standard height and one is of smaller height, and the use of these two forms of abutting *r* has not been studied in detail. Even the four examples detected in the present collation do not agree with each other on this issue (see Appendix 3). In each case, an *r* is preceded by an *e*, and the only known rule is to use an abutting form *r* after an *e*.

One case, I 282vb 25 (29/2v) (*Job* 9:19), involves a correction required by this rule; a non abutting *r* is used after *e* in *querit*[*ur*] in the earlier version, and this is later replaced by an abutting and shorter *r* (see Figure 2).

The other three cases all involve the use of a double *rr* after *e*; this rule of the use of abutting *r* is observed in the original version, but a variant occurs, nevertheless. I 259va 42 (26/9+1v) (4 *Esdras* 16:24) (2 *Esdras* 16:24 in the *Apocrypha*) shows a change from "shorter *r* – standard *r*" to "standard *r* – standard *r*;" I 281rb 39 (29/1r) (*Job* 4:14) changes from "standard *r* – standard *r*" to "standard *r* – shorter *r*;" and II 185va 42 (19/4v) (2 *Maccabees* 11:7) changes from "standard *r* – shorter *r*" to "shorter *r* – shorter *r*". The latter two examples have one thing in common that only one copy was found to show the earlier version in the present collation. The *r*s are printed perfect in both cases, and so they are unlikely to be examples of the replacement of a defective type *r*.[9] These examples are found in different text units, and were presumably allocated to different press-crew teams: B1, B3, and D1, respectively. This may have reflected the preferences of the press-crew(s), although even on the same page the use of shorter *r* does not seem to be perfectly standardized. But the fact that these exchanges seem to have happened without an apparent typographical reason (such as a defective or worn type) may suggest that there is a unknown rule of composition or preferences of the person who made these changes.

3.1.3. Category F variants

Figure 3. Change of contractions on f. II 27ra 22-24

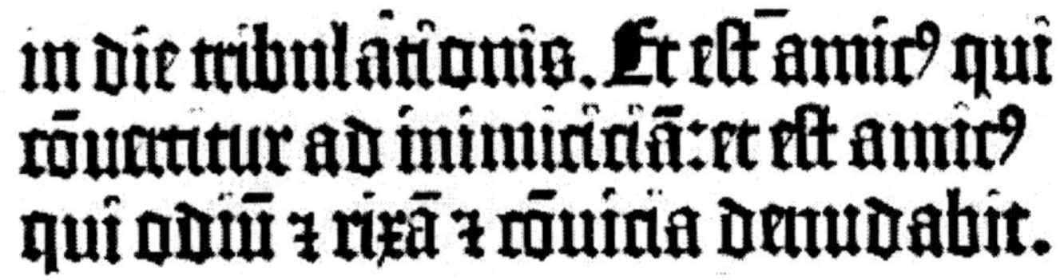

in die tribulationis. Et est amic⁹ qui couertitur ad inimicicia: et est amic⁹ qui odiū ⁊ rixā ⁊ couicia denudabit.

a. P27 (British Library), with permission of the British Library Board

---

9   This shorter *r* is not a single defective piece of type, because several shorter *r*s are found on one page in some cases.

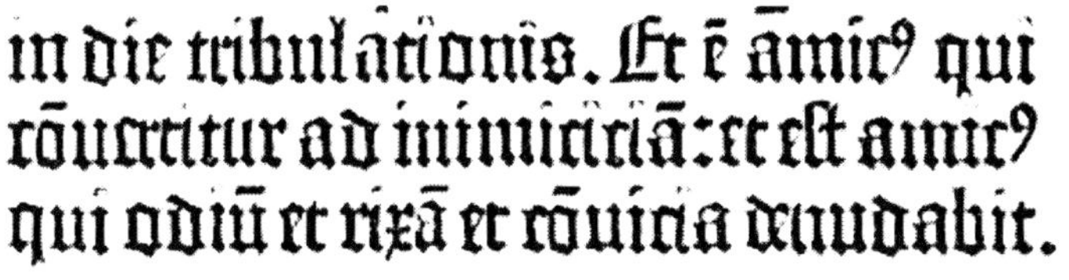

> in die tribulationis. Et ē amic⁹ qui
> conuertitur ad inimiciā: et est amic⁹
> qui odiū et rixā et conuicia denudabit.

b. P13 (Bayerische Staatsbibliothek München [2 Inc.s.a. 197])

II 27r (3/7r) (*Ecclesiasticus* 6) (*Sirach* 6 in *NRSV*) exhibits seven variants within a page, four of which fall into category F. Two of them, which occur on lines a22 (see the first line of Fig. 3) and a36 (see the first line of Fig. 4), are assumed to have been made for purposes of justification; in both cases, the final letter of the line protrudes from the column ending in the earlier versions, while in the corrected versions a word is abbreviated in order to create enough space so that the final letter is perfectly printed within the column.

However, there is no apparent reason for the following two variants. In the earlier version copies, *P16* and *P27*, II 27ra 24 reads *qui odiu*[m] [*et*] *rixa*[m] [*et*] *co*[n]*uicia denudabit*, and contains two abbreviated Tironian forms of the word *et*. In the other copies (*P13, P14, P15, P17, P22, P25, P29, P30, P33, P35, P46, V6, V10*, and *V11*), both *et*s are spelled out, and the two letters *de* are changed into a ligatured *(de)*, so that the passage reads *qui odiu*[m] *et rixa*[m] *et co*[n]*uicia (de)nudabit* (see the last line of Fig. 3). The reason why this change was made is not clear, because even the earlier version did not break any known composition rule, and it had a justified line ending.[10] The change may have been made because the line in the earlier version may have seemed a little too spacious to the person responsible for the emendation, and so this may have reflected a personal preference.

Figure 4. Change of contractions on f. II 27ra 36-39

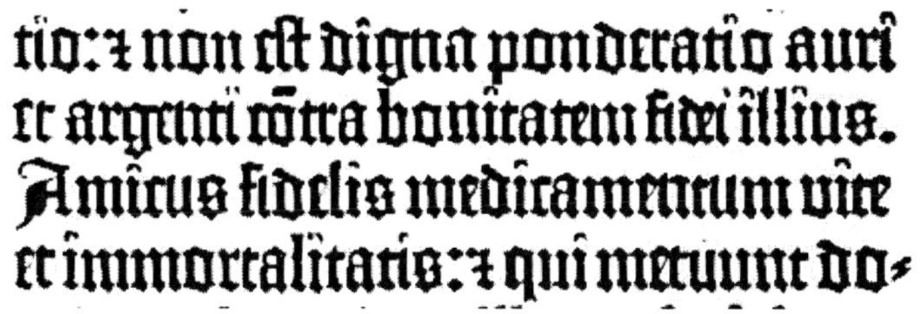

> tio: ⁊ non est digna ponderatio auri
> et argenti contra bonitatem fidei illius.
> Amicus fidelis medicamentum vite
> et immortalitatis: ⁊ qui metuunt do⸗

a. P27 (British Library), with permission of the British Library Board

---

10 A full stop protrudes outside the column, but it accords with the basic compositional rule as mentioned in 2.4.

> tio:et non e digna ponderatio auri
> et argenti cotra bonitatem fidei illius.
> Amicus fidelis medicamentum vite
> et immortalitatis: et qui metuunt do-

b. P13 (Bayerische Staatsbibliothek München [2 Inc.s.a. 197])

Fifteen lines below this, on line a39, we find another, similar change in the use of a contraction (Fig. 4). In *P16* and *P27*, the text after the colon reads [*et*] *qui metuunt do=* with an abbreviated Tironian '*et*'. In the other copies (*P13, P14, P15, P17, P22, P25, P29, P30, P33, P35, P46, V6, V10,* and *V11*), this has been changed to *et qui metuunt (do)=*, where the *et* has been expanded and the final letters *do* have been ligatured. Compared to the next line, this line in the second version is very slightly better justified. This change is similar to the preceding example on line a24, and in both cases the *et* is spelled out, and the letter *d* is ligatured with the next letter. This may have been done to ensure a very small justification, or it may have reflected the preference of the person who made the change, or both.

3.2. False corrections

Four variants are probably examples of miscorrection, that is, false corrections that run contrary to the corrector's intention.[11] Since they belong to categories F and G, these changes, although unnecessary, must have required a certain level of Latin literacy. Four category C variants on II 35v, described above (3.1.1), can be also included among the false corrections.

a) Example 1: I 250vb 33 (26/1v) (4 *Esdras* 6:7) (2 *Esdras* 6:7 in the *Apocrypha*) – Category F

---

11 There is one more possible example of false correction of the "category F" kind, occurring on I 291va 37 (30/1v) (*Job* 39:10). The second word on this line appears as *rinocerota* in the earlier version copy, *P20*, which is grammatically correct. In *P16, P23, P27, P29, P30, P33, P35, P39, V6, V8, V10,* and *V11*, however, this word has been replaced with *rinocerota*[m], in which the letter *ā* has appears with a suspension mark above it. Here it should be remembered that a facsimile of *P20* was consulted in this study; there is a high possibility that the suspension mark was deleted in the original of *P20*, as it was in *V6*, and that there is thus no trace of it in the photographic facsimile. This possible change is worth recording until it can be confirmed by examination either of the original or of a high resolution image.

On I 250v a variant is detected on line b33. In *P39*, the first word of this line is *iniciu*[*m*] with a suspension mark above the final letter *u* which is used in order to show the omission of the nasal *m*. In *P33*, however, type without a suspension mark is used to print *iniciu*, which does not make sense. Since the abbreviation marks are integral to the letters, and it is very unlikely that the mark was completely broken away by accident, they must represent two distinct types.

P13, *P16*, *P17*, *P28*, *P30*, and *P38* are identical to *P39* (*iniciu*[*m*]) in this regard, whereas the remaining paper and all the vellum copies are identical to *P33* (*iniciu*).[12] Another simple typographical correction of inserting punctuation on this page strongly suggests that *P39* and its companions represent the earlier version. Thus, this change seems to be an example of a false correction. A "corrector" in fact made the text worse. It may have been caused by an unfinished attempt to spell out *inicium*, considering that this line has enough space for the change.[13]

b) Example 2: II 30vb 1 (3/10v) (*Ecclesiasticus* 15:14) (*Sirach* 15:14 in *NRSV*) – Category F

The fourth word on the first line of II 30v gives another example. In *P46*, and only there, this word is printed *illu*[*m*], with the *ū* bearing a suspension mark, which is textually correct. In the other copies, however, the *u* appears without a suspension mark, forming the word *illu*.[14]

Because the erroneous setting is found in all the vellum copies, it can be stated with considerable confidence that *P46* represents the original version. There are two possible explanations for the misprint. First, the false correction may have been the consequence of an abortive attempt to change *illū in* into *illum i*[*n*]. Second, the next word, *in*, might have been mistaken for an *m*, and the "corrector" may have attempted to change *illu*[*m*] *m* to *illum* by deleting a superfluous *m*, even though it was in fact *illu*[*m*] *in* in the original version.

c) Example 3: II 200va 32 (20/9v) (*Matthew* 19:12) – Category G

On II 200v, a variant appears on line a32. In the eight copies examined (*P15*, *P22*, *P23*, *P25*, *P27*, *P29*, *P30*, and *P33*), the third word on this line is *castraveru*[*n*]*t*. In the other paper and all the vellum copies, however, *crastraveru*[*n*]*t* is printed. The former version is the correct word here, and it is also presumed to represent the earlier version; this again must therefore be a false correction.

---

12   In the three copies – *P27*, *V1* and *V10* – a mark was added by hand above the final letter *u*.
13   I am grateful to Dr. Needham for this suggestion.
14   A suspension mark has been added by hand in copies *P16*, *P17*, *P23*, *P29*, and *P30*, for correction.

d) Example 4: II 302vb 32 (30/8v) (*James* 3:2) – Category G

On II 302v, line b32 contains a variant. The third and fourth words on this line are *In m[u]ltis*; the appearance of the *l* with a hook indicates that a preceding *u* is abbreviated. Five copies have these words – *P20, P25, P27, P29* and *P35*. In the fourteen other copies, however, the fourth word is represented differently, and reads *In in[u]ltis*; the *m* has been replaced by an *i* without an upper bow or bar and an accompanying *n*, whilst the space between the preceding full stop and the *l* has been slightly narrowed. The correct words here are *In m[u]ltis*, but reading in the vellum copies suggests that this is found in the earlier version, whereas the erroneous *In in[u]ltis* appears in the later version. Considering that the *m* and the *in* in the *B42* fount look very similar, both consisting of three vertical strokes, this difference might have been caused by bad inking or by the wearing out of the type *m*. The change in the spacing between the period and the *l* suggests, however, that the types *m* and *in* were physically exchanged. The most probable explanation is that this is an example of false stop-press correction.

3.3. Accidental changes

Several changes may be evidence of simple accident; for example, pieces of type may well have been pulled out during either inking or printing and put back upside down. This kind of accident could easily have happened, especially with *u* and *n* (as in examples 1 and 2, below). These accidental changes were not corrected and were thus transmitted as the final version of the text.

In addition, some of the category A variants (changes in spacing) are presumed to have occurred unintentionally – these variants can be divided into shifted types and drifting types. Shifted types, and the resulting variants, have been discussed by scholars working on later printed books. For instance, Greg has discussed the probable origin of the six kinds of shifts found in the *First Quarto* of Shakespeare's *King Lear*, and has demonstrated that the shift of types tended to occur at the time of correction (Greg 1940: 36–38). Blayney, studying the same work, focused on the pulled type, has argued that "[t]he continuous operation of the press often loosens the quoins, and when a forme is press-corrected the unlocking and re-locking *on the press itself* sometimes leaves a few lines sufficiently loose to permit accidental pulling" [italics in the original] (Blayney 1982: 206). A similar kind of accident is presumed to have happened in examples 3 and 4, below.

a) Example 1: I 106ra 25 (11/5r) (*Joshua* 8:25) – Category G

A difference on I 106r shows up on line a25. In *P14, P16, P17, P23, P27, P30*, and *P42*, the first word is continued from the previous line to form *(homi= /) num*. In the remaining paper and all the vellum copies, this word is printed *(homi= /)*

uum, and the first *u* is shorter than the second. Clearly, the former spelling (*hominum*) is correct. However, the erroneous version is presumed to be the later of the two because the vellum copies show this version, whereas *P14* and its companions – with the correct reading – belong to the earlier setting. This should not be considered an intended correction, but an incidental change. This type *n* may have come loose in the forme at some point, and then was put back in upside down. The difference in height of two *u*s in the later version also supports this speculation.

b) Example 2: I 291ra 34 (30/1r) (*Job* 38:3) – Category B

On I 291r of first version copies (*P15*, *P28*, *P29*, *P35*, *P36*, *P39*, and *P44*), the first word on line a34 is correctly printed *Accinge*. In *P33*, this word is erroneously printed *Acciuge*. These are printed using the same type, although the word is printed the right way up in *P39*, and inverted in *P33*. Most copies, *P13*, *P14*, *P16*, *P17*, *P20*, *P23*, *P25*, *P26*, *P27*, *P33*, *P38*, *P42*, *V1*, *V2*, *V4*, *V6*, *V7*, *V8*, *V9*, *V10*, and *V11*, agree with *P33*. Therefore, this is assumed to be another accidental variant.

c) Example 3: II 217ra 9 (22/6r) (*Mark* 15:40) – Category H

The first and the second word on line a9 of II 271r are not separated, and are printed *(iaco=/) biminoris* in *P16*, *P17*, *P29*, *P30*, and *P33*. In the other copies of later version, they are correctly separated to form *(iaco=/) bi minoris*. However, *P30* shows still a small space between *bi* and *minoris*; *P15*, which presented the earlier version on line b10, shows the corrected version here. Taking these details into account, as well as the facts that this is the first word on the line and that a stop-press correction is made at the adjacent line in the right column, this may have been an incidental change rather than an intentional one. This area of the forme may have come loose when a correction was made to the adjacent line; alternatively, this word division may indeed have been corrected by the press-crew, who may have inserted inadequate spacings between *i* and *m* to accidentally make a superfluous space in the line and allow the types to drift.

d) Example 4: II 253vb 35 (26/2v) (*Romans* 11:7) – Category G

On II 253v there is a variant on line b35. In *P27* and *P30*, the fifth word is misprinted as *querbat*. In the other eighteen copies, the missing *e* is added to correctly form the word *quere(ba)t*, with the *ba* in ligature. This is a justified correction. However, it brought about another subtle point of difference; the ligatured type *ba* is slanted anti-clockwise in all of the corrected-version copies. This inclination should be regarded as an accidental change. Of course, it could be that the type face was slanting in the first place. But it might have come about when the type became slanted, because an inadequate number of spaces were inserted at the time of correction.

4. The hands of the press-crew

These examples illustrate an aspect of the changes made to the text in the hands of the press-crew at the first printing shop. In addition to typographical improvements, grammatical and textual corrections, and intentional changes – some of which came about for discernible reasons and some for unknown ones – we find a few false corrections and some variants that have occurred by accident. When the press was stopped to allow the press-crew to make a correction, additional errors were sometimes introduced. The final product is therefore a mixture of both intentional changes and involuntary, incidental changes.

Here it should be noted that many mistakes still remain uncorrected; even a simple typographical mistake such as the omission of a period or the inversion of a type tends to be left uncorrected, even when it appears on the same page as a corrected mistake. On the other hand, there are pages and quires where contractions have been changed for the sake of a very slight justification, and where subtle deviations from the composition rules have been carefully amended (albeit sometimes following a misapprehension, as in the case of II 35v as shown in 3.1.2.).

These stop-press variants are therefore presumed to reflect the habits, tastes, care, diligence, and degree of literacy of the press-crew. At present it would be premature to identify each press-crew based on the stop-press variants that have been detected so far, but the present results suggest that the kinds of stop-press variants in the *B42* might serve as a clue to help identify a press-crew, just as spelling habits and distinctive uses of typefaces have served in the identification of compositors/scribes.[15]

A greater accumulation of examples of stop-press variants is essential if we are to pursue this work further. Furthermore, the compositors' work should be studied in detail. We need to learn about spelling habits, the ways in which compositors selected particular letter shapes, their occasional indifference to, or misunderstanding of, the composition rules, and their tendency to make certain grammatical mistakes. Comparing these characteristics with stop-press variants, and analyzing them in conjunction with the preceding studies, will eventually allow us to identify compositors and press-crews at work in the earliest printing shop.

---

15 For example, scholars have revealed that some distinctive uses of the letter *a* forms help identify compositors in Caxton's printing shop (Hellinga 1982: 59–62; Tokunaga 2005: 152–157).

Acknowledgements

Grateful acknowledgement is made to each institution for kindly giving me permission to examine the original copies of the *B42*, and/or to use and reproduce digital images from them. My special thanks go to the *HUMI Project* of Keio University. Without the digital images that *HUMI* has produced and lent to me, this study could never have been undertaken. I owe Mrs. Doreen Simmons and Dr. Jeremy Lowe my thanks for their help in polishing my English. Despite all the help I have received, I am solely responsible for any errors remaining in this article.

References

Agata, Mari
    2003   "Stop-press variants in the *Gutenberg Bible*: The first report of the collation", *The Papers of the Bibliographical Society of America* 97, 2: 139–165.
    2006   Stop-press variants in the *Gutenberg Bible*. [Unpublished Ph.D. dissertation, Keio University.]

[*Bible*]
    1989   *The holy Bible containing the Old and New Testaments with the Apocryphal / Deuterocanonical Books: Newly revised standard version with Apocrypha.* Oxford: Oxford University Press.

Blayney, Peter W. M.
    1982   *The texts of King Lear and their origins.* Cambridge: Cambridge University Press.

Dziatzko, Karl
    1890   *Gutenbergs Früheste Druckerpraxis, Sammulung Bibliothekswissenschaftlicher Arbeiten.* Volume 4. Berlin.

Gaskell, Philip
    1972   *A new introduction to bibliography.* Oxford: Clarendon Press. [Reprinted with corrections, 1974]

Greg, Walter W.
    1940   *The variants in the First Quarto of King Lear.* London: Bibliographical Society.
    1950–1951   "The rationale of copy-text", *Studies in Bibliography* 3: 19–36.

Hellinga, Lotte
    1982   *Caxton in focus: The beginning of printing in England.* London: British Library.

Needham, Paul
    1985a   "The paper supply of the *Gutenberg Bible*", *The Papers of the Bibliographical Society of America* 79, 3: 303–374.
    1985b   "Division of copy in the *Gutenberg Bible*: Three glosses on the ink evidence," *The Papers of the Bibliographical Society of America* 79, 3: 411–426.

1986 "A *Gutenberg Bible* used as printer's copy by Heinrich Eggestein in Strassburg, ca. 1469", *Transactions of the Cambridge Bibliographical Society* 9: 36–75.

Powitz, Gerhardt
1990 *Die Frankfurter* Gutenberg-Bibel*: Ein Beitrag zum Buchwesen des 15. Jahrhunderts.* Frankfurt am Main: V. Klostermann.

Schwab, Richard N. – Cahill, Thomas A. – Kusko, Bruce H. – Eldred, Robert A. – Wick, Daniel L.
1987 "The proton milliprobe ink analysis of the Harvard *B42*, Volume II", *The Papers of the Bibliographical Society of America* 81, 4: 403–432.

Schwenke, Paul
1900 *Untersuchungen zur Geschichte des ersten Buchdrucks: Festschrift zur Gutenbergfeier herausgegeben von der Koeniglichen Bibliothek zu Berlin. Am 24. Juni 1900.* Berlin: Behrend.
1923 *Johannes Gutenbergs zweiundvierzigzeilige Bibel: Ergänzungsband zur Faksimile-Ausgabe.* Leipzig: Insel-Verlag.

Tokunaga, Satoko
2005 "Early English printing and the hands of compositors", *International Journal of English Studies* 5, 2: 149–160.

Weber, Robertus (ed.)
1994 *Biblia sacra iuxta vulgatam versionem.* Stuttgart: Deutsche Bibelgesellschaft.

Appendix 1

Copies collated[16]

SOURCE: Data from Paul Needham, "The Paper Supply of the Gutenberg Bible," The Papers of the Bibliographical Society of America 79, no.3 (1985): 355-358.

	Data	Copy No.	Library	Level
Primary	digital	P16	Mainz, Gutenberg Museum (Kraus copy)	comprehensive collation
	digital	P27	London, British Library (George III copy)	comprehensive collation
	digital	P29	Vienna, National Bibliothek	comprehensive collation
	digital	P33	Cambridge, University Library	comprehensive collation
	digital	P39	Tokyo, Keio University Library (v. 1)	comprehensive collation
	digital	P46	Mainz, Gutenberg Museum (Laubach) (v. 2)	comprehensive collation
	digital	V6	Gottingen, Niedersächsische Staats- und Universitätsbibliothek	comprehensive collation
	digital	V10	London, British Library (Grenville)	comprehensive collation
	digital	V11	Vatican, Vatican Library (Barberini copy)	comprehensive collation
Secondary	digital facsimile	P25	Pelplin, High Priests' Seminary Library	spot-check
	digital facsimile	P30	Austin TX, University of Texas Library	spot-check
	digital facsimile	V8	Washington, D.C., Library of Congress	spot-check (&supplied data)
	paper facsimile	P20	Paris, Bibliothèque Mazarine	spot-check
	paper facsimile	P35	Burgos, Biblioteca Pública de Burgos	spot-check

16 P13, P16, P23, P25, P27, P33, P39, P46, V10, and a copy in the National Library of Scotland were digitized by or with the technical assistance of the *HUMI* Project of Keio University.

paper facsimile	V7	Berlin, Staatsbibliothek zu Berlin	spot-check
#	P13	Munich, Bayerischen Staatsbibliothek	spot-check (&supplied data)
#	P14	Frankfurt am Main, Universitätsbibliothek Frankfurt am Main	spot-check
#	P15	Aschaffenburg, Hofbibliothek	spot-check
#	P17	Stuttgart, Württembergische Landesbibliothek	spot-check
#	P22	Oxford, Bodlean Library	partial spot-check
#	P26	Princeton NJ, Scheide Library	partial spot-check (&supplied data)
#	P28	New York, Morgan Library & Museum 19206	partial spot-check (&supplied data)
#	P38	New York, Morgan Library & Museum 12 (OT)	partial spot-check (&supplied data)
#	P42	Kassel, Landesbibliothek und Murhardsche Bibliothek der Stadt Kassel	spot-check
#	P44	Paris, Bibliothèque nationale de France (Cremer)	partial spot-check (&supplied data)
#	V1	Paris, Bibliothèque nationale de France	partial spot-check (&supplied data)
#	V4	Fulda, Landesbibliothek (vol. 1)	spot-check
#	V9	New York, Morgan Library & Museum 13	partial spot-check (&supplied data)
#	V12	London, Lambeth Palace Library (NT)	partial spot-check
#	P23	Manchester, Rylands	spot-check (&supplied data)
	P36	New York, New York Public Library	partial spot-check (supplied data)
	V2	San Marino CA, Henry E. Huntington Library	partial spot-check (supplied data)

Appendix 2

Variant categories

	Categories	Vol. 1	Vol. 2	Total
A	Changes in spacing	120	40	160
B	Inversion of a type	10	5	15
C	Different shapes of the same letter	8	20	28
D	Correction of punctuation	6	4	10
E	Change between upper/lower case	0	1	1
F	Use of contraction	6	6	12
G	Misspelling	13	27	40
H	Word division	2	8	10
I	Addition of words	1	0	1

(Number of variants)

Appendix 3

Replacement of an abutting *r*

Folio (quire)	1st state	1st state copies	2nd state	2nd state copies
I 259va 42 (26/9+1v)	the first *r* of *terra* is abutting and shorter	P15, P17, P20, P23, P25, P27, P28, P30, P35, P38, P39, P42, P44	both *rs* are abutting forms of the standard height	P13, P14, P16, P26, P29, P33, P36, V1, V2, V4, V6, V7, V8, V9, V10, V11
I 281rb 39 (29/1r)	two *rs* of *rr* in *perterrita* are abutting forms of the standard height	P39	the second *r* of *rr* is abutting and shorter	P13, P14, P15, P16, P17, P20, P23, P25, P26, P27, P28, P30, P33, P35, P36, P38, P42, P44, V1, V2, V4, V6, V7, V8, V9, V10, V11
I 282vb 25 (29/2v)	a standard *r* of the primary form is used in *querit*[*ur*]	P14, P15, P25, P26, P27, P28, P33, P35, P44	an abutting and shorter *r* is used	P13, P16, P17, P20, P23, P30, P36, P38, P39, P42, V1, V2, V4, V6, V7, V8, V9, V10, V11
II 185va 42 (19/4)	the first *r* of *ferre* is standard; the second is shorter (both abutting)	P27	both *rs* are abutting and shorter	P13, P14, P15, P16, P17, P20, P22, P23, P25, P29, P30, P33, P35, P46, V6, V7, V8, V10

A textual analysis of the overlooked tales in de Worde's *Canterbury Tales*[1]

Satoko Tokunaga, Keio University

Chaucer's *Canterbury Tales* enjoyed great popularity in fifteenth-century print culture, a fact borne out by the existence of four successive editions of the work: Two published by William Caxton ([1476–1477], *STC* 5082; [1483], *STC* 5083), and one each by his followers, Richard Pynson ([1492?]; *STC* 5084) and Wynkyn de Worde ([1498], *STC* 5085). When Caxton reprinted his first edition (hereafter Cx^1), he introduced woodcut illustrations of the pilgrimage as well as textual revisions (Dunn 1939; Bordalejo 2002). Pynson, basing his text on Caxton's second edition (Cx^2), adopted a new series of woodcut illustrations, and also changed the layout slightly by arranging the prose texts into double columns. Both printers thus strove to add new elements to their editions, probably with the aim of attracting a wider readership.

It is now generally accepted that when de Worde printed his 1498 edition (hereafter *Wy*), he used Cx^2 as his principal text, but that at times he also consulted a manuscript as an additional source – it is even possible that he printed his version directly from this manuscript (for overview, see Hellinga 2007; Partridge 2007). However, the existing scholarship on *Wy* is still slight and somewhat fragmentary. The chart in Appendix 1 illustrates the tale order of *Wy*, and also shows the source/sources used by de Worde for each tale (*i.e.* Cx^2 and/or a manuscript), where there is scholarly consensus on this matter.[2] As the chart shows, roughly half of de Worde's text has so far received in-depth textual scrutiny, whilst the remaining tales need further examination.[3] If we are properly to understand the

---

1 This paper is based on part of my doctoral thesis; for further discussion of the sources used by de Worde for the 1498 edition of the *Canterbury Tales*, see Tokunaga 2005. I am grateful to Professor Toshiyuki Takamiya, who first motivated me to pursue this study. Also, I would like to acknowledge my greatest thanks to Dr Jeremy Lowe, Dr Takako Kato, Professor A. S. G. Edwards, Dr Lotte Hellinga and the editors of this volume for reading earlier versions of this draft and giving me invaluable comments.

2 In conducting my preliminary textual study of *Wy*, I used a computer programme called *Collate 2*, which Peter Robinson of the *Canterbury Tales Project* produced and developed. I am thankful to Professor Robinson for allowing me to use both this system and the transcription of the witnesses. I am also indebted to Dr Barbara Bordalejo for instructing me in using the system. The manuscript sigils, tale divisions and line numbers used in this paper are, therefore, based on those adopted by the *Canterbury Tales Project*. But I have also relied on the collation results and "constant groups" of manuscripts established by Manly and Rickert in the tales where the transcriptions of the manuscripts were not ready yet for conducting the textual collation using *Collate 2*.

3 William Hutmacher attempted a textual comparison of *Wy* and Cx^2, from the "General Pro-

compositional background of *Wy*, then, it is essential that we complete this textual assessment. The present paper therefore provides the first ever complete textual analysis of these neglected tales of *Wy*, and aims to establish the identity of de Worde's copy text (or texts) as well as determine his editorial methodology.

In this article I examine the collation results of *Wy* and Cx^2 by comparing them with manuscript readings, in order to determine whether these variants were derived from a manuscript source or not. When variants do not agree with any of the extant manuscripts, they are categorized as unique. The groupings of the other variants are then classified based on whether the readings are shared by what Peter Robinson has termed the "O group witnesses" or, rather, not (Robinson 1997). For example, when a variant agrees with *Ellesmere [El]*, *Hengwrt [Hg]*, and the other majority of "O group witnesses", it is highly likely that the reading comes from the archetype in the textual history of the *Canterbury Tales*. In general, there are too many manuscripts that contain such an archetypical reading to allow us to identify a particular manuscript (or group of manuscripts) available to de Worde. However, when variants do not agree with *Hg* and/or *El*, they often provide useful information because they tend to show a particular textual affiliation for the reading. We have to remember, however, that textual variants are not always generated as a result of references to an extra source. The text was transmitted in printed books through the hands of the editors/compositors in each printing house; editors who, occasionally, exercised their own editorial judgment, or introduced mechanical errors.

Appendix 2 presents all the textual differences of *Wy* from Cx^2 that are supported by manuscript readings, and which are examined in this paper. Because my primary concern is to discern whether de Worde used Cx^2 as his sole copy text or not, I have eliminated those textual differences that conform to what W. W. Greg has termed "accidental variants" (Greg 1950–1951), *i.e.*, the compositors' spelling differences and their graphemic distinctiveness in writing, as well as obvious typographical errors caused by the conversion of printing types, and any corrections of Cx^2's typos. Also, I do not include de Worde's modernization of three particular lexical items – *clepe* (*call*), *eke* (*also*), and *mykel* (*moche*) – because the modernization of these words is constant throughout in *Wy*, as will be discussed in detail below.

---

logue" and to the "Franklin's Tale". Hutmacher, however, merely presented where *Wy* differs from Cx^2 and did not conduct a further analysis of the textual variants that existed between Cx^2 and *Wy* against manuscript readings. This paper therefore re-examines these tales. For a similar reason, the "Knight's Tale", of which only the first 116 lines were examined (Greg 1924), is included in the analysis below.

1. Tales based on a single source

1.1. "Reeve's Prologue" (L2) and "Tale" (RE)

The "Reeve's Prologue" (66 lines) shows no variations from Cx^2. Of the 404 lines of the "Reeve's Tale", only eight show variation from Cx^2, four of which are variants unique to *Wy* (RE 72, 109, 227, and 357). There are four variants which have manuscript support, and Bo^1, Ph^2, and *Nl* are the only extant manuscripts that share *Wy*'s readings more than once (see RE 115, 126, and 270). These variants are, however, omissions of a word and a letter, and seemingly due to the compositor's carelessness. The other variant is likewise minor (in RE 151 *hys* to *her*), and it is unlikely that these variants were introduced from a source other than Cx^2.

1.2. "Cook's Prologue" (L3) and "Tale" (CO)

No doubt this section was faithfully reprinted from Cx^2, because the "Prologue" (fourty lines) has no variation from Cx^2, and the "Tale" (fifty-eight lines) has only one variant unique to *Wy* (CO 40).

1.3. "Wife of Bath's Tale" (WBT)

In the "Wife of Bath's Tale" (1,237 lines), besides five unique variants, *Wy* has only four substantive divergences from Cx^2. Three of these variants agree with *Hg* and *El*, while the other is supported by Cx^1 and its affiliation. One example in WBT 1231 is a substantial change from *And* to *In*, which agrees with *Hg*, *El*, and the major manuscripts; but from the low number of textual differences it is apparent that *Wy* was reset from Cx^2.

1.4. "Friar's Prologue" (L10) and "Tale" (FR)

The "Friar's Prologue" (thirty-six lines) has only two variants from Cx^2 (including one unique reading). There is therefore no doubt that the text was faithfully reprinted from Cx^2. In the "Friar's Tale" (365 lines), *Wy* diverges from Cx^2 fourteen times, and six of these variants are unique to *Wy*. Although the other eight variants have some manuscript support (FR 66, 92, 96, 103, 251, 282, 311, and 347), they are very trivial changes (such as *thys* to *the* and *the* to *this*), and the distribution of the manuscripts that share these variants is too fragmentary to allow any close identification. It is therefore unlikely that de Worde introduced these variants from a manuscript source.

1.5. "Clerk's Tale" (CL)

There are twelve variants unique to *Wy* (CL 10, 20, 51, 113, 130, 298, 324, 337, 433, 517, 550, and 645) and ten variants shared by the manuscripts. Only one variant is shared by both *Hg* and *El* (CL 708); the other nine variants that disagree with *Hg* and *El* show only trivial differences between *Wy* and Cx^2 (CL 73, 79, 448, 449, 618, 802, 834, 971, and 1057), and no particular manuscript and/or manuscript group shows a consistent pattern of agreement with these variants. It is therefore certain that *Wy* was reprinted from Cx^2 throughout this section.

1.6. "Lenvoy of Chaucer" (L13) and "Words of the Host" (L14)

There are no variants in these sections.

1.7. "Merchant's Prologue" (L15) and "Tale" (ME)

There is no variation in the "Merchant's Prologue". In the following "Tale", *Wy* has thirty-four variants, and fourteen variants have manuscript support. Four of these variants agree with the majority of manuscripts, including *Hg* and *El*, but they are trivial changes, such as the transposition of two words and the deletion of a single word (ME 46, 685, 1062, and 1133). Of the ten variants which are not shared by *Hg* and *El*, two variants are worth noting (ME 73 *hous* to *hondis*; ME 116 *as* to *after*); but the distribution of the variants among the manuscripts is too scattered to allow the identification of a particular manuscript or group of manuscripts. The variants with manuscript authority must therefore be accidental. Moreover, most of the textual changes throughout this section are omissions, which only result in a corruption of the rhyme (see ME 303, 946, and 1011), or the transposition of words (ME 46 and 1133). These changes could probably have been introduced by the editor/compositor without recourse to an extra source other than Cx^2, and the "Merchant's Tale" from *Wy* must be a reprint of Cx^2, with some changes made by the editor/compositor.

1.8. "Man of Law's Endlink" (L8)

This section must have been printed from Cx^2, since it has no substantial variant from it.

1.9. "Squire-Franklin Link" (L20)

In the "Squire-Franklin Link", *Wy* has only two variants; but the changes are merely a trivial transposition and the deletion of a minor word (*that*) respectively, which can be easily explained away as compositorial error.

1.10. "Franklin's Tale" (FK)

In the "Franklin's Tale", three variants have the support of *Hg* and *El* (FK 25, 624, and 756), but in the other cases the distribution of the manuscripts that share

Wy's readings is very random (FK 78, 196, 333, 376, 439, 641, 778, 840, 857, and 875), and so it can be concluded that *Wy* was based on Cx^2 in this section.

1.11. "Second Nun's Prologue and Tale" (NU)

In this section, *Wy* textually diverges from Cx^2 in fourteen lines, six of which are unique to *Wy* (NU 26, 32, 36, 69, 76, and 51). Moreover, five of the eight variants which have manuscript support are mere omissions of single words, which were most likely introduced by the compositor's carelessness (see NU 169, 175, 384, 493, and 508). The manuscript that most frequently agrees with *Wy*'s variants is Ha^3, but the number of agreements is too low to allow for identification. Thus, we can conclude that the "Second Nun's Prologue and Tale" were reprinted from Cx^2, with some compositorial changes.

1.12. "Canon's Yeoman's Prologue" (L33) and "Tale" (CY)

In the "Prologue", there are two variants in *Wy*, but neither is substantive. In the "Tale" (762 lines) there are twenty-four variants, eighteen of which are unique to *Wy*, whereas six have manuscript support (CY 21, 140, 172, 279, 363, and 720). Two of the unique variants involve the modernization of words (CY 335: *kidyth* to *sheweth*; CY 571 *thou* to *you*), but there is little indication that there are similar editorial alterations in the other variants, except for CY 720, where Caxton's unique reading *he* is corrected to *be*. We can therefore conclude that *Wy* was printed from Cx^2 with some revision, though without reference to a manuscript source.

1.13. "Pardoner's Prologue and Tale" (PD)

This section, which is 640 lines in total, has eight textual variations from Cx^2. Of these eight, there are three variants that have manuscript support, and all of them are trivial; *e.g.*, a transposition (PD 95 and 250), and an addition (of p^l: PD 337). The small number of variants thus confirms that this section is a reprint of Cx^2.

1.14. "Shipman's Tale" (SH)

In this tale, *Wy* has 16 textual differences from Cx^2, eight of which have manuscript support (SH 29, 42, 123, 169, 186, 290, 291, and 373). All of the eight variants are trivial changes, such as omissions, additions, and transpositions of single words or letters, so de Worde's "Shipman's Tale" must have been based on Cx^2.

1.15. "Monk's Prologue" (L29)

The "Monk's Prologue" of *Wy* has only three variants from Cx^2; two are unique to *Wy* and the other one is the omission of *haue* in Cx^2. *Wy*'s reading agrees with *Ii*, but this must be a coincidence and this section seems to have been reprinted from Cx^2.

1.16. "Man of Law's Prologue" (L7) and "Tale" (ML)

There is only one variant in the "Man of Law's Prologue" (in line 38, *the* is omitted), so undoubtedly *Wy* is a reprint of Cx^2 here. The "Man of Law's Tale" (1,064 lines) has twenty-five variants in total: Ten are unique to *Wy* (ML 191, 266, 386, 415, 416, 465, 627, 629, 845, and 950), whereas fifteen are shared by manuscript authorities. Of these fifteen variants, six agree with *Hg*, *El*, and the other major manuscripts (ML 42, 80, 525, 616, 783, and 915), but all of the variants could easily have been introduced by the editor/compositor: There are transposition (ML 42, 783), word omission (ML 80, 525), and word substitution (*tyme* for *tyde* in ML 616; *moders* for *moder* in ML 915). Of the remaining nine variants, which do not agree with either *Hg* or *El*, seven variants involve omission (ML 484, 515, 568, 621, 761, 991, 1014), one involves substitution (in ML 659 $þ^e$ for *this*), and one involves addition (in ML 1055 *the* is added to *to ground*). It is interesting that five of these nine variants that do not agree with *El* and *Hg* do agree with Ra^2; but there is no other regular recurrence of a particular manuscript that agrees with *Wy*'s variants. It seems reasonable to consider that de Worde used Cx^2 as his base text here, sometimes making textual changes to it.

In fact, of *Wy*'s variants that agree with *Hg* and *El*, one case shows that de Worde was a careful reader and editor:

This fals knyght þt hath this treson wrought
Bereth hyr in hond she [Custance] hath do thys thyng
But natheles there was grete mornyng
Among the pepyl & sayden they can not gesse
That she hadde *not* do so gret a wickednesse (Cx^2: ML 521–25)

These lines describe a scene where Custance stands accused by a knight of killing Hermengyld, the wife of Alla, the king of Northumberland. The people do not believe that Custance, who is a pious Christian woman, murdered her beloved Hermengyld; in fact, the accusation is a deception contrived by the knight, who has fallen in love with Custance. Cx^2's inclusion of *not* in ML 525 is therefore inappropriate here. The witnesses that contain *not* are only Cx^1, *Ne*, Tc^1 (*not do*), and *He* (*do non*); thus it appears that Caxton simply copied and retained the erroneous reading from Cx^1, whereas de Worde was careful enough to eradicate it. The correction in ML 525 was thus probably a result of de Worde's own editorial tinkering, where he paid considerable attention to the context of the narrative.

2. Tales based on multiple sources: "Knight's Tale" (KT)

The textual analysis conducted above has confirmed that the tales examined were reset from Cx^2, occasionally involving revisions of Cx^2, though presumably without manuscript support. De Worde's "Knight's Tale", however, shows some exceptional variants which suggest that de Worde could well have referred to a manuscript source alongside Cx^2. In fact, de Worde's reliance on a manuscript source is not exceptional at all. As the previous scholarship has established, de Worde consulted a manuscript as an additional source to Cx^2, or even printed his text directly from it in several tales of the latter half of the volume (see Appendix 1).

In an article published in 1924, Greg analyzed the first 116 lines of the "Knight's Tale" in the incunabula editions. Greg recognized 18 readings where *Wy* differs both from Cx^2 and Pynson's first edition, among which there were three, he assumed, that "might have been made by an attentive reader but might equally be derived from any manuscript except Tt2" (Greg 1924: 756–757). He further suggests that two specific readings out of these 18 might, if derived from a manuscript, have come from Ad^1, Ad^3, En^3, Ha^3, Sl^1, *El* and *Hg*; or possibly En^2, Ha^1, Ha^2, or *Gg*. Greg's remarks, however, are based on the analysis of the first 116 lines of the tale only, whereas the following analysis presents a textual comparison of the entire text of the "Knight's Tale" between *Wy*, Cx^2 and the extant manuscripts.

According to my collation, in the analysis of the results of de Worde's "Knight's Tale", which has 2,244 lines, there are thirty-one lines in *Wy* that show substantive textual variations from Cx^2. Twelve of these are unique to *Wy* (KT 1, 73, 242, 482, 948, 1043, 1049, 1426, 1829, 2129, 2182, and 2191), whereas the remaining nineteen variants are supported by manuscript readings. This number of textual divergences from Cx^2 in the "Knight's Tale" is not as high as in the cases of, for example, the "Tale of Sir Thopas", where scholarship has established that de Worde printed his version directly from a manuscript source (Garbáty 1978). According to my own data, there are forty-eight substantive variants (including five unique readings) in the "Tale of Sir Thopas" (in total 194 lines); and variants occur at the rate of almost one every four lines. The number of textual differences from Cx^2 in de Worde is comparably much smaller in the "Knight's Tale", but the nature of these variants deserves further analysis.

When the variants agree with *Hg*, *El*, and the majority of the other "O group witnesses", these variants may have been derived from the archetype and/or disseminated across groups of manuscripts within the textual tradition; however, they are not helpful in allowing us to discern whether a particular reading is characteristic of a specific manuscript or group of manuscripts. In contrast, variants which are not shared by *Hg* and/or *El* may shed some light on the affiliation of the variants to the textual tradition of the *Canterbury Tales*. As for the "Knight's Tale" in *Wy*, there are nine textual differences from Cx^2 that do not agree with *El* and *Hg*

(KT 726, 1334, 1361, 1456, 1610, 1821, 2152, 2163, and 2170). The manuscripts that most frequently agree with the variants in *Wy* are *Py* (four times), *Bo¹* and *Ph²* (three times), and *Tc¹* (three times), but the number of agreements might be too low, and the manuscript groups that share these readings too scattered, to allow us to identify a particular manuscript or manuscript group as de Worde's source.

Nonetheless, the textual divergences of *Wy* from *Cx²* in the "Knight's Tale" explicitly indicate that de Worde strove to make some revision to his master's text, by introducing archetypical readings. Of the nineteen variants between *Wy* and *Cx²*, more than half agree with *Hg*, *El* and the majority of the related manuscripts (KT 3, 427, 445, 471, 552, 764, 808, 1386, 1911, and 1964). Most of these variants are substantive in the sense that they contribute to semantic changes in the text, and it is hard to attribute these changes simply to the editor/compositor's personal preference for one form over another. For example, in KT 427 *Cx²* reads *Thou mayst say thou hast wysedom & manhede*, whereas in *Wy*, as in *Hg*, *El*, *Ch*, *Cp*, and *La*, *Cx²*'s *say* is replaced by *syn*; similarly, at KT 445, where *Cx²* reads *That sayde se o cruel goddes that gouerne*, *Wy* reads *Then sayd he o cruell goddes that gouerne* (emphasis added), which is supported by *Hg*, *El*, *Ch*, *Cp*, *Dd*, *Gg*, *Ha⁴*, *La*, and many other manuscripts. At KT 808, *Cx²*, like *Cx¹*, reads *So strau[n]ge it [the destiny] is þ' though the world hath sworn*; but *straunge* in this context is inappropriate, and so in *Wy straunge* is replaced with *strong*, an appropriate emendation, following the lead of significant manuscripts, including *Hg*, *El*, *Ch*, *Cp*, *Gg*, *Ha⁴*, and *La*. Given the number of manuscript witnesses to this reading, the appearance of "strong" in *Wy* is clearly archetypical.

A further interesting example of such variations appears at KT 471: *Cx²* has the reading *And thourgh hym vnhappy and eek wood*, for which *Wy* reads *And eek thurgh Iuno Ialous and eke wood* (emphasis added). *Wy*'s reading is the same as most of the other manuscripts, including *Hg*, *El*, *Ch*, *Dd*, *Cp*, *Ha⁴*, *Gg*, and *La*. In contrast, according to Manly and Rickert, the only sources for the reading *hym vnhappy* at KT 471 are *Cx¹*, *Cx²*, and *Tc²*. This indicates that Caxton did not make any corrections to this sentence in *Cx¹*, despite the fact that he made a number of other textual revisions throughout his edition, using a manuscript source that presumably retained archetypical readings. Thus it is most likely that, like Caxton, de Worde had access to a manuscript which contained archetypical readings. In preparing his version, de Worde presumably compared the text of *Cx²* with that of a manuscript, and decided that some parts of *Cx²* in the "Knight's Tale" needed further textual revisions.

In this paper I have been able to confirm that de Worde made use of *Cx²* as the copy text for setting the majority of the verse texts, texts which up to now have escaped scholarly scrutiny. These texts have been thoroughly examined in this paper. The tales into which de Worde introduced an additional source have also now been safely established; these sections are in the "Knight's Tale", the "Prologue to Sir Thopas", the "Tale of Sir Thopas", the "Thopas-Melibee Link", the "Tale of Melibee", the "Monk's Tale", the "Nun's Priest's Prologue", the "Parson's Tale", and the "Retraction".

Now that we have established which copy texts de Worde adopted for all the tales, we can attempt to give an overview of how he prepared the whole of the *Canterbury Tales*. One of the main reasons why early printers such as de Worde adopted a manuscript source was in order to achieve textual completeness. For example, when de Worde reprinted Caxton's *Morte d'Arthur* (STC 802, 803), he supplemented his text with a manuscript source in places where Caxton's copy (STC 801) had missing leaves (Mukai 2000). In the case of the *Canterbury Tales*, however, de Worde adopted readings from a manuscript even when a copy of Caxton's edition was not deficient, as the analysis of the "Knight's Tale" has illustrated.

At this point, I would like to address the fact that de Worde's editorial praxis in producing *Wy* was the opposite of Caxton's approach when he prepared the text of Cx^2: While Caxton's corrections are scarce towards the end of the volume, especially in the prose texts, de Worde hardly used his manuscript source at all in the first half of *Wy*, but depended heavily upon it towards the end. De Worde could easily have reprinted the whole text of Cx^2 as it was, but he did not. In my view, de Worde might well have intended to complete what his master had left unfinished. As is well known, Caxton was asked to make corrections to Cx^1 by a *gentylman* who lent him a manuscript, but Caxton presumably had to work in great haste, so that he had to give up the process of adding corrections to the majority of the pages towards the end of the volume (Dunn 1939). It is most possible that de Worde, who was working as a foreman of Caxton, observed that his master had had to abandon the project. When preparing his version of the *Canterbury Tales*, then, de Worde borrowed a Chaucerian manuscript, possibly with the aim of completing Caxton's revisions. At first, de Worde might have planned to revise the whole volume, starting with the "Knight's Tale", but he found this too laborious a task, and so he decided instead to limit his work to those tales that Caxton had hardly touched.

It may well seem that de Worde simply followed his master's lead, but he was certainly no mere copyist: In fact, he clearly exercised his own editorship in preparing the *Canterbury Tales*. In this context, it might be worth mentioning de Worde's modernization of words in the *Canterbury Tales*. When we examine the entire text of de Worde's edition, we see that de Worde regularly changed or modernized words most attentively. Most strikingly, de Worde consistently substituted certain words throughout multiple tales, or sometimes even throughout the entire volume. Specifically, he changed *clepe, eke, ylke, thee/thou*, and *mykel*, replacing them with *call, also, sayd, you*, and *moche* respectively. For example, in the "Miller's Tale", *the(e)* in Cx^2 is replaced by *you* (MI 98), and *ye* (MI 112) in

Wy. Other examples are: The word *swynke*, which appears several times in the "General Prologue" (GP), and which is replaced by various different words in different contexts, each of which is contextually appropriate: In GP 21 *Wy* reads *goo* for *wenden* in Cx^2; GP 100 *carf* in Cx^2 is substituted with *keruid* in *Wy*; at GP 186 *swynke* is replaced by *besy*, and at GP 542 by *labur*; and at GP 533 *swynker* in Cx^2 is substituted by *labourer* – and so on. In particular, whereas Cx^2 contains *mykel/mykyl* in several tales, this word does not appear at all throughout the text of *Wy*. The linguistic provenance of *mykel/mykyl* is northern England, and so the form was probably deemed inappropriate for de Worde's intended readership, and so de Worde emended all instances of it in Cx^2.[4] These examples show that de Worde exercised editorial skills in preparing his text, probably with the aim of making the language more comprehensible to his intended contemporary readership.

The current study has attempted to re-envisage de Worde as a textual transmitter in his own right; an editor who played an important role in the textual tradition of the *Canterbury Tales*. The concept of editing which de Worde practiced was, nevertheless, far different from the editorial practices later exercised in early-modern England, for example, by William Thynne, who assembled and compared multiple sources to establish a sophisticated text. What de Worde sought was, nevertheless, a modernizing project: His aim was clearly not to preserve or restore the language, syntax, or style of Chaucer's original text. Instead, he shaped and defined the text for his own audiences, with the intention of completing his master's work.

References

Baker, Donald C. (ed.)
    1979   *A Variorum edition of the works of Geoffrey Chaucer, II, part 10: The "Manciple's Tale"*. Norman and London: University of Oklahoma Press.
    1983   *A Variorum edition of the works of Geoffrey Chaucer, II, part 12: The "Squire's Tale"*. Norman and London: University of Oklahoma Press.
Blake, Norman F.
    1997   "The Project's lineation system" in: Norman Blake – Peter Robinson (eds.), 5–14.

---

[4] The same tendency to replace *mykel/mykyl* by *moche* has been detected by Lotte Hellinga in de Worde's first edition of the Nicholas Love's translation of *Speculum Vitae Christi* printed in 1494 (*STC* 3261); see (Hellinga 1997: 153–155); and see also, for example, Edwards 1980 where he points out that de Worde himself probably made more than three hundred changes to Stephen Hawes's *Example of Vertu* between the 1509 and 1530 editions, specifically for the purpose of the modernization of language, syntax and style.

Blake, Norman F. – Peter Robinson (eds.)
    2002   *The Canterbury Tales Project occasional papers volume II*. (Office for Humanities Communication Publications 9.) London: Office for Humanities Communication.

Bordalejo, Barbara
    2002   The manuscript source of Caxton's second edition of the *Canterbury Tales* and its place in the textual tradition of the *Tales*. [Unpublished Ph.D. dissertation, De Montfort University.]

Boyd, Beverly
    1984   "William Caxton", in: Paul G. Ruggiers (ed.) 13–34.

Boyd, Beverly (ed.)
    1983   *A Variorum edition of the works of Geoffrey Chaucer, II, part 20: The "Prioress's Tale"*. Norman and London: University of Oklahoma Press.

Corsa, Helen Storm (ed.)
    1987   *A Variorum edition of the works of Geoffrey Chaucer, II, part 17: The "Physician's Tale"*. Norman and London: University of Oklahoma Press.

Dunn, Thomas F.
    1939   The manuscript source of Caxton's second edition of the *Canterbury Tales*. [Unpublished Ph.D. dissertation, University of Chicago.]

Edwards, Anthony Stockwell Garfield
    1980   "Poet and printer in sixteenth century England: Stephen Hawes and Wynkyn de Worde", *Gutenberg Jahrbuch* 55: 82–88.

Garbáty, Thomas J.
    1978   "Wynkyn de Worde's 'Sir Thopas' and other tales", *Studies in Bibliography* 31: 57–67.

Greg, Walter W.
    1924   "The early printed editions of the *Canterbury Tales*", *Publications of the Modern Language Association* 39, 4: 737–761.
    1950-1951   "The rationale of copy-text", *Studies in Bibliography* 3: 19–36.

Hellinga, Lotte
    1983   "Manuscripts in the hands of printers", in: J. B. Trapp (ed.), 3–11.
    1997   "Nicholas Love in print", in: Shoichi Oguro – Richard Beadle – Michael G. Sargent (eds.), 143–162.

Hellinga, Lotte (ed.)
    2007   *Catalogue of books printed in the XVth century now in the British Library. Part XI, England*. 't Goy-Houten: Hes & De Graaf.

Hutmacher, William F.
    1978   *Wynkyn de Worde and Chaucer's* Canterbury Tales: *A transcription and collation of the 1498 edition with Caxton2 from the* General Prologue *through the* Knight's Tale. (Costerus NS 10.) Amsterdam: Rodopi.

Manly, John M. – Edith Rickert (eds.)
    1940   The text of the *Canterbury Tales*: Studied on the basis of all known manuscripts. 8 vols. Chicago: University Chicago Press.

Mukai, Tsuyoshi
    2000   "De Worde's 1498 *Morte Darthur* and Caxton's copy-text", *Review of English Studies* New Series 51: 24–42.
Oguro, Shoichi – Richard Beadle – Michael G. Sargent (eds.)
    1997   *Nicholas Love at Waseda: Proceedings of the International Conference 20–22 July 1995*. Cambridge: Brewer.
Partridge, Stephen Bradford
    2007   "Wynkyn de Worde's manuscript source for the *Canterbury Tales*: Evidence from the glosses", *The Chaucer Review* 41, 4: 325–359.
Pearsall, Derek (ed.)
    1983   *A Variorum edition of the works of Geoffrey Chaucer, II, part 9: The "Nun's Priest's Tale"*. Norman and London: University of Oklahoma Press.
Plummer III, John F. (ed.)
    1983   *A Variorum edition of the works of Geoffrey Chaucer, II, part 7: The "Summoner's Tale"*. Norman and London: University of Oklahoma Press.
Prendergast, Thomas A. – Barbara Kline (eds.)
    1999   *Rewriting Chaucer: Culture, authority, and the idea of the authentic text, 1400–1602*. Columbus: Ohio State University.
Ransom, Daniel J.
    2000   "Prolegomenon to a print history of the 'Parson's Tale': The novelty and legacy of Wynkyn de Worde's text", in: David Raybin – Linda Tarte Holley (eds.), 77–93.
Ransom, Daniel, et al. (eds.)
    1993   *A Variorum edition of the works of Geoffrey Chaucer, II, part one A: The "General Prologue"*. Norman and London: University of Oklahoma Press.
Raybin, David – Linda Tarte Holley (eds.)
    2000   *Closure in The Canterbury Tales: The role of the "Parson's Tale"*. (Studies in Medieval Culture 41.) Kalamazoo: Medieval Institute.
Robinson, Peter
    1997   "A stemmatic analysis of the fifteenth-century witnesses to the *Wife of Bath's Prologue*", in: Norman Blake – Peter Robinson (eds.), 69–132.
Robinson, Peter (ed.)
    1996   *The* Wife of Bath's Prologue *on CD-ROM*. Cambridge: Cambridge University Press.
    2004   *The* Miller's Tale *on CD-ROM*. Leicester: Scholarly Digital Editions.
Ross, Thomas W. (ed.)
    1983   *A Variorum edition of the works of Geoffrey Chaucer, II, part 3: The "Miller's Tale"*. Norman and London: University of Oklahoma Press.
Ruggiers, Paul G. (ed.)
    1984   *Editing Chaucer: The great tradition*. Norman, OK: Pilgrim.

Tokunaga, Satoko
    2001   "The sources of Wynkyn de Worde's version of the *Monk's Tale*". *The Library*, 7th ser. 2: 223–235.
    2005   The textual transmission of the *Canterbury Tales*: The case of Wynkyn de Worde. [Unpublished Ph.D. dissertation, Keio University.]
Thomas, Paul (ed.)
    2006   The Nun's Priest's Tale *on CD-ROM*. Birmingham: Scholarly Digital Editions.
Trapp, J. B. (ed.)
    1983   *Manuscripts in the fifty years after the invention of printing: Some papers read at a colloquium at the Warburg Institute on 12–13 March 1982*. London: Warburg Institute, University of London.
Vaughan, Míceál F.
    1999   "Creating comfortable boundaries: Scribes, editors, and the invention of the *Parson's Tale*", in: Thomas A. Prendergast – Barbara Kline (eds.), 45–90.

Appendix 1

Source studies of de Worde's 1498 edition of the *Canterbury Tales*

Textual segment	Source(s) used for *Wy*	Reference[5]
"General Prologue"	Cx^2	Ransom *et al.* (eds.) 1993
"Knight's Tale"	Cx^2 and ms (only first 116 lines examined)	Greg 1950–1951
"Miller's Prologue" and "Tale"	Cx^2	Ross (ed.) 1983
		Robinson (ed.) 2004
"Reeve's Prologue" and "Tale"		
"Cook's Prologue" and "Tale"		
"Man of Law's Prologue" and "Tale"		
"Wife of Bath's Prologue"	Cx^2	Robinson 1997
"Wife of Bath's Tale"		
"Friar's Prologue" and "Tale"		
"Summoner's Prologue" and "Tale"	Cx^2	Plummer III (ed.) 1983
"Clerk's Tale"		
"Lenvoy of Chaucer"		
"Words of the Host"		
"Merchant's Prologue" and "Tale"		
"Man of Law's Endlink"		
"Squire's Tale"	Cx^2	Baker (ed.) 1983
"Squire-Franklin Link"		
"Franklin's Tale"		
"Second Nun's Prologue and Tale"		
"Canon's Yemon's Prologue" and "Tale"		
"Physician's Tale"	Cx^2	Corsa (ed.) 1987
"Physician/Pardoner Link"	Cx^2	Corsa (ed.) 1987
"Pardoner's Prologue and Tale"		
"Shipman's Tale"		
"Shipman/Prioress Link"	Cx^2 and ms	Boyd (ed.) 1983
"Prioress's Tale"	Cx^2 and ms	Boyd (ed.) 1983
		Hellinga 1983, (ed.) 2007
"Prologue to Sir Thopas", "Tale of Sir Thopas", "Thopas-Melibee Link"	ms	Garbáty 1978
"Tale of Melibee"	ms	Garbáty 1978
		Hellinga 1983, (ed.) 2007
		Partridge 2007 (on glosses)

---

5   In addition to these studies cited here, Hutmache has conducted a textual comparison between *Wy* and Cx^2 from the "General Prologue" to the "Franklin's Tale".

"Monk's Prologue"		
"Monk's Tale"	Cx^2 and ms	Tokunaga 2001
"Nun's Priest's Prologue"	ms	Pearsall (ed.) 1983
		Thomas (ed.) 2006
"Nun's Priest's Tale" and "Endlink"	Cx^2	Pearsall (ed.) 1983
		Thomas (ed.) 2006
"Manciple's Prologue" and "Tale"	Cx^2	Baker (ed.) 1979
"Parson's Prologue"	Cx^2	Ransom 1999
"Parson's Tale"	ms	Hellinga 1983, (ed.) 2007
		Ransom 1999
		Partridge 2007 (on glosses)
"Retraction"	ms	Vaughan 1999

Appendix 2

Collation results of de Worde's *Canterbury Tales*[6]

Appendix 2 includes the collation results of the tales of the *Canterbury Tales* from Cx^2 and *Wy* which are examined in this paper. The base text is Cx^2 and variants are *Wy*'s readings with manuscript supports; "+" indicates that there are more witnesses supporting the reading of *Wy*. *Wy*'s variants from Cx^2 are categorized and listed into three groups:

Wy with *Hg-El*: Variants agree with *El*, *Hg* and majority of other manuscripts.
Wy with *Hg/El*: Variants agree with either *El* or *Hg*.
Wy-not-*Hg-El*: Variants do not agree with *El* and *Hg*.

"Reeve's Tale" (RE)[7]
Wy-not-*Hg-El*
  <RE 115/A 4035> *that*] omit. *Wy* Cx^1 / b Bo¹ Bo² Cn En¹ En³ Fi Ha³ Ht Ii Lc Mc Nl Py Ra³ Sl¹ Sl² Tc¹ To
  <RE 126/A 4046> *Thys*] *The Wy* / *Nl*
  <RE 151/A 4071> *hys*] *her Wy* / *Pw*
  <RE 270/A 4190> *abreyde*] *brayd Wy Ad³ Dd* / *Ha⁵* Bo¹ Ma

---

6   The data presented in this Appendix are the collation results generated by using the *Canterbury Tales Project*'s system. However, I also made a substantial use of Manly and Rickert's "Corpus of Variants", and adopted their records of variants when the transcriptions of all the manuscripts were not available for running the *Collate 2*.
7   The base text is Cx^2, and the representatives of variants are from *Wy*.

"Wife of Bath's Tale" (WBT)
Wy with *Hg-El*
<WBT 981/D 1008> *quyte wel*] *wel quyte Wy Hg El Ad³ Bo² Cn Cp Dd*+
<WBT 1209/D 1236> *I haue*] *haue I Wy Hg El Ad³ Bo² Ch Cp Dd Gg La*+
<WBT 1231/D 1258> *And*] *In Wy Hg El Ad³ Bo² Ch Cp Dd Gg La*+
*Wy-*not-*Hg-El*
<WBT 1097/D 1124> *vs folowe hem*] *hem folowe vs Wy Cx¹* / b̲ *Hk*

"Friar's Prologue" (Link 10)
Wy with *Hg-El*
<L10 9/D 1273> *I se ye*] *I saye Wy Hg El Ad³ Ch Cp Ds¹La*+

"Friar's Tale" (FR)
Wy with *Hg-El*
<FR 66/D 1366> *there I may the*] *thre I the may Wy Hg El Ad³ Bo² Ch Cp Gg Ha⁴ La*+
*Wy-*not-*Hg-El*
<FR 92/D 1392> *baylle*] *baylyf⁸ Wy Cp Gg Ht La Ra³*
<FR 96/D 1396> *baylle*] *baylyf Wy Ht La Ra³*
<FR 103/D 1403> *thys*] *the Wy* / *Ad¹ En³ Nl Ph³ Ra¹ Ry² Ld²*
<FR 251/D 1551> *thy*] *my Wy Ad³* / *Ad¹ Bw Ps Si To*
<FR 282/D 1581> *the*] *this Wy* / *Ha³ Ld² Mc Ra¹*
<FR 311/D 1610> *than*] omit. *Wy* / *Ha³ He Ii Ra³*
<FR 347/D 1646> *had*] omit. *Wy* / *Ad¹ En³*

"Clerk's Tale" (CL)
Wy with *Hg-El*
<CL 708/E 708> *wayted*] *wayteth Wy Hg El Ad³ Bo² Ch Cp Dd Gg La*+
*Wy-*not-*Hg-El*
<CL 73/E 73> *and strong*] *a strong Wy Cx¹* / *Cn Mg Ne Tc²*
<CL 79/E 79> *In*] *I Wy* / *He*
<CL 448/E 448> *nys*] *is Wy Ch Cp Ds¹ En¹ Ht La* / *Ad¹* Bo̲¹ *Bw* c̲ *Cn Dl En² Fi Ha² Ha³ Hk* Lc̲ *Ld¹ Ln* Mc̲ *Nl Ph⁴* Ps̲ Pw̲ *Ra² Ra³ Ra⁴ Ry¹ Ry² Si Sl¹ Tc¹ Tc²*
<CL 449/E 449> *ofte tyme*] *oft tymes Wy* / *Ad²*
<CL 618/E 618> *vp on*] *vpon a Wy Cx¹ Dd Ds¹ En¹ Ht*
<CL 802/E 802> *pope*] *popes Wy Ad³ En¹ Gg Ht* / *Ad²* Bo̲¹ (eras. *Bo¹*) C̲n̲ *Ha⁴ Ld²* Mc̲ *Mm Np Ph⁴ Ra² Ra⁴ Ry¹ Si*
<CL 834/E 834> *I was*] *was I Wy Hl⁴* / E̲n̲³ *Ha³ Tc¹*
<CL 971/E 971> *no*] omit. *Wy* / *Fi La Ld¹ Nl Ra⁴*
<CL 1057/E 1057> *her in armys took*] *in his armys toke Wy* / *Sl² Tc²*

---

8   Manly and Rickert do not record *baylyf* as a variant.

"Merchant's Tale" (ME)
Wy with *Hg-El*
    <ME 46/E 1290> *not hym*] *hym nat Wy Hg El Bo² Ch Dd Gg Ha⁴*+
    <ME 685/E 1929> *calle*] *to call Wy Hg El Ch Gg*+
    <ME 1062/E 2306> *to*] omit. *Wy Hg El Ad³ Bo² Ch Cp Dd Gg Ha⁴ La*+
    <ME 1133/E 2377> *you yeue*] *yeue you Wy Hg El Ad³ Bo² Ch Dd Gg Ha⁴*+
Wy-not-*Hg-El*
    <ME 73/E 1317> *hous*] *hondis Wy Sl²*
    <ME 116/E 1360> *as*] *after Wy Bo² Ds¹ He Hk Sl² / Cn Gl Ii Ld¹*
    <ME 303/E 1547> *in*] omit. *Wy Cx¹ Gg Ha³ He Ii* (not in Manly – Rickert 1940) *La Ne Pn Tc²*
    <ME 449/E 1693> *That thys mayde whyche that may hyghte*] *That this mayde whyche that mayus Wy Dl Ld¹*
    <ME 700/E 1944> *Thys bylle had*] *This byll hath Wy Cx¹ Ii Tc²*
    <ME 812/E 2056> *ne no wordly*] *ne to no worldly Wy Ch Cp Dl En² Ha² Ha³ La Lc Ld Ln Mg Mm Ne Nl Ph³ Pw Ry¹ Ry² To¹ / Sl²* (not in Manly – Rickert 1940)
    <ME 884/E 2128> *may men*] *men may Wy Ps Tc¹ / Hk Ii*
    <ME 946/E 2190> *my*] omit. *Wy Tc¹*
    <ME 1011/E 2255> *that*] omit. *Wy Ha⁵ Py*
    <ME 1107/E 2351> *not*] *no Wy Ch Py*

"Squire-Franklin Link" (L20)
Wy-not-*Hg-El*
    <L20 31/F 703> *sir hoost quod he*] *quod he syr hoste Wy Ht Ps / Tc¹*
    <L20 34/F 706> *that*] omit. *Wy Dl Fi Gl Ln Nl Pw Ra² Ra³ / Ha² Sl¹ Tc¹*

"Franklin's Tale" (FK)
Wy with *Hg-El*
    <FK 25/F 733> *was*] *were Wy Hg El Ad³ Ch Gg La*+
    <FK 624/F 1332> *forto*] *to Wy Hg El Ad³ Bo² Cn Cp Dd Gg Ha⁴ La*+
    <FK 756/F 1466> *to*] omit. *Wy Hg El Ad³ Bo² Ch Dd Gg Ha⁴*+
Wy-not-*Hg-El*
    <FK 78/F 786> *on*] *of Wy Cx¹ Ha² He Ii Ne / Ad¹ En³ Ha³ Hk Nl Tc²*
    <FK 196/F 904> *of*] omit. *Wy Bo² Ds¹ Fi / En¹*
    <FK 333/F 1041> *ye*] *thou Wy Ad¹ Bo²* (not in Manly – Rickert 1940) *En³ Gg Ha⁵ Ma Mg Mm* (not in Manly – Rickert 1940) *Ph³ Ps / Gl To¹*
    <FK 376/F 1084> *this [...] this [...]*] *his [...] his [...] Wy Bo¹ Cp Dl En² Ha² La Lc Ld¹ Ld² Ma Mm Ph² Ps Pw Ry² Se / Sl² Ii Mg Nl Sl²*
    <FK 439/F 1147> *as*] omit. *Wy Cx¹ Pn Bw Fi Ha⁵ Hk Ii Ln Ne Ps Ra³ / He Tc² Gl Ha³ Nl To*
    <FK 641/F 1349> *it*] omit. *Wy Cx¹ Hk Ne / Ha³ Tc¹*

<FK 778/F 1488> *anone*] omit. *Wy Ry[1]*
<FK 840/F 1556> line missing] *Wy Fi* / <u>c</u>
<FK 857/F 1573> *I ges*] *as I ges* *Wy Cn Dl Ma* / *Gl Ra[3]*
<FK 875/F 1591> *me*] omit. *Wy* / *To*

"Second Nun's Prologue and Tale" (NU)
Wy with *Hg*/*El*
   <NU 493/G 493> *O cecily*] *O* omit. *Wy Hg Ad[3] Ch Ds[1] En[1] Ha[4] La Ra[3]*+
Wy-not-*Hg*-*El*
   <NU 32/G 32> *wretchys*] *wretchyd* *Wy* / *Ps*
   <NU 169/G 169> *right*] omit. *Wy Bo[2] Cp Ht La* / <u>Bo</u>[1] <u>En</u>[2] <u>En</u>[3] *Fi Ha[2] Hl[3] Ii* <u>Lc</u> *Ld[1] Mc Nl* <u>Pw</u> *Ra[2] Ry[1]* <u>Ry</u>[2] *Sl[1]*
   <NU 175/G 175> *right as that I*] *ryght as I* *Wy Gg* / *Ha[3] Hl[3] Tc[1]*
   <NU 384/G 384> *al*] omit. *Wy* / *Bw Ii Ln Mc Nl Ra[2]*
   <NU 508/G 508> *his*] omit. *Wy Ds[1] En[1] Ra[3]* / <u>Cn</u> *Fi Gl Ld[1]* (space) *Pw Ry[2]* (space Ry[2]) *Tc[1] To*
   <NU 510/G 510> *do not*] *do no* *Wy Cx[1]* / <u>Cx</u>[1] *Ha[3]*
   <NU 516/G 516> *was it do*] *it was do* *Wy* / *Ha[3]*

"Canon's Yeoman's Prologue" (L33)
Wy-not-*Hg*-*El*
   <L33 54/G 607> *it*] omit. *Wy* / <u>b</u> *Cn Ha[3]*
   <L33 166/G 719> *thynges*] *Wy* / *Nl To*

"Canon's Yeoman's Tale" (CY)
Wy-not-*Hg*-*El*
   <CY 21/G 740> *For*] *So* *Wy Cp* / *Nl*
   <CY 140/G 859> *wol I*] *I wol* *Wy* / <u>En</u>[3]
   <CY 172/G 891> *folke*] *folkes* *Wy* / *Hk*
   <CY 279/G 998> *is*] *it is* *Wy Cp* / *Ph[3]*
   <CY 363/G 1082> *to*] omit. *Wy Ph[3]*
   <CY 720/G 1439> *he*] *be* *Wy Ad[3] Ch Cx[1] Ds[1] El En[1] Gg Ha[4]*+

"Pardoner's Prologue and Tale" (PD)
Wy-not-*Hg*-*El*
   <PD 95/C 423> *I woll*] *woll I* *Wy Ht* / *Ad[2] Ht*
   <PD 250/C 578> *ye mowe*] *mow ye* *Wy* / *Dl* <u>En</u>[3] *Ld[2] Mm Nl Ps Py*
   <PD 337/C 665> *was*] *þ[t] was* *Wy* / *Gl Ii Ra[3]*

"Shipman's Tale" (SH)
Wy with *Hg*-*El*
   <SH 169/B 1359> *this*] *thus* *Wy Hg El Ad[3] Bo[2] Ch Cp Dd Gg Ha[4] La*+

Wy-not-*Hg*-*El*
    <SH 29/B 1219> *so*] omit. *Wy Cn Ma Ps*
    <SH 42/B 1232> *dure*] endure *Wy Nl* / *Gl*^{1} *Gl*^{2} *Ht Ii La Ld*^{1} *Ln Ps Ra*^{3} *Sl*^{2}
    <SH 123/B 1313> *am I of drede*] *I am of dred* *Wy Pn Ad*^{1} *Bo*^{1} *Cn Dl En*^{2} *En*^{3}
    Fi Ha^2 *Ma Mm Nl Ph*^{2} *Ry*^{2} *To* / *Bw Lc Mg Pw Ph*^{3} *Py Ra*^{2} *Ld*^{2} *Sl*^{1}
    <SH 186/B 1376> *must I*] *I muste* *Wy Ps To*
    <SH 290/B 1480> *goldeles*] *goodles* *Wy Ad*^{1} *Ad*^{3} *En*^{3}
    <SH 291/B 1481> *in*] *at* *Wy Cx*^{1} *Ii Ne Nl Se*
    <SH 373/B 1563> *redy*] *redyly* *Wy* / Lc *Ln*

"Monk's Prologue" (Link 29)
Wy-not-*Hg*-*El*
    <L29 57/B2 3135> *haue*] omit. *Wy Ii*

"Man of Law's Prologue" (L7)
Wy with *Hg*-*El*
    <L7 38/B 38> *at the leest*] *at leest* *Wy Hg El Bo*^{2} *Ch Cp Ds*^{1}*Ha*^{4} *La*+

"Man of Law's Tale" (ML)
Wy with *Hg*-*El*
    <ML 42/B 140> *sellen her hem*] *sellen hem her* *Wy Hg El Bo*^{2} *Ch Cp Dd Gg La*+
    <ML 80/B 178> *þ*^{1}] omit. *Wy Hg El Bo*^{2} *Ch Cp Dd Gg Ha*^{4}+
    <ML 525/B 623> *hadde not do*] *had do* *Wy Hg El Bo*^{2} *Ch Cp Gg Ha*^{4} *La*+
    <ML 616/B 714> *tyde*] *tyme* *Wy Hg El Bo*^{2} *Cx*^{1} *Cp Ch Dd Gg Ha*^{4} *La*+
    <ML 783/B 881> *it telle*] *telle it* *Wy Hg El Bo*^{2} *Ch Cp Dd Gg Ha*^{4} *La*+
    <ML 915/B 1013> *moder*] *moders* *Wy Hg El Bo*^{2} *Ch Cp Dd Gg Ha*^{4}+
Wy-not-*Hg*-*El*
    <ML 484/B 582> *euer vs waytith*] *euer wayteth* *Wy Ht* / *Ha*^{2} *Nl* Ra^2
    <ML 515/B 613> *here before ye me haue herd*] *here before ye haue herde* *Wy* / Bo^1 *Dl Ha*^{1} *Hk* Lc Mc *Pw Py* Ra^2 *Ry*^{1} *Tc*^{1}
    <ML 568/B 666> *wryten*] omit. *Wy* / *Tc*^{1}
    <ML 621/B 719> *so*] omit. *Wy* / *Hk Ra*^{1}
    <ML 659/B 757> *this lettre*] *þ*^{e} *letter* *Wy* / *Ht* (not recorded in Manly – Rickert 1940) / *Ln Nl Py* Ra^2
    <ML 761/B 859> *lytyl*] omit. *Wy* / *To*
    <ML 991/B 1089> *so souereyn*] *souereyn* *Wy* / Mc
    <ML 1014/B 1112> *none*] omit. *Wy Cx*^{1} *Bo*^{2} *La* / b *Dl Fi Lc* Mc Mm *Nl Ox*^{2} *Ph*^{3} Ps *Py* Ra^2 *Se To*
    <ML 1055/B 1153> *to*] *to the* *Wy* / *Ha*^{1} *Ra*^{2}

"Knight's Tale" (KT)

Wy with *Hg-El*

    <KT 3/A 861> *thebes*] Athenes *Wy Hg El Ch Cp Dd Gg Ha^4 La*+

    <KT 427/A 1285> *say*] syn *Wy Hg El Ch Cp La*+

    <KT 445/A 1303> *That*] Then *Wy Hg El Ch Cp Dd Gg Ha^4 La*+ | *se*] he *Wy Hg El Ch Cp Dd Gg Ha^4 La*+

    <KT 471/A 1329> *And thourgh hym vnhappy*] And eek thurgh Iuno Ialous *Wy Hg El Ch Cp Dd Gg Ha^4 La*+

    <KT 552/A 1410> *And alone*] And al allone *Wy Hg El Ch Cp Dd Gg Ha^4 La*+

    <KT 764/A 1622> *ither*] eche *Wy Hg El Ch Cp Ha^4 Gg La*+ | *hath*] had *Wy Hg El Ch Cp Gg Ha^4 La*+

    <KT 808/A 1666> *strau[n]ge*] strong *Wy Hg El Ch Cp Gg Ha^4 La*+

    <KT 1386/A 2244> *and*] and in *Wy Hg El Cp Dd Ha^4 La*+

    <KT 1911/A 2771> *payne*] paynes *Wy Hg El Ad^3 Ch Cp Dd Gg Ha^4 La*+

    <KT 1964/A 2828> *Or*] Of *Wy Cx^1 Hg El Ad^3 Ch Cp Dd Gg Ha^4 La*+

Wy-not-*Hg-El*

    <KT 726/A 1584> *the*] omitted *Wy Py*

    <KT 1334/A 2192> *at*] after *Wy* / <u>Bo</u>^{1} *Dl* <u>En</u>^{2} *Fi Ha^2 Ha^3 Ii* <u>Lc</u> *Ld^1 Ln Ma^2 Ps* <u>Pw</u> *Py* <u>Ry</u>^{2} *Se Sl^1 Tc^1*

    <KT 1361/A 2219> *knelyth*] knelyd *Wy La* / *Ht La Ld^2 Ln Py Tc^1*

    <KT 1456/A 2314> *hath suche loue*] suche loue hath *Wy* / <u>Bo</u>^{1} *Dl*

    <KT 1610/A 2468> *castis*] castelles *Wy* / <u>Bo</u>^{1} *Bw*

    <KT 1821/A 2679> *vp on*] vnto *Wy Pn* / <u>En</u>^{2} *Fi Ha^2* <u>Lc</u> *Ld^1 Ln* <u>Pw</u> *Py* <u>Ry</u>^{2} *Sl^1*

    <KT 2152/A 3016> *Thys*] Thus *Wy* / *Dl Ll^1 Sl^2*

    <KT 2163/A 3027> *wel*] <u>omit</u>. *Wy Cx^1* / <u>b</u> *Nl Ra^1 Tc^1*

    <KT 2170/A 3034> *thyng*] thynges *Wy* / *Ll^1* <u>Ra</u>^{2}

Compounds and code-switching: Compositorial practice in William Turner's *Libellus de re herbaria novvs*, 1538[1]

Roderick W. McConchie, University of Helsinki

1. Introduction

This paper considers the interpretation of type-setting practice in a Latin-English work by William Turner, the *Libellus de re herbaria novvs* of 1538, published by John Byddell (Bydell).[2] The book itself, a modest quarto collated Ai^r-Bii^v, lists the herbs with their names in Greek, Latin and English, and gives brief descriptions of them. The matrix text is Latin, as is the title-page and the epistle to the reader. The title-border consists of five flower panels, appropriately chosen for the subject, but not very well matched and apparently not designed as a set for this production. A dedication to Thomas Patinson appears at the end of the work.

Turner faced particular problems in compiling his botanical works, first in what to include and whether to be inclusive in the sprit of the the German pioneer, Otto Brunfels (1464–1534), or whether to adhere to the traditional list of Dioscorides. He felt obliged to list plants unknown in England and those which had no recognized name in English, and thus had to neologize (see Rydén 1994; McConchie 2002: 277, 283). Some of these new terms and descriptive compounds became established in English, as Rydén has shown. Since the *Libellus* was a multilingual text, there was also the question of whether it was desirable to mark foreign terms in some way in the text, and if so how, especially in a text which is almost lexicographic in the richness of its botanical terminology, Turner's botanical works having indeed been described as "polyglot lexicons of herbs" (Lancashire 2004: 20).[3] The conventional way of doing this was to use italics to distinguish such terms from a matrix text in blackletter by using a different fount, often italic where the foreign language was Latin. The solution adopted in the *Libellus*, was however, idiosyncratic, as we shall see. I also consider the relation of the solution to this problem eventually adopted to other conventions of printing, showing the difference between this work and some others which adopted different and more conventional solutions.

---

1 My thanks to the Varieng Centre of Excellence, funded by the Finnish Academy, and to an anonymous referee for very helpful remarks and suggestions.
2 Three copies of this work are mentioned in *STC*: One in the British Library, the second in the Library of the Museum of History and Science, Oxford, and the third in private possession.
3 I have argued elsewhere that it should be regarded in this light; see McConchie (2002: 277–278).

2. English compounds

Knowing whether a word in early modern English was regarded as a compound or not is not always a straightforward matter, and was not necessarily simplified by the advent of movable type. In considering possible compounds as they appear in early printed books, we must consider the conventions of type-setting as well as the other linguistic evidence which comes to hand, such as the written record of a particular lexeme, the type of compound, and whether it derives from an earlier form, or is borrowed or neologized. Many considerations, however, not all pertinent to accurate linguistic representation, might affect the way in which a compositor worked, including line justification and page layout, an idiolect or dialect differing from that of the author, spelling conventions imposed by the printing house, and so on.

In the fairly recent modern edition of Turner's *Libellus* by Rydén, Helander, and Olsson, a remark is made about the difficulty of deciding in many instances "whether a compound plant name is printed in one or two words" (1999: 13). My contention is that some consideration of the practices adopted by Byddell's printing-house will help resolve the great majority of them. In general, the editors of the *Libellus* have not commented on the actual layout and production of the book, rather against the spirit of their own comment on the view that "orthographic habits mirror current ideas of etymology and word-relations" (18). One might well add that in this case typographical conventions are also relevant to lexical questions. A typical instance is that on page 60, where, under *Cynorrhodos*, the editors transcribe *swetebrere* for what is obviously *swete brere* in the original printed text, while on the same page they render *brere tre* as two words between which the spacings are no larger than between *swete* and *brere* in the previous example. The regular practice for the Latin text in this work is the conventional one of using an en space or less and, in a cramped line, omitting spaces on one or both sides of punctuation marks.

Figure 1. Swete brere (sig. Aiv^v)

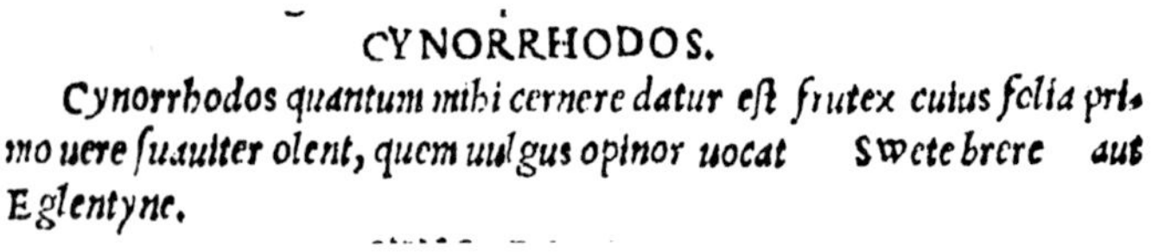

CYNORRHODOS.
Cynorrhodos quantum mihi cernere datur eſt frutex cuius folia pri-
mo uere fuauiter olent, quem uulgus opinor uocat   Swete brere   aut
Eglentyne.

Note: All figures have been taken from Early English Books Online [http://eebo.chadwyck.com/home] PDF images of the works concerned. The upright capitals are typical of italic founts prior to the middle of the sixteenth century (Dowding 1998: 45).

In fact, there appear to be only two really ambiguous cases in this text, each of a somewhat different kind. The first is *Hallywaterstrycle Disshewashinges* (*Hippvris*, sig. Bij^r) and the second is the term *esp tre* (sig. Biiij^v) and *heptre* (sig. Aiiij^v) (Rydén *et al.*'s readings). The real question is how consistently compounds are treated, and how they relate to other compositorial rules in this text.

The first matter can probably be resolved by considering the effect of the long *st* ligature of *stryncle*. There is a suggestion of a space, but the lower, left-pointing descender makes it look less obvious than it might be.[4] Where there is no space before this ligature, the kerned descender bends in under the previous letter, as in *nostrata* and *bistortis*, five lines from the bottom of the previous page. It does not do so here. Moxon, writing in the following century, points out in *Mechanick Exercises* that the proper use of the thin-space is to justify the line, not to separate words, but Byddell's compositor, or compositors, seem to have had other principles in mind, as we shall see. As Moxon remarks "Thin-spaces being intended and Cast only that the Compositor may Justifie his Lines the Truer, and not to serve for convenient distinction between Words; yet do some Compositors too often commit this error, rather than put themselves to the trouble of Spacing out a Line" Moxon continues by adumbrating the problems of setting too wide and too close (Moxon 1677: II, 215).

The other problem is created by the *w* of *water*, which looks a bit odd. The most important point here is that this *w* is not native to the italic fount used, which obviously had no *w*, presumably being French or possibly Italian in origin.[5] The *w* used looks awkward, clearly having a larger *x*-height than the rest of the fount, and often rides a bit too high and on occasions too low. It also recurves strongly to the top left.[6] On balance, *hallywater stryncle Dysshewasshynges* seems the best reading, given that the insertion of this *w* always leaves a slightly larger gap to each side of it than the regular letters in this fount.

Figure 2. Hallywater stryncle (sig. Bij^r, detail)

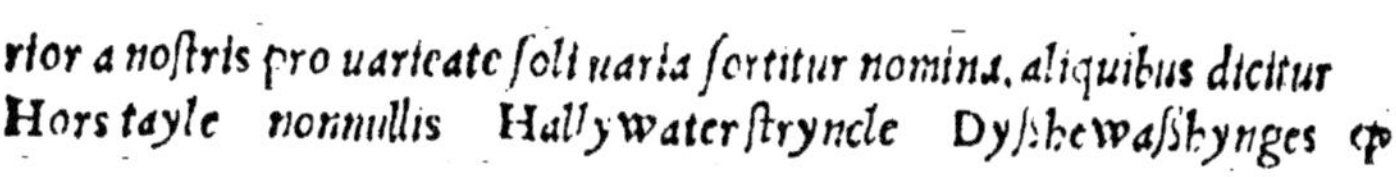

rlor a noſtris pro uaricate foli uaria fortitur nomina, aliquibus dicitur Hors tayle nonnullis Hallywaterſtryncle Dyſhewaſhynges cp

The *esptre*/*heptre* problem is perhaps best considered in the light of the practice elsewhere in the book. All the terms involving *tre* are separated by a space, except for these two, and in both these cases the lines in which they occur are rather

---

4   This may be a hair-space; presumably what Moxon describes as a "thin-space" (1677: 215), which was one-fifth of an em (*OED s.v.* 'thin-space').
5   The *k* has also been imported to make up this composite fount.
6   This *w* is clearly not the same in the black-letter fount used on sig. Aij^r.

cramped. In the case of *esptre*, under *Populis alba*, two and possibly three abbreviations have been used to justify the line and retain the long-space marking – one deletion of the space either before or after a comma, one tilde to delete *n*, and possibly the deletion of a space altogether between the last two words. The line thus reads:

Populus alba,a grecis λευκ[ι] dicitur ab a[n]glis   an aspe aut an esptre.

Figure 3. esptre (fol. Biv^v, detail)

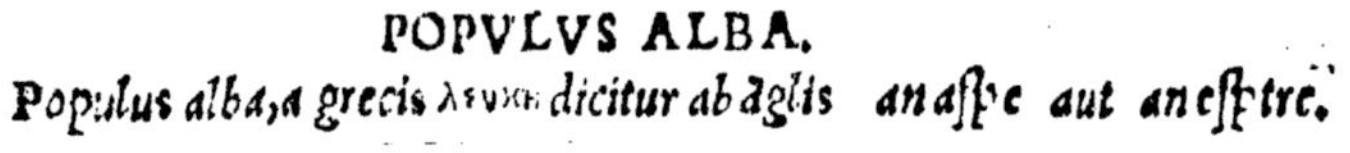

POPVLVS ALBA.
Populus alba,a grecis λευκα *dicitur ab aglis   an aspe aut an esptre.*

But is it not odd that such long spaces occur in an obviously cramped line? It would have been so much easier to use a shorter space. Moxon points out the undesirability of such a practice: "These wide Whites are by Compositors (in way of Scandal) call'd Pidgeon-holes, and are by none accounted good Workmanship, unless in such cases of necessity, as aforesaid" (Moxon 1677: II, 215). Moxon's "necessity" is exceeding the limit of three extra white spaces per line to achieve justification (Moxon: 1677: II, 214). This surely suggests that in the present case the spaces were being treated as an important typographical marking principle, as well as suggesting that the *esptre*, representing the words next most amenable to having the space between them removed to conserve the other principle, should not be perceived as a genuine compound, at least not in the compositor's view. In the case of *heptre* (*Cynosbatos*), there was no space available anywhere else in the line, unless the *tre* of *brere tre* was to drop to the next line and stand alone, being the last word of the entry. The shortest overhang of this kind elsewhere is the four-letter-long *pane* of *Allicampane* on sig. Bi^v, so that presumably this one would have broken another typesetting convention.[7] The compositor's obvious desire to rob *esptre* in order to preserve the marking of the code-switch from Latin to English brings us to the next major point, which is that rules governing the spacing of compounds gives way before a more important rule where necessary in this text.

---

[7] Some other evidence from mid sixteenth-century books suggests that weakly-stressed second lexical elements of compounds and those in the process of being cliticized may be spelt as one word (Rissanen 1999: 196, 201), but potential compounds in Turner's *Libellus* seem to have been treated pretty consistently otherwise.

3. Code-switching

Another, more general consideration about this work is that it follows a consistent policy of using the largest available spaces to bracket the English words in the text wherever a code-switch occurs, thus marking them visually as not Latin. This, as we shall see, is followed with remarkable consistency, and overrides some more conventional rules. The spacing between elements of a compound pretty consistently employs the smallest space, one quarter of a quad, or an em space; a further point is that where a short Latin word comes between two English ones, as occurs under *Filix* and *Daphoides*, a space of an intermediate size is sometimes used to the left of the Latin word, and a longer one to the right, again creating a characteristic marking. There are some variations in this pattern, but these are probably to be explained by the requirements of right justification, provided the spaces remain sufficiently long. However, the practice of marking an English term by inserting a long space is considered important enough to override right justification on sig. Bij[r] under *Hippvris*, where there is a very visible space at the end of the line after *dicitur* and before *Hors tayle*, as well as under *Intubum*, after the word *suckery*.[8]

Figure 4. Unjustified lines, sig. Bij[r]

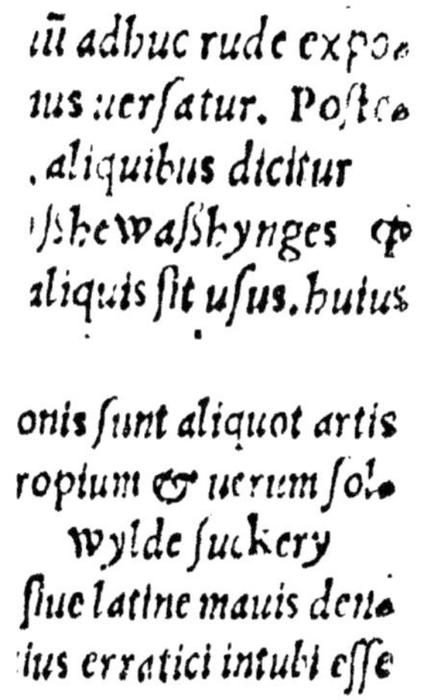

iū adhuc rude expoe
ius uerſatur. Poſtce
aliquibus dicitur
'ſhewaſshynges ꝙ
aliquis ſit uſus. huius

onis ſunt aliquot artis
roptum & uerum ſol
wylde ſuckery
ſluc latine mauis denu
ius erratici intuli eſſe

This patterning may be represented as follows, letting L = Latin word, E = English word; *l* = long quad, *m* = medium quad, and *s* = short quad. The basic patterns employed are:

---

8   All measurements here should thus be taken as relative, not absolute.

1. L / E / L
2. L / E s E / L
3. L / E m(l) L m(l) E l

The brackets indicate fairly common variants in these patterns. It is not all that unusual to omit a space between words in the running text either, presumably for reasons of justification. There is also a strong tendency to leave large spaces in pattern three around the embedded Latin word if it is long or if there is more than one word, as sometimes happens. If there is a single, short, embedded Latin word, there is usually a pattern of medium-long or long-medium on either side of it, but not long-long.[9]

4. The spacing employed

I now consider the spaces used to introduce and close English words and phrases in more detail, leaving aside the medial ones for the moment. The English words in the text were identified and the spaces before and after them measured at very large magnification using the *Gimp* image manipulation programme (http://www.gimp.org/). This allowed large-sized images to be measured accurately to derive relative sizes, which were then reduced to approximately the original size. In calculating the overall averages, *etc.*, line breaks were ignored. Removing the twenty-four line breaks, left 238 of the original 262 measurements. For consistency's sake the measurements were taken from the nearest edges of the actual letter rather than the presumed edge of the type itself. An em in this fount appears to be approximately 1.9 mm. in width, although it did seem that the "100%" pdf images available varied somewhat in size, making this measurement a little uncertain.[10]

The results show that the disparity between the largest and the smallest gap is considerable, ranging from 6.7 mm to 0.4 mm. The spread is shown in Chart 1:

---

9 "It is generally observed by Work-men as a Rule, That when they Cast Quadrats they Cast them exactly to the Thickness of a set Number of m's or Body [...] The reason is, that when the Compositor Indents any Number of Lines, he may have Quadrats so exactly Cast that he shall not need to Justifie them either with Spaces of other helps" (Moxon 1677: 174).

10 My thanks to Turo Vartiainen for taking these measurements.

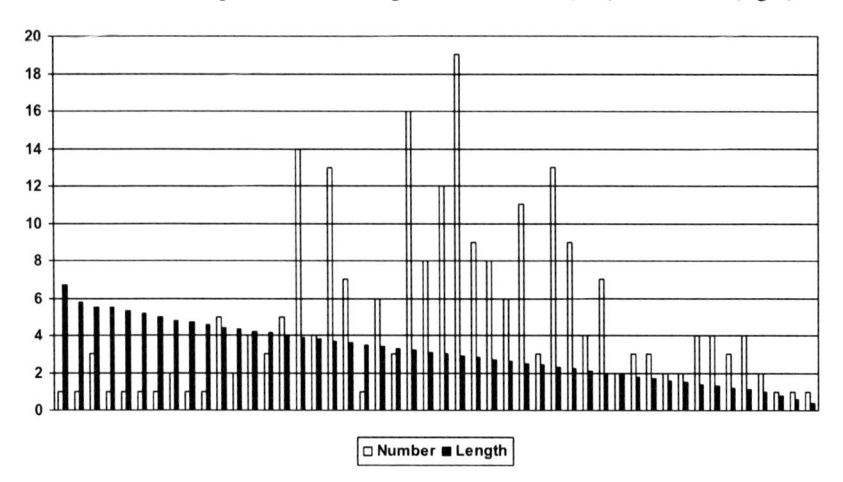

Chart 1. Number of spaces at each length from 6.7 mm (left) to 0.4 mm (right)

The chart also shows a large number of different measurements, forty-eight in all, which is far greater than one might expect from the employment of simple measures such as combinations of ems and ens. Three ems and one en would roughly account for the largest gap, 6.7 mm. Dividing the figures derived by 1.9 expressed to two decimal places still produced forty-eight different numbers, but this was reduced to thirty at one decimal place. These have been charted above. The assumption that only en and em quads were used to create the spaces would mean that only eighteen combinations in all could be used to produce the spaces. Since this does not account for the figures, this suggests either that Byddell used thin spaces as well, or perhaps that there were quads of more irregular length available to him. On the whole, however, the largest numbers cluster around 1.5 and 2 ems. The other apparent cluster is at about 1.3 ems (an em plus a thin space?).

There was at least one clear distinction within this spacing system when a synonym was introduced. The word *aut* 'or' occurred sixty-four times in this function. The average length of the spaces before *aut* turned out to be substantially less on average than that for all spaces – 1.96 as against 2.99. The spaces following *aut* average slightly less at 1.77.[11]

The measurements taken were also divided into groups suggested by combinations of em and en spaces as follows (em=1.9mm, 3.8mm, 4.7mm; en=0.95mm). This yielded the following results:

---

11 It is possible that the *or* in *a wylde heptre, or a brere tre* under *Cynosbatos* is an error for *aut*, but it may be Turner's oversight, since the compositor has treated it as being within a piece of English text, using the normal spacing.

1.9–2.85 (1 em—1 em + an en): Forty-two
2.85–3.8 (em+en—2ems): Eighty-nine
3.8–4.7 (2 ems—2 ems plus and en): Thirty
4.7 and over: Five

Analysis of the words or phrases marked as English in this way thus shows that:

(1) no English word or phrase is introduced by an en space;

(2) only one is introduced by a space interpreted here as no more than an em (*comfrey*, under *symphytum*, which measures 1.9). The remainder are larger, as shown above. Relatively shorter spaces generally either precede or follow words such as *aut, sed, vocant*, or *dicitur* following the first English term.

Neither is the spread even across the whole text. There is an apparent tendency for the larger spaces to cluster in the final pages of the text and to swing more erratically between the largest and the smallest gaps. The second-largest spacing appears only rarely before the middle of the text, although this might suggest some uncertainty on the part of the compositors as to what rule to follow. If the basic question at issue was justification, one might expect a more random distribution. These trends are resolved when initial spaces are charted separately from final spaces, since these charts appear much more randomly distributed than the combined chart. There is no evidence that particular quads lengths were running low, the only obvious clustering of a particular length being a short run of successive long final spaces on sig. Bii^v-Biii^r (*Lichen–Macer*) and another, more intermittent one of initial spaces on sig. Ci^{r-v} (*sampsucum–verbena*).

There is one glaring exception to this policy, however, the first page of the main text (sig. Aij^r). Here, the English words are mostly not separated by long spaces at all, though middle-sized ones precede two of the thirteen. The English words themselves are distinguished here simply by being set in black-letter, a practice perfectly familiar to such works as dictionaries throughout the century. However, this practice does not continue onto the next page, possibly representing a change of policy in the printing-house. Perhaps circumstances did not justify resetting the first page following the change of mind. It is also possible that the blackletter was needed for another job, since 1538 was one of his busiest years (Pollard *et al.* 1976-1991, 3: 35), but this would be to abandon a long-standing convention.

Figure 5. Sig. Aii^r (detail)

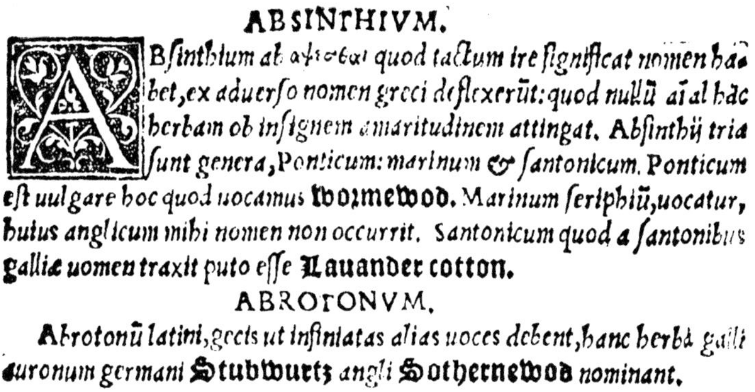

> **ABSINTHIVM.**
> B*finthium ab* ἀψίσθαι *quod tactum ire fignificat nomen habet, ex aduerfo nomen greci deflexerūt: quod nullū aī al hāc herbam ob infignem amaritudinem attingat.* Abfinthij *tria funt genera, Ponticum: marinum & fantonicum.* Ponticum *eft uulgare hoc quod uocamus* wo2mewoo. *Marinum feriphiū, uocatur, huius anglicum mihi nomen non occurrit.* Santonicum *quod a fantonibus gallie uomen traxit puto effe* Lauander cotton.
> **ABROTONVM.**
> *Abrotonū latini, grecis ut infinitas alias uoces debent, hanc herbā galli duronum germani* Stubwurtz *angli* Sothernewoo *nominant.*

This typographical marking might, however, have been done at Turner's insistence. It seems less likely to have been a practice familiar to Byddell's workshop or to a particular compositor working there, and indeed runs against the conventions of the time. Judging by the way Turner signed his dedication to Thomas Patinson (sig. Cii^v) *Londini apvd Ioannem Bydellum*, he was present at Byddell's printing-house and perhaps was living in his house at the time – a not unusual circumstance.

5. Further typographical considerations

Another striking point is that the black-letter fount used on this opening page is obviously not the one from which the *w* in the rest of the text was imported. That which appears on sig. Aii^r is upright, with a very high first stem which ends in a modest ascender, stems parallel, and a second *v* which is noticeably smaller than the first, while the imported *w* is more even in height and has a strongly recurved final stem, whereas that in the first is straighter. The three stems in the first *w* all begin at different heights. The imported *w* also forms two very clear *v*s at the bottom, where the one on sig. Aii^r forms two curves. Byddell probably felt that this *w* looked more at home in the italic fount than the upright one with parallel stems of uneven height.

The matters canvassed in this paper suggest a solution to another problem, the reading by Rydén *et al.* of the compound *Varispowder* on sig. Bij^v.

Figure 6. Varispowder, sig. Bij^v

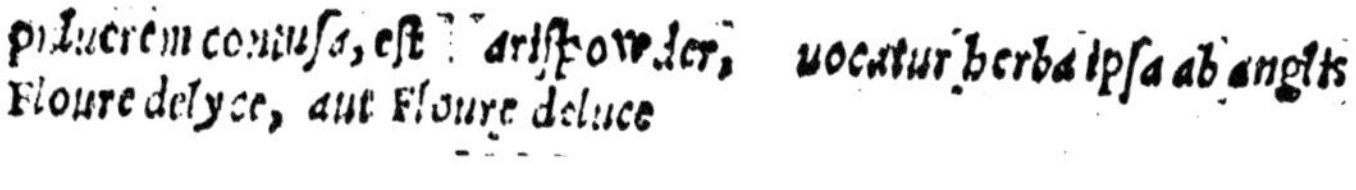

p*ı Lucrem contusa, eft* arıspowder, *uocatur herba ipfa ab anglis* Floure delyce, *aut* Floure deluce

As it stands, varis represents a nonce-word. If this reading is correct, then it is possibly the only exception to the rule that a long space precedes the English word, but this seems unlikely Further, the capital *V* is faint, apparently has long serifs, and is not the same shape as the normal capital *V* in this fount, having a vertical left-hand stroke, and a sloped right-hand stroke. Normally, this fount has a *V* with two sloped strokes. It also appears to be very slightly taller. In any case, since the reading *arispowder* would be more satisfactory, being an obvious variant of *orris*, and hence the powdered root of various iris species, mainly *iris germanica, florentina*, and *pallida*, I would suggest that this is not a capital *V* at all, and that *arispowder* is the correct reading. In fact this "letter" neatly occupies precisely the space preceding the English word which the compositor has found so important. Perhaps the edge of a slipped or misplaced quad has left a mark on the paper. In any case, the height to paper was obviously incorrect – the type possibly not being hammered down accurately before printing, so that it somewhat resembles a compartment line on a typographed postage stamp. Such horizontal compartment lines occur frequently at the top and bottom of pages in this text in any case, so that the *V* is more likely to be a space partially filled by the result of poor or hasty presswork.

6. Comparison with other works

Returning to the original question of compounds, a brief survey of some other works printed by Byddell reveals nothing similar to the treatment of these words in the *Libellus*. The Lilly grammar (1538), for example, distinguishes the Latin translations and glosses by using Roman type, but treats the spacing quite haphazardly, sometimes very short, sometimes quite long, and now and then left justified to the right of the English. Page layout seems to be the paramount consideration in this case. A few separated compounds occur in the *Institutions in the lawes of Englande* (1538) such as *gauel kynde* (sig. Cvii^v) and *free holde* (sig. Aii^v), but there is nothing regular:

Figure 7. '*free holde*' *Institutions in the lawes of Englande*, 1538, sig. Aii^v

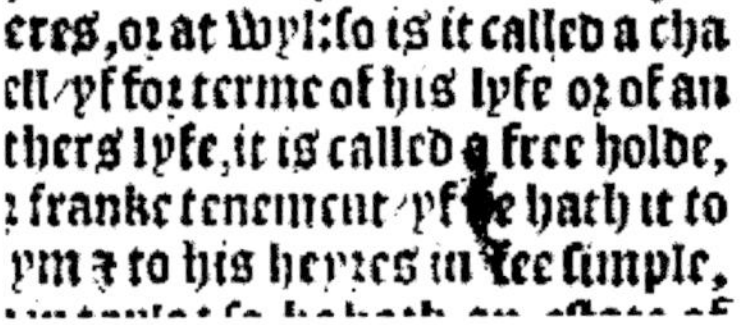

eres, or at wylifo is it called a cha
ell yf for terme of his lyfe or of an
thers lyfe, it is called a free holde,
i franke tenement yf e hath it to
ym to his heyres in fee simple,

Some other works printed by Byddell reveal nothing similar to the treatment of these words in the *Libellus*, so that we may speculate that Turner himself may have imposed this treatment of "foreign" words having seen the first page, but that Byddell was unwilling to reset it.

A brief survey of some other works which deal with similar subjects or whose publishers might perhaps have found this arrangement convenient, revealed no similarities. The most obvious place to seek similar treatment is Turner's own later work, *The names of herbes* (1548), but this work is printed entirely conventionally, except that all names in whatever language are in black-letter, like the rest of the text, being distinguished only by rather inconsistent capitalization.

Figure 8. The entry in *The names of herbes* (1548) corresponding to that for 'Populus alba' in the *Libellus* (see Fig. 3)

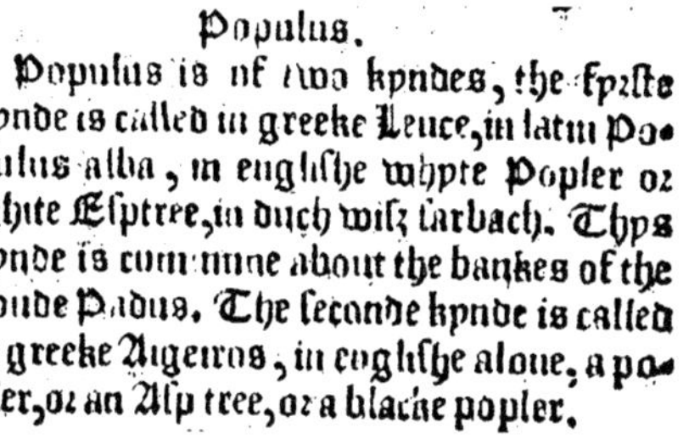

> Populus.
> Populus is of two kyndes, the fyrste kynde is called in greeke Leuce, in latin Populus alba, in englishe whyte Popler or whyte Esptree, in duch wiß tarbach. Thys kynde is cummune about the bankes of the flonde Padus. The seconde kynde is called in greeke Aigeiros, in englishe alone, a popler, or an Asp tree, or a blacke popler.

The differential treatment of the compound 'asp-tree' (*Esptree/Asp tree*) here seems to arise from the exigencies of line justification. Turner's *Herball* (1551), his *magnum opus* published by Mierdman in Cologne, does not show this feature either. Neither do the editions of Elyot's dictionary, first published in the same year as the *Libellus*, which contrast black-letter with Roman type, although one could speculate that this use of spacing might be appropriate to dictionary typography. The same applies to the *Ortus vocabulorum* (1500/1516), which uses black-letter throughout; but the *Ortus* does sometimes use spaces inconsistently; see sig. Aiiij[r] *Accercitus*, sig. Pviii[v] *Fusillus*, etc. The *vertuose boke of distyllacyon* (1527), a text entirely in black-letter, does not either, although it does use spacing to mark off upper-case letters used for sub-divisions. The *Promptorium paruulorum* (1499/1508) uses full-stops, with or without normal spaces and black-letter throughout. This seems to be a conventional layout. The version of Stanbridge's *Accidentia* published by Byddell in 1538 has a convention which is somewhat reminiscent of that in Turner in that headwords and their glosses are separated by at least an em space, but this work also justifies groups of entries within
a page as well, which causes much variation. Right justification gives way to this practice as well, in that such short left-justified lines are not fully justified.

Figure 9. Stanbridge's *Accidence* (sig. Cii^v, detail)

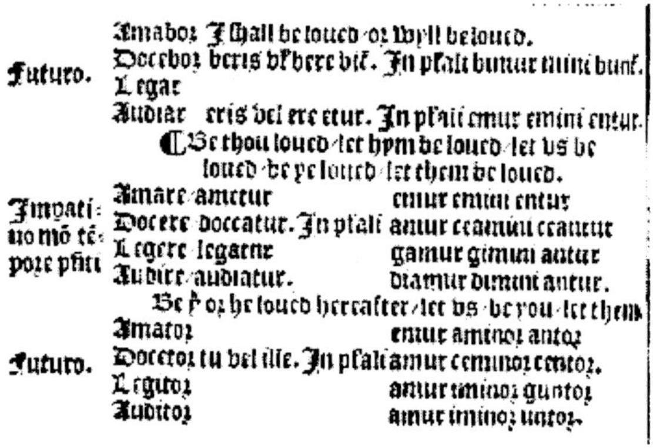

This layout is not apparent in the 1495 edition by Wynkyn de Worde.

7. Conclusions

Byddell's compositor has abandoned the original and conventional distinction between italic and black-letter used on the first page of the work for a distinction based entirely on length of spacing. This has meant occasional abandonment of more familiar conventions such as the right justification of lines, as well as the introduction of a *w* and *k*, which would have been native to a black-letter fount, into the italic fount. We might thus speculate about whether Turner himself wanted the text to look more learned by being entirely in italics. This was normal enough for languages conventionally regarded as learned such as Latin, but if this was Turner's intention, then he must have wanted the English to appear equally learned. A move to stress the significance of either the book itself or the language of the code-switches by typographical means would be of considerable significance as an innovation in the 1530s. The shift from the conventional technique of discriminating code-switches to the new one is ultimately inexplicable, as is the failure to correct what had already been done on the first sheet. It is rendered the more inexplicable by the fact that, because the first forme cannot have been locked up when the change was made, the disruption caused by the correction would have been less. The decisions may have been either ideological or simply pragmatic choices made in a printing house of limited means, but it is hard to see why the printer should shift from a familiar method to one so markedly idiosyncratic, especially since the compositors would inevitably spend more time setting it.

References

1. Early printed books (all *STC* numbers refer to the second edition).

Anonymous
    1538   *Institutions in the lawes of Englande.* J. Byddell. STC 9290.

Brunschwig, Hieronymus
    1527   *The vertuose boke of distyllacyon of the waters of all maner of herbes with the fygures of the styllatoryes, fyrst made and compyled by the thyrte yeres study and labour of the moste co[n]nynge and famous master of phisyke, Maister Iherom bruynswyke.* Laurence Andrewe. STC 13435.

Elyot, Thomas
    1538   *The dictionary of syr Thomas Eliot knyght.* Thomas Berthelet. STC 7659.
    1542   *Bibliotheca Eliotae Eliotis librarie.* London: Thomas Berthelet. STC 7659.5.

[Galfridus, Anglicus]
    1499   *Incipit liber q[ui] dicitur Promptorium paruulorum siue clericorum.* Richard Pynson. STC 20434.
    1500   *Ortus. Vocabulorum. Westminster:* Wynkyn de Worde. STC 13829.
    1516   *Ortus Vocabulorum. Westminster:* Wynkyn de Worde. STC 13833 [incomplete].

Lilly, William
    1538   *Guillelmi Lilii Angli rudimenta Paruulorum Lilii nuper impressa. London:* J. Byddell, STC 15610.

Stanbridge, John
    1495   *Accedence Westminster:* Wynkyn de Worde. STC 23153.4.
    1538?   *Accidentia ex Stanbrigiana editione nuper recognita & castigata lima Roberti Whitintoni Lichfeldiensis in Florentissima Oxoniensis academia laureati.* John Byddell STC 23152.3.

Turner, William
    1538   *Libellus de re herbaria novvs.* John Byddell. STC 24358.
    1548   *The names of herbes in Greke, Latin, Englishe, Duche. and Frenche.* S. Mierdman for J. Day and W. Seres. STC 24359.
    1551   *A new herball, wherin are conteyned the names of herbes.* Cologne: S. Mierdman. STC 24365.

2. Secondary sources

Coleman, Julie – Anne McDermott, (eds.)
    2004   *Historical dictionaries and historical dictionary research: Papers from the International Conference on Historical Lexicography and Lexicology, at the University of Leicester, 2002.* Lexicograhica series maior 123. Tübingen: Max Niemeyer Verlag.

Dowding, Geoffrey
 1998 *An introduction to the history of printing types.* New Castle, Del. and London: British Library and Oak Knoll Press.

Duff, Gordon E.
 1948 *A century of the English book trade.* London: The Bibliographical Society.

Fisiak, Jacek (ed.)
 2002 *Studies in English historical linguistics and philology: A festschrift for Akio Oizumi.* (Studies in English Medieval Language and Literature 2) Frankfurt am Main: Peter Lang.

Kastovsky, Dieter (ed.)
 1994 *Studies in Early Modern English.* Berlin: Mouton de Gruyter.

Lancashire, Ian
 2004 "Lexicography in the early modern English period: The manuscript record", in: Julie Coleman – Anne McDermott, (eds.), 19–30.

McConchie, Roderick W.
 2002 "Doctors and dictionaries in sixteenth-century England", in: Jacek Fisiak (ed.), 267–292.

Moxon, Joseph
 1677 *Mechanick exercises, or, the doctrine of handy-works.* II, 12.

Pollard, Alfred W. – Gilbert R. Redgrave – William A. Jackson – Frederic S. Ferguson – Katharine F. Pantzer (eds.)
 1976-1991 *Short-title catalogue of books printed in England, Scotland and Ireland.* 3 vols., London: The Bibliographical Society.

Rissanen, Matti
 1999 "Isn't it or is it not? On the order of postverbal subject and negative particle in the history of English", in: Ingrid Tieken-Boon van Ostade – Gunnel Tottie – Wim van der Wurff (eds.), 189–205.

Rydén, Mats
 1994 "William Turner and the English plant names", in: Dieter Kastovsky (ed.), 349–370.

Rydén, Mats – Hans Helander – Kerstin Olsson
 1999 *William Turner Libellus de re herbaria novus 1538. Edited with a translation into English.* (Skrifter utgivna af Kungliga Humanistiska vetenskapssamfundet i Uppsala 50.) Uppsala: Almqvist & Wiksells.

Tieken-Boon van Ostade, Ingrid – Gunnel Tottie – Wim van der Wurff (eds.)
 1999 *Negation in the history of English.* Berlin: Mouton de Gruyter.

Weiss, Adrian
 1990 "Font analysis as a bibliographical method: The Elizabethan play-quarto printers and compositors". *Studies in Bibliography* 43: 95–164.

Index of manuscripts

Aberystwyth,
   National Library of Wales,
      Peniarth 392 D: Hengwrt 10, 73–90, 157–160, 162–164, 171–176
Alnwick,
   Alnwick Castle,
      Duke of Northumberland 455 .... 159, 171–176
Austin,
   University of Texas, HRC 43: Cardigan 171–175
Cambridge,
   Corpus Christi College 61 82
   Corpus Christi College 140 17
   Corpus Christi College 198 .... 77, 90
   Corpus Christi College 201 17
   Corpus Christi College, Parker 147 .... 111, 116, 119–121
   Emmanuel College 34 .... 112, 116, 117, 119, 121, 122
   Emmanuel College 108 .... 112, 116–119
   Fitzwilliam Museum, McClean 181 .... 98–100, 104, 171–176
   Gonville & Caius College 343/539 .... 112, 116, 119, 121, 122
   Magdalene College, Pepys 15 .... 112, 115–117, 119, 120, 122
   Magdalene College, Pepys 2073 .... 112, 116–119
   Peterhouse College 75.I 81
   Peterhouse College 118 .... 17, 18, 23–26
   Trinity College, B.15.17 .... 75, 81–84, 86–87
   Trinity College, R.3.2 .... 74, 75
   Trinity College, R.3.3 .... 158, 160, 171–176
   Trinity College, R.3.15 .... 164, 172, 173
   University Library, Dd.4.24 .... 164, 171–176
   University Library, Gg.4.27 .... 82, 163, 164, 172–176
   University Library, Ii.3.26 .... 96, 98, 99, 101, 104, 161, 171–176
   University Library, Ll.1.13 .... 111, 112, 115, 116, 118, 119, 121, 122
   University Library, Mm.2.15 .... 126, 172–175
Cheltenham,
   Phillipps Library 8137 .... 98–101, 104, 172–175
Chicago,
   University of Chicago Library 564: McCormick .. 98–104, 171, 172, 174, 175
Dallas,
   Southern Methodist University,
      Bridwell Library 7 .... 111, 116, 119–121

Dumfries,
   Archive Centre, WMF18 (Wigtown Burgh Court Book) 95
Exeter,
   Cathedral Library 3501 (Exeter Book) 16, 22, 33, 50
Geneva,
   Bodmer Library 48 (Bodmeriana) 98–100, 104, 159, 164, 173, 175
Glasgow,
   Hunterian Museum U.1.1 .... 173, 174
   University Library, Hunter 3 23
   University Library, Hunter 95 15
   University Library, Hunter 328 17
   University Library, Hunter 497 .... 15, 28
Hatfield,
   Marquess of Salisbury's Library, Cecil Papers, Box S/1 .... 74, 75
Hereford,
   Cathedral Library, O.vii.1 111
Holkham,
   Holkham Hall 667 (Earl of Leicester) 98, 99, 101, 104, 172–175
Lichfield,
   Lichfield Cathedral 29 .... 96, 98, 99, 104, 171–176
Lincoln,
   Cathedral Library 110 172–176
London,
   British Library,
       Additional 5140 .... 163, 172, 173, 175
       Additional 35286 .... 78, 83, 84, 86, 163, 171–176
       Cotton Claudius B.iv 47, 51
       Cotton Vespasian D.xxi 34
       Cotton Vitellius A.xv 17, 29
       Cotton Vitellius C.v 32, 40, 43, 46
       Egerton 2622 .... 17, 23–25, 27–28
       Egerton 2726 171–174
       Egerton 2863 .... 98, 99, 101, 104, 163, 172–176
       Egerton 2864 .... 98, 104, 163, 171–175
       Guildhall Library 5370 74
       Harley 1239 163
       Harley 1758 .... 98, 100–102, 104, 163, 172–176
       Harley 2253 .... 56, 67, 68
       Harley 3271 .... 32, 40, 44–46
       Harley 5908 172
       Harley 7333 .... 161, 163, 171–174, 176
       Harley 7334 .... 77, 164, 172–176

Index of manuscripts

Harley 7335 .... 98, 99, 104, 171, 173
Lansdowne 455 111
Lansdowne 851 172–176
Royal 1 B.vi 98–101, 104, 172–176
Royal 17 D.xv 172–175
Royal 18 C.ii 104
Sloane 5 .... 10, 53–71
Sloane 340 .... 17, 18, 23–27
Sloane 1685 .... 163, 171–176
Sloane 1686 .... 171–173, 175, 176
Royal College of Physicians 388 .... 171, 173–176
Manchester,
 John Rylands University Library, English 80 .... 111, 112, 116–119
 John Rylands University Library, English 113 .... 171, 173–175
Naples,
 Royal Library xiii.B.29 172
New Haven,
 Yale University,
  Beinecke Library 360 109
New York,
 Morgan Library, M.249 .... 172, 173, 175
 Morgan Library, M.400 .... 112, 116–119
 Public Library, MA 64 .... 111, 112, 116, 117, 119, 120, 122
 Public Library, MA 65 .... 112, 116, 119
 Public Library, MA 66 111
Oxford,
 Bodleian Library,
  Barlow 20 .... 98, 99, 101, 104, 172–176
  Bodley 277 127
  Bodley 343 .... 12, 32, 36, 38–40, 51
  Bodley 414 .... 159, 164, 171–176
  Bodley 686 171–175
  Bodley 790 28
  Christ Church College 145 .... 112, 115–119
  Christ Church College 146 .... 112, 116, 119–120
  Christ Church College 152 .... 164, 172–176
  Corpus Christi College 198 .... 77, 90, 164, 172–176
  e Museo 232 109
  Fairfax 2 .... 108, 109
  Fairfax 3 82
  Hatton Donat. 1 171–176
  Junius I 28

Laud Misc. 381 51
Laud Misc. 509 .... 32, 34–37, 40, 47, 48, 50, 51
Laud Misc. 600 .... 98, 100, 101, 104, 172–176
Laud Misc. 739 .... 98–102, 104, 172–176
New College, D 314 .... 162, 172, 173, 175
Queen's College 388 .... 112, 116, 117, 119
Rawl. poet. 141 .... 172, 175, 176
Rawl. poet. 149 .... 162, 172–176
Rawl. poet. 223 171–175
Rawl. poet. C 172
Trinity College 49 173

Paris
    Bibliothèque Nationale,
        Fonds anglais 39 .... 98–101, 104, 172–176

Philadelphia,
    Free Library of Philadelphia 39 107
    Rosenbach Museum and Library 1084/1 .... 98–101, 104, 172–175
    Rosenbach Museum and Library 1084/2 175

Princeton,
    Firestone Library 100: Helmingham 98, 100, 102, 104, 162, 172–173
    William H. Scheide 12 .... 111, 116, 119–121
    William H. Scheide 13 .... 112, 116, 119, 120

San Marino, California,
    Huntington Library,
        El 26.A.17 82
        El 26.C.9: Ellesmere 10, 73–90, 157–176
        HM 140 172

Sussex,
    Petworth House 7 171–176

Tokyo,
    Takamiya 22 172
    Takamiya 24 172–175
    Takamiya 32: Delamere 172–176

Warminster,
    Longleat House 29 108
    Longleat House 257 176

Index of names

Abdon (saint) 41
Ælfric of Eynsham 5, 12, 31–47, 49–52, 126
Æthelmar the Stout 33
Æthelred II (king, "the Unready") 51
Æthelthryth (saint) 41
Æthelwold of Winchester 31, 33
Agata, Mari 10, 135, 137, 151
Alcuin of York 45
Alexander, Jonathan J. G. 123, 124
Almeida, Francisco Alonso 68
Ames, Joseph 127, 132
Anne (saint) 49
Arundel, Thomas 125
Ascham, Roger 130
Baker, Donald C. 166, 170
Barnhouse, Rebecca 50, 51
Beadle, Richard 167, 168
Beal, Peter 87, 88
Bede, the Venerable 42, 126
Benskin, Michael 55, 66, 67, 80, 87–89, 105
Benson, Larry Dean 66, 67, 82, 88
Bischoff, Bernhard 107, 123
Black, John Bennett 130, 132
Black, Merja Riitta 53, 56, 66
Blake, Norman F. 66, 67, 77, 79, 88, 89, 92, 105, 106, 166–168
Blayney, Peter W. M. 148, 151
Boëthius, Anicius Manlius Severinus 131, 133
Bordalejo, Barbara 157, 167
Bosworth, Joseph 61, 66
Boyd, Beverly 167, 170
Brassington, William Salt 129, 130, 132
Brodin, Gösta 61, 66
Brook, George L. 56, 67
Brunner, Karl 64, 65, 67
Brunschwig, Hieronymus 189

Brunsfel, Otto 177
Buchanan, George 131
Bugaj [Kopaczyk], Joanna 95, 105
Burchfield, Robert 16, 19, 28
Burrow, John Anthony 65, 67
Byddell, John 11, 177–179, 183, 185–188
Cahill, Thomas A. 152
Caie, Graham D. 107, 123, 124
Calle-Martín, Javier 5, 10, 15–17, 22, 28
Campbell, Alistair 64, 66, 67, 70
Carlson, Leland H. 132
Caxton, William 9, 28, 150, 151, 157, 161, 162, 164, 165, 167, 168
Cerquiglini, Bernard 9, 13
Chambers, Raymond W. 50
Charlemagne 41
Chassant, Alphonse 96
Chaucer, Geoffrey 9, 10, 28, 49, 55, 66–68, 73, 74, 76–78, 81–84, 88–90, 106, 157, 160, 165–168
Choulant, Ludwig 61, 67
Chrysostom, John 41
Clanchy, Michael T. 107, 123
Clemens, Raymond 18, 28, 107, 117, 123
Clemoes, Peter A. M. 38, 41–44, 50
Cole, C. Robert 132, 134
Coleman, Julie 189, 190
Conner, Patrick W. 33, 50
Coron, Antoine 137
Corsa, Helen Storm 167, 170
Cotton, Robert Bruce 43, 47
Cranmer, Thomas 127
Crawford, Samuel John 34, 36, 41, 50
Cromwell, Oliver 47
Crowley, Robert 12, 126, 127, 128, 130
Cynewulf 32

Index of names

Davenport, Cyril 129, 130, 132
David (biblical character) 48
Davis, Norman 55, 64, 67, 88
de Corbeil, Gilles 17
De Hamel, Christopher 107, 123
De Worde, Wynkyn 5, 9, 124, 157–159, 161–171, 188
Deansley, Margaret 126
Denholm-Young, Noël 15, 28
Díaz-Vera, Javier 28
Dioscorides, Pedanius 177
Dollerup, Cay 105
Domitian, *see* Domitianus
Domitianus, Titus Flavius 42
Donaldson, Ethelbert Talbot 75
Donatus, Aelius 92, 95
Dossena, Marina 13, 67
Dove, Mary 108–110, 116, 117, 121, 123
Dowding, Geoffrey 178, 190
Doyle, Andrew Ian 73, 74, 76, 77, 79, 80, 88
Dryden, John 28, 89, 106
Duff, Gordon E. 190
Dunn, Thomas F. 157, 165, 167
Dunstan (saint) 31
Dziatzko, Karl 139, 151
Edgar (king, "the Peaceable") 47
Edward IV (king) 125, 129, 133
Edwards, Anthony Stockwell Garfield 157, 166, 167
Eisner, Sigmund 110, 123
Eldred, Robert A. 152
Elizabeth I (queen) 47, 129, 130–134
Elton, Geoffrey R. 125, 132
Elyot, Thomas 187, 189
Eusebius of Caesarea 40–42
Felix of Crowland 34
Ferguson, Frederic S. 190
Fisher, Jane L. 65, 67
Fisher, John H. 65, 67
Fisiak, Jacek 190
Flaccus, Quintus Horatius 133
Fletcher, William 129, 130, 132
Flower, Robin 33, 50
Forshall, Josiah 108, 124, 127, 133
Förster, Max 50
Fowler, David C. 126, 128, 133
Fristedt, Sven L. 128, 133
Frolova, Olga 5, 12, 125, 129
Fry, Elizabeth 133
Fuchs, Hero 126
Galfridus, Anglicus 189
Garbáty, Thomas J. 163, 167, 170
Gaskell, Philip 135, 151
George (saint) 41
Gibson, Margaret T. 123, 124
Gneuss, Helmut 43, 50
Godden, Malcolm 28, 42, 50
Goodwin, William Watson 53
Gough, John 126, 127
Gower, John 74, 90
Graham, Timothy 18, 28, 47, 51, 107, 117, 123
Gray, Douglas 28, 64, 67, 88, 89
Greg, Walter W. 9, 13, 135, 138, 148, 151, 158, 163, 167, 170
Griesbach, Johann J. 113
Griffiths, Jeremy 87, 88, 124
Gutenberg, Johannes 5, 10, 136, 151, 152
Hanna, Ralph 75, 77, 80, 88
Hawes, Stephen 166, 167
Haymo of Halberstadt 42
Hector, Leonard C. 15, 28
Helander, Hans 178, 190
Hellinga, Lotte 127, 133, 134, 150, 151, 157, 166, 167, 170
Henry VI (king) 130, 131
Henry VII (king) 129
Henry VIII (king) 125, 127, 129, 131, 133
Hentzner, Paul 130
Herbermann, Charles George 125, 133
Hieronymus, Sophronius Eusebius 41, 126

Hladký, Josef 16–18, 22, 28
Hoad, Terry 28
Holley, Linda Tarte 168
Hoochstraten, Johannes 127
Horace, *see* Flaccus, Quintus Horatius
Horobin, Simon C. P. 75, 76, 81–84, 87, 88
Hudson, Anne 126–127, 130, 133
Hunt, Richard William 56, 68, 123
Hutmacher, William F. 157, 158, 170
Ingham, Patricia 67
Irvine, Susan 36–39, 51
Jackson, William A. 190
James I and IV (king) 129, 131
Jenkins, Elizabeth 130, 133
Jerome, *see* Sophronius Eusebius Hieronymus
John (apostle) 40–46
Kane, George 75, 114, 124
Kastovsky, Dieter 190
Kato, Takako 157
Ker, Neil R. 36, 37, 45, 51, 56, 67, 89
Keynes, Simon 33, 51
King, John M. 128, 133
Klauser, Theodor 109, 124
Kline, Barbara 168, 169
Kopaczyk, Joanna 5, 11, 91, 105
Krygier, Marcin 105, 106
Kusko, Bruce H. 152
L'Isle, William 12, 47–51
Laing, Margaret 55, 66–68, 80, 88, 89, 92, 94, 105
Lancashire, Ian 177, 190
Langland, William 75, 81, 128
Lapidge, Michael 51
Lass, Roger 12, 13, 64, 67, 92, 94, 105
Lee, Sidney 126, 134
Lee, Stuart 48, 51
Lelamour, John 5, 10, 53, 61, 68
Lilly, William 186, 189
Lindberg, Conrad 127, 133
Love, Nicholas 166–168

Lowe, Jeremy 151, 157
Lucy (saint) 41
Lutz, Angelika 16, 28
Lydgate, John 55
Macer, Aemilius 15, 53, 68
MacErlean, Andrew Alphonsus 133
Madden, Frederic 108, 124, 127, 133
Malory, Sir Thomas 49
Manly, John M. 73, 77, 89, 98, 102, 106, 157, 164, 167, 171–173, 175
Marsden, Richard 34, 35, 51
Martin, Charles Trice 93, 94, 106
Mary I (queen) 47, 133
Mary (saint) 37
Massey, Bernard W. A. 18, 28
McConchie, Roderick W. 5, 11, 177, 190
McDermott, Anne 189, 190
McIntosh, Angus 53, 55, 66–68, 74, 80, 87, 89, 91, 92, 105
McNiven, Peter 137
Michael (saint) 39
Mierdman, Steven 187
Miller, J. David 113, 114, 124
Miranda-García, Antonio 16, 22, 28
Mitchell, Bruce 68, 69
Moody, Michael E. 132, 134
Mooney, Linne 74, 75, 77, 81, 83, 84, 87–89, 110, 124
More, Thomas 127
Moreno Olalla, David 5, 10, 53, 54, 61, 68
Mossé, Fernand 60, 63–65, 68, 70
Moxon, Joseph 179–180, 182, 190
Mukai, Tsuyoshi 165, 168
Mustanoja, Tauno F. 68, 70
Needham, Paul 137–140, 147, 151, 153
Nevalainen, Terttu 88, 90
Nicholas of Lynn 123
Nicholas of Lyre 129
Nichols, Stephen 9, 13
Nicolas of Hereford 126

O'Keeffe, Katherine O'Brien 51
Ogilvie-Thomson, Sarah J. 108, 109, 124
Oguro, Shoichi 167, 168
Oizumi, Akio 190
Oldcastle, Sir John 125
Olsson, Kerstin 178, 190
Orchard, Andy 51
Owen, Charles 98, 106
Pace, Edward Aloysius 133
Pahta, Päivi 88, 90
Pallen, Condé Bénoist 133
Pantzer, Katharine F. 190
Parker, Matthew 47–49, 51
Parkes, Malcolm B. 22, 28, 74, 76, 77, 79, 80, 88, 89, 107, 124
Parr, Catherine 131
Partridge, Stephen Bradford 108, 124, 157, 168, 170
Patinson, Thomas 177, 185
Paul the Deacon 40–42, 44–46
Paul, Thomas 169
Pearsall, Derek 124, 168, 171
Peikola, Matti 5, 10, 107, 109, 110, 116, 121, 122, 124
Pemberton, Caroline 130, 133
Petti, Anthony G. 22, 28, 74, 81, 89, 94, 96, 100, 101, 106
Pinkhurst, Adam 5, 10, 73–77, 79–84
Plummer, John F., III 168, 170
Plutarch of Chaeronea 133
Pollard, Alfred W. 127, 134, 184, 190
Pope, John C. 36, 38, 41, 43, 44, 51
Powell, Marcy S. 18, 29
Powitz, Gerhardt 138, 152
Prendergast, Thomas A. 168, 169
Purvey, John 126, 131, 132
Pynson, Richard 157, 163
Quentell, Peter 126
Ramsey, Roy Vance 74, 89
Rand Schmidt, Kari Anne 81, 83, 89, 121, 124

Ransom, Daniel J. 168, 170
Raybin, David 168
Redgrave, Gilbert Richard 127, 134, 190
Revard, Carter 56, 68
Reveney, Denis 123, 124
Richardson, Malcolm B. 65, 67
Rickert, Edith 74, 77, 89, 98, 102, 106, 157, 164, 167, 171–173, 175
Rickert, Margaret 77
Rissanen, Matti 88, 90, 180, 190
Roberts, Jane 93, 95, 96, 106
Robinson, Pamela 81, 89
Robinson, Peter M. W. 78, 88, 89, 91, 94, 95, 97, 105, 106, 157, 158, 166–168, 170
Rodríguez Álvarez, Alicia 68
Rogos, Justyna 93, 106
Rohde, Eleanor Sinclair 53, 68
Rolle, Richard 109, 124
Ross, Thomas W. 168, 170
Rufinus of Aquileia 40, 41, 45
Ruggiers, Paul G. 88, 89, 167, 168
Rutkowska, Hanna 9
Rydén, Mats 177–179, 185, 190
Rymer, Thomas 125, 134
Rypins, Stanley 17, 29
Salesbury, William 128
Samuels, Michael L. 53, 55, 56, 66–68, 74–77, 82, 87–90, 105
Sargent, Michael G. 167, 168
Sawyer, Peter H. 32, 51
Sayle, Charles E. 127, 134
Schoeffer, Peter 126
Schwab, Richard N. 139, 152
Schwenke, Paul 139, 140, 152
Scott, Kathleen L. 77, 90
Sennes (saint) 41
Seymour, Michael C. 98, 106
Shahan, Thomas Joseph 133
Shailor, Barbara A. 109, 124
Shakespeare, William 148
Siebert, Frederick S. 125, 134

Index of names

Sigefyrth 33
Sigeweard 32–34, 36, 38, 40, 43–46
Sikorska, Liliana 105, 106
Simmons, Doreen 151
Skeat, Walter W. 41, 52
Smetana, Cyril 41, 52
Smith, Jeremy J. 76, 82, 89, 90
Solopova, Elizabeth 78, 89, 91, 94, 95, 97, 106
Somer, John 124
Spenser, Edmund 47
Stanbridge, John 187–189
Stanley, Eric G. 88, 89
Stephen, Leslie 126, 134
Stephen (saint) 41, 45, 46
Stevens, Martin 88, 90
Stubbs, Estelle 77–80, 90
Swain, Larry J. 5, 12, 31
Swan, Mary 51, 52
Taavitsainen, Irma 88, 90
Tabor, Stephen 137
Takamiya, Toshiyuki 157
Talbot, Charles H. 53, 68
Talbot, Robert 51
Tannenbaum, Samuel A. 22, 29
Tanselle, G. Thomas 91, 106
Tatlock, John S. P. 73, 90
Thaisen, Jacob 5, 9–11, 73, 83, 90, 92, 105
Thynne, William 166
Tieken-Boon van Ostade, Ingrid 190
Tokunaga, Satoko 5, 9, 150, 152, 157, 169, 171
Toller, Thomas Northcote 61, 66
Tottie, Gunnel 190
Trapp, J. B. 125, 133, 134, 167, 169
Treharne, Elaine 51, 52
Trevelyan, George Macaulay 125, 134
Trevisa, John 126
Tudor, Margaret 131

Turner, William 5, 11, 177, 178, 180, 183, 185–190
Turville-Petre, Thorlac 65, 67
Tyndale, William 126
Ullerston, Richard 127
Van der Wurff, Wim 190
Vander Meulen, David L. 91, 106
Vartiainen, Turo 182
Vaughan, Míceál F. 169
Voigts, Linda Ehrsam 110, 124
Wagner, Bettina 137
Wallace-Hadrill, Anne 67
Walpole, Horace 130, 131, 134
Warton, Thomas 130, 134
Watson, Andrew G. 88, 89
Weber, Robertus 152
Weiss, Adrian 190
Whytlaw-Gray, Alianore 53, 55, 61, 68
Wick, Daniel L. 152
Williams, Neville 131, 134
Williamson, Keith 67, 89, 105
Willson, David Harris 131, 134
Withers, Benjamin C. 50, 51
Woodward, Daniel H. 88, 90
Wright, Joseph 60, 61, 68
Wright, Laura 75, 90
Wulfgeat 33
Wulfhad (saint) 36
Wulfstan 37–40
Wulfstan II 36
Wulfstan of Worcester 36
Wulfstan the Homilist 36
Wycliffe, John 5, 10, 12, 125–128, 130, 133, 134
Wynne, John Joseph 133
Youngs, Fr. J. 125, 134
Załuski, Andrzej Stanisław 132
Załuski, Józef Andrzej 132
Zettersten, Arne 105

Index of terms

abbreviation 5, 11, 16, 73, 78, 91–106, 108, 111, 113, 114, 117, 118, 120, 121, 147, 180
abutting form 140, 141, 143, 144, 155
accidental textual variants, *see* text, variation
Acts of the Apostles 31, 35
affixation 18
annotation of manuscripts 51, 54
Apocalypse 41, 42, 45, 46
apocrypha 41, 124, 133, 142, 144, 146, 151
Apollonius of Tyre 17, 19, 22, 26, 28
archetype 82, 83, 110, 121, 158, 163, 164
audience 9, 11, 32, 34–36, 40, 42, 43, 45–47, 49, 50, 76, 91, 93, 109, 127, 166
autograph 61, 81–83
Benedictine Reform 31, 34
Beowulf 17
Bible 5, 10, 12, 31, 34, 36, 38, 40, 45–48, 107–124, 125–135, 135–155
Bishop's Bible 131
blackletter 177, 184, 187
Boece 82
Book of Acts, see Acts of the Apostles
Book of Genesis 34–36, 50, 51
Book of Judges 34
Book of Operation 15
Book of Revelation, see Apocalypse
book stamp 125–134
Canterbury Tales Project 78, 88, 91, 95, 97, 98, 105, 157, 167, 171
Canterbury Tales 9, 10, 73–106, 108, 124, 157–176
Canticles 108
capital letter 34, 55, 117, 141, 178, 186, 187
capitularia, *see* table of lessons

catchword 79, 80
Catholic Homilies 37, 41–46, 50
Cerne Abbas 31
Chancery Standard 65, 67, 75
charter 32, 33, 51
collation 9, 113, 135–139, 143, 144, 151–153, 157, 158, 163, 167, 171
Cologne 126, 187, 184
colon 22, 23, 141, 146
colophon 10, 53, 54
column 23, 55, 83, 110, 115, 137, 141, 142, 145, 149, 157
common prayer 109
compilation 44, 51, 60, 61
composition rule 140, 141, 143, 145, 150
compositor 5, 9, 79, 135, 139, 140, 143, 150, 152, 158–162, 164, 177–190
compounding 15, 16, 18, 20, 21, 24, 25, 177–190
Confessio Amantis 74, 76, 82, 88, 90
constrained selection 55
constraint 10, 27, 73, 79, 81, 83, 110
 functional 73, 81, 84
 spatial 10, 19, 22, 23, 27, 73, 76, 79, 81, 84, 107–124
 temporal 73, 81, 84
contraction 94, 96, 138, 144–146, 150, 155
copy text 13, 135, 151, 158, 164, 167, 168, *see also* exemplar
copying space 5, 107–124, *see also* constraint, spatial
Corinthians 113, 143
correction 5, 10, 35, 50, 61, 120, 122, 135–155, 158, 162, 164, 165, 188
 false 142, 146, 147, 150
 stop-press 10, 135, 137–140, 148–151

De Assumptione Mariae 44
De Doctrina Sancti Gregorii, see *Visio Sancti Pauli*
De haeretico comburendo 125
De Initio Creaturae 45
De Sancta Trinitate et de Festis Diebus per Annum de Septiformi Spiritu 43, 44
De Ueteri Testamento et Novo 38
De Urinis 17
De Virginitate 44
De Viribus Herbarum 44, 61
decoration (of texts) 53, 80, 129, 157
devotional text 35, 39, 40, 49
dialect 20, 36, 53–56, 60, 61, 65, 66, 68, 83, 84, 87, 94, 95, 102, 128, 178
dialectology 13, 67, 68, 89, 91, 105
dissemination (of texts) 45, 46
double hyphen 22, 23, 141
early printed books 48, 178, 189
East Midlands 65
Ecclesiasticus, see *Sirach*
edification (purpose of text) 45, 46, 125
editing 28, 32, 94, 97, 106, 166, 168
edition 5, 9, 11–13, 16, 17, 32, 38, 41, 42, 47–49, 54, 55, 68, 73, 77, 89–91, 103, 104, 111, 123, 127, 128, 131–133, 136, 142, 157, 163–170, 178, 187–189
  digital 5, 17, 90, 91, 103, 104, 168, 169
em 179, 181–184, 187
emendation 48, 136, 145, 164
en 178, 183, 184
Equatorie of the Planetis 81–83, 89
Esdras 144, 146
Example of Vertu 166
Excerptiones de arte grammatica anglice 31
exemplar 38, 45, 54, 55, 59–61, 65, 66, 79, 84, 92, 108, 114, 115, 117, 120–122, see also copy text

Exeter Book 16, 22, 33, 50
explicit 54, 68, 110–117, 119, 120, 122
Eynsham 5, 31–33
Fachliteratur 53
Faerie Queene 47
Fates of the Apostles 32
First Quarto 148, 151
foliation 142
formality 10, 81, 84
forme 148, 149, 188
fount 97, 140, 148, 177–179, 182, 185, 186, 188
  italic 179, 185, 188
General Prologue 74, 121, 166, 167, 168, 170
Geneva Bible 131
genre 40, 46, 49, 107, 109, 114, 123
Glasgow University Library 15, 17
gloss 35, 50, 51, 67, 108, 124, 126, 151, 168, 170, 171, 186, 187
  indexing 108
  marginal 35, 108
glossary 50, 67
glossator 35
gospel 17, 112, 113, 126, 130
graphemics 11, 21, 78, 91–94, 99, 104, 158
Gutenberg Bible 5, 10, 135, 137, 151–153
handwriting 5, 11, 15–29, 73, 80, 107–108
  compressed 108
Harley Lyrics 56, 65, 67–70
Heptateuch 34, 35, 47, 50
heraldic insignia 129, 130
herbal 5, 10, 11, 53, 65, 66, 68, 177, 187, 189, 190
Herbary 15
Hereford 53–56, 61, 111, 126
Herefordshire 10, 53, 66
hexameral tradition 31
Hexateuch 34, 35, 47, 50, 51

Historia Ecclesiastica 40, 41
History of the Holy Rood Tree 37
holograph, *see* autograph
homily 12, 33, 34, 37–47, 49–51
Hours of the Virgin 109
Humanities Media Interface Project (*HUMI*) 136, 151, 153
Hunterian Collection 17
hyphen 19, 22, 23, 28, 141
iconicity 10, 73
Imperial Public library 132
incipient standard 38, 108, 109, 111–117, 120–123, 189, *see* standardization
incipit 38, 108, 109, 111–117, 120–123, 189
incunabula 163
inflection 20, 22, 24, 95, 102, 105
ink 34, 80, 110, 150, 151
Interrogationes (Alcuin) 45
Job 144, 146, 149
Joshua 34, 148
justification (of lines) 138, 141, 145, 146, 150, 178, 180–182, 184, 187, 188
King James Bible 48, 131
King Lear 148, 151
Latin "pocket" *Bible* 107
Latin 10, 11, 18, 35–37, 39–46, 49, 51, 53, 61, 93, 96, 106–107, 109, 110, 123, 124, 126, 129–131, 133, 136, 141, 146, 177, 178, 180–182, 186, 188, 189
leather 129, 130
lectio brevior potior 11, 113, 124
lectionary 114
Lelamour's Herbal 53–71
Leominster 56
Letter of Alexander the Great to Aristotle 17
Letter of Christ to Abgar 41
Letter to Sigeweard 5, 12, 31–52
Letter to Wulfgeat 33–35

Libellus de Veteri Testamento et Novo 31
library, personal 33
Lichfield Cathedral 104, 130
Life of St. Christopher 17
Linguistic Atlas of Late Medieval English (*LALME*) 53, 54, 68, 74, 89, 91, 95, 102, 105
linguistic profile 53, 74, 75, 82, 83, 86
literacy 33, 134, 142, 146, 150
literatim copying 55
littera, doctrine of 11, 13, 92, 93, 96, 98, 102, 103, 134
litteral substitution sets 94, 105
Lives of Saints 37, 41, 52
localization (of text from language) 10, 94
Lollardy 12, 125–128, 132, 133
London 10, 17, 28–29, 32, 34, 40, 43, 44, 46, 50–54, 56, 67, 68, 74, 75, 77, 78, 82–84, 87–90, 104, 106, 111, 123, 124, 126, 130, 132–134, 151, 153, 154, 166–169, 189, 190
long space 180, 181, 184, 186
Lord's Prayer 37, 39
Ludlow 56
Mainz 136, 153
margin 10, 15, 16, 19, 21, 22, 27, 48, 73, 80, 81, 107, 108, 115, 120, 122, 136
Mass 109, 121
material
  used as writing support 80, 107
  vellum 80, 137–139, 147–149
matrix text 177
Mercia 45
miscellany 46, 56
mise-en-page 110, 123, 124
morphology 10, 15–21, 23–27, 54, 55, 59, 60, 62, 63, 65, 67
Morte d'Arthur 49, 165

Natale Innocentium Infantum 42
National Library of Russia 5, 12, 125, 127, 131, 132
New Testament 38, 42, 47, 50, 110, 116, 124, 128, 130, 133, 151
nobility 31, 33, 34
North Midlands 54, 66
North 54, 66, 166
octavo 34, 129
Office of the Dead 109
Old Testament 38, 47, 50, 133, 151
ordinatio 107, 124
orthography 10, 11, 15, 16, 19, 21, 27, 36, 37, 40, 73–76, 78–84, 90, 128, 178
Oxford English Dictionary 60, 69, 179
paleography 11, 12, 34, 88, 89, 116, 120
paraphrase (poetical restatement of Biblical content) 34, 41, 126
Parson's Tale 76, 78, 108, 165, 168, 169, 171
Peasants' Revolt 125
Penitential Psalms 109
pericope 109, 110, 112, 113, 117, 118, 121, 122
phonology 10, 15, 16, 18–21, 23–26, 34, 59, 67, 92, 105
Piers Plowman Electronic Archive 91, 95, 106
Piers Plowman 75, 88, 114, 124, 128
preacher's marks 39
preaching (function of text) 35, 39, 40
prefixation 15, 16, 20, 21, 24–27
press crew 10, 135, 140, 143, 144, 149, 150
printing house 135, 138, 158, 178, 184, 185, 188
Privy Seal warrant 23
Protestant Reformation 47, 48, 125
Psalms 109, 126, 131, 132

Psalter 90, 108
Psalter-Hours 109
punctuation 16, 19, 22, 23, 28, 113, 135, 141, 147, 155, 178
quad 181, 183, 184, 186
quire 48, 74, 79, 80, 108, 139, 140, 142, 143, 150, 155
reading 21, 35, 39, 40, 53–55, 60, 61, 107, 110–115, 117–122, 131, 148, 189, 157–159, 161–165, 171, 179, 185, 186
redactor 32, 38–40, 44
revision 157, 161, 163–165
royal 5, 15, 51, 76, 104, 111, 125, 129, 130, 132, 134
rubrication 34, 35, 80, 107, 108, 110, 113
ruling 23, 79
running head 80, 107
Sanctorale 121
scientific text 44, 56, 110, 124
Scotland 105, 131, 153, 190
scribal hand 11, 15–17, 26, 28, 34, 35, 37, 45, 53, 54, 74, 77, 81, 89, 97, 98, 102, 106, 135, 139, 142, 147, 150, 152, 158, 167
scribe 9–12, 15, 16, 18–27, 33, 34, 39, 43–45, 49, 53–56, 58–61, 65, 66, 68, 73–76, 79–81, 83, 84, 88–90, 92–95, 101, 104, 107–109, 114, 115, 117, 120–123, 135, 150, 169, *see also* paleography, textual transmission
script 16, 50, 73, 84, 98, 102, 106, 110, 141, *see also* paleography
  Gothic 141
  hierarchy of 73, 84
  scriptura continua 18
  textualis 110
scriptorium 27, 35, 45
Sermo Lupi ad Anglos 37
sermon 34, 35, 37–47, 109
Shropshire 56, 61

Sirach 143, 145, 147
space, insufficient, *see* constraint, spatial
spacing 138, 148, 149, 155, 178–184, 186–188
Staffordshire 61
standardization 10, 15, 26, 65, 75, 84, 141, 144
stationer 110
suffixation 11, 15, 20–22, 24–27
syllable boundary 16, 27
table of lessons 5, 11, 107, 109, 110, 114, 116, 122
Temporal Homilies 44–46
Temporale 112, 117, 121
text
   omission 19, 35, 108, 120, 122, 147, 150, 159–162
   relationship 98, 110, 111, 114, 115, 117, 118, 120, 122
   textual analysis 5, 121, 157, 158, 163
   textual transmission 5, 9, 31, 32, 38, 43, 46, 49, 66, 107, 108, 110, 111, 114, 115, 118, 120–123, 166, 169
   transposition 78, 160–162
   unique reading 159, 161, 163
   variation 9–11, 110, 111, 135, 138, 142, 148, 149, 158–161, 163–164
   word substitution 94, 105, 162
The Crafte of Nombrynge 17
The Cure of Enpostumes 17
The Grave 37
The Hours of the Cross 109
transcription 5, 11, 48, 53–55, 73, 78, 91–95, 97, 98, 100–104, 106, 142, 157, 167, 171, 178
translation 12, 15, 17, 34–36, 40–42, 44–49, 51, 53, 61, 70, 64, 66, 68, 83, 88, 94, 110, 116, 125–133, 166, 186, 190, *see also* scribe
Treatise on the Astrolabe 82
Treatise on Urines 17
Troilus and Criseyde 74, 82
Type III 75, 83, 84, *see also* standardization
Type IV 75, *see also* standardization
type
   ligature 142, 145, 146, 149, 179
   movable type 136, 178
   thin space 179, 183
typeface 150
typesetting 180
typography
   conventions 10, 11, 178, 180, 185
   error 141, 150, 158
vernacular translation 12, 48
vernacularization, *see* vernacular translation
Visio Sancti Pauli 37
Vita sancti Guthlaci 34
Vulgate 48, 124, 126, 133, 136, 142
Westminster 9, 74, 75, 82–84, 189
Wonders of the East 17
woodcut illustrations, *see* decoration (of texts)
Worcester 36, 61, 102
Worcestershire 102
word-division
   principle 10, 16, 20, 24, 26
word division
   anomalous 15, 18–20, 22–24, 27
   line-final 5, 10, 15, 16, 18, 19, 22, 27, 28
word formation 17, 20
Worms 126
writing area 79, 116
Wycliffite Bible 5, 10, 12, 108, 110, 116, 122, 124–128, 130, 132, 133
Załuski Library 132

Notes on Contributors

Mari Agata is Associate Professor in the Faculty of Letters, Keio University, Japan. Her research has focussed on book history in general, and incunabula and the transition from manuscript to print in particular. Her publications and conference presentations have mainly addressed early prints of the Bible, especially the *Gutenberg Bible*. Digitization of books and the application of digital technology to analytical bibliography are other areas of interest to her.

Javier Calle-Martín is Reader in English Historical Linguistics in the Department of English at the University of Málaga, Spain. His research interests range from historical linguistics to palaeography, codicology, manuscript transmission and authorship attribution studies. He has published in specialized journals such as *Neuphilologische Mitteilungen* (2004), *Folia Linguistica Historica* (2005), *Literary and Linguistic Computing* (2007), *Studia Neophilologica* (2007) and the *Review of English Studies* (2008). He is currently the leading researcher of a project funded by the Autonomous Government of Andalusia (P07-HUM02609) and aimed at (a) the electronic editing of late Middle English *Fachprosa* and (b) the compilation of an annotated corpus of mediaeval science in the vernacular.

Olga Frolova, a historian, graduated from the Department of Medieval History at the University of St. Petersburg, Russia, in 1987 and specializes in sixteenth century English history. Since 1987, she has worked in the Department of Western European books at the National Library of Russia. She is the author of numerous articles dealing with different aspects of older English and European book culture, among them seventeenth-century English almanacs, the English Royal library, and sixteenth-century English books. She has also published on the history of book collecting in western Europe and Russia.

Joanna Kopaczyk is Assistant Professor (*adiunkt*) at Adam Mickiewicz University in Poznań, Poland. She is a contributor to the Canterbury Tales Project and has taken part in digitizing "The Man of Law's Tale". She uses paleography as a tool for reading original texts and comparing them with editions and corpus transcriptions. Her monograph on *Middle Scots Inflectional System in the South-West of Scotland* (Bugaj 2004, Peter Lang) was based on the earliest extant manuscript of burgh court records from the area. Currently, she is working on a post-doctoral project dealing with the language of Scottish burghs in light of discourse-specific lexical bundles and their link to text-type standardization.

Joanna is also interested in the linguistic history of Scottish diasporas in the Baltic region, with emphasis on Poland and Prussia.

Roderick W. McConchie, PhD, Docent, is a University Lecturer at the University of Helsinki, Finland. His current interests include Early Modern English lexicography, book history, and early Middle English prefixation. He published a monograph on Early Modern English medical terminology entitled *Lexicography and Physicke* in 1997, and has more recently published several articles on the prefix dis- in Middle English and George Motherby's 1775 medical dictionary, and co-edited conference proceedings and a collection of essays. He was until recently a member of Varieng, The Centre of Excellence for the Study of Variation, Contacts and Change in English, and organized the two HEL-LEX conferences held in 2005 and 2008 in Finland.

David Moreno Olalla is Lecturer at the University of Málaga, Spain. His main areas of research include plant-lore in mediaeval England, manuscript studies, and Middle English dialectology, although he dabbles occasionally in Old and Early Modern English. He is interested in the mediaeval interpretation of (post-) classical sources for the creation of vernacular herbals, and in the identification and diffusion of plant-names throughout the ME *Sprachgebiet*. He is currently working on an annotated edition of a hitherto unpublished translation into Middle English of the Latin poem *De viribus herbarum*, and on a monograph about the scribal phrase *plenus amoris* that appears in the colophon of many mediaeval MSS.

Matti Peikola is Adjunct Professor of Philology in the Department of English, University of Turku, Finland, and currently Academy Research Fellow funded by the Academy of Finland. He specializes in manuscript and textual studies with a focus on Late Middle and Early Modern English writing, especially texts associated with the Wycliffite/Lollard movement. He has recently published articles on manuscripts of the *Wycliffite Bible*, for example in *Journal of the Early Book Society* and in *Medieval Texts in Context* (Routledge, 2008), and is one of the associate editors of *Records of the Salem Witch-Hunt* (Cambridge University Press, 2009).

Hanna Rutkowska has been Assistant Professor (*adiunkt*) in the School of English at Adam Mickiewicz University, Poznań, Poland since 2001. In 2003 she published *Graphemics and morphosyntax in the Cely Letters (1472–1478)* (Peter Lang), a monograph based on her doctoral dissertation. She has been involved in the *Man of Law's Project* at Adam Mickiewicz University, Poznań, transcribing the extant witnesses of Geoffrey Chaucer's *Man of Law's Tale* since 2007. She is currently working on her post-doctoral project dealing with the orthographic standardization in English on the basis of several sixteenth- and seventeenth-century editions of *The kalender of sheperdes*, benefiting from a post-doctoral project grant (N N104 055438) from the Polish Ministry of Science and Higher Education, 2010–2012.

Larry J. Swain is Assistant Professor of English in Medieval and Renaissance Literature at Bemidji State University, United States of America. Among his academic interests are all matters concerning medieval manuscripts and textual culture, biblical literature and exegesis, and sources of medieval literary culture, oral and written, especially in Anglo-Saxon England. He is currently the editor in chief of *The Heroic Age: A Journal of Early Medieval Northwestern Europe* and is working on a volume for *Sources of Anglo-Saxon Literary Culture*.

Jacob Thaisen taught in the School of English at Adam Mickiewicz University, Poznań, Poland, but is now Associate Professor of Literacy Studies at the University of Stavanger, Norway. His work falls in the intersection of the history of the English language with textual and manuscript studies. It has focused on the scribal tradition of Chaucer's *Canterbury Tales* and more recently on probabilistic modelling of Middle English manuscript orthography. Humanities computing is another area of interest, and he is currently coordinating work financially supported by the Polish Ministry of Education on an electronic corpus which includes all the known late-medieval copies of Chaucer's *Man of Law's Tale* so as to permit scholars to trace the flow of linguistic variants through about a century of its manuscript tradition.

Satoko Tokunaga is Assistant Professor in the Faculty of Letters, Keio University, Japan (from 2007), and a visiting fellow of Corpus Christi College, Cambridge (2010-2011). She has been studying early English printing, mainly Caxton and de Worde, and is now making a catalogue of early English books housed in Japanese libraries. Her publications have appeared in journals such as *International Journal of English Studies, Poetica* and *The Library*.

Studies in English Medieval Language and Literature

Edited by Jacek Fisiak

Vol. 1 Dieter Kastovsky / Arthur Mettinger (eds.): Language Contact in the History of English. 2nd, revised edition. 2003.

Vol. 2 Studies in English Historical Linguistics and Philology. A Festschrift for Akio Oizumi. Edited by Jacek Fisiak. 2002.

Vol. 3 Liliana Sikorska: In a Manner of Morall Playe: Social Ideologies in English Moralities and Interludes (1350–1517). 2002.

Vol. 4 Peter J. Lucas / Angela M. Lucas (eds.): Middle English from Tongue to Text. Selected Papers from the Third International Conference on Middle English: Language and Text, held at Dublin, Ireland, 1–4 July 1999. 2002.

Vol. 5 Chaucer and the Challenges of Medievalism. Studies in Honor of H. A. Kelly. Edited by Donka Minkova and Theresa Tinkle. 2003.

Vol. 6 Hanna Rutkowska: Graphemics and Morphosyntax in the *Cely Letters* (1472–88). 2003.

Vol. 7 The *Ancrene Wisse*. A Four-Manuscript Parallel Text. Preface and Parts 1–4. Edited by Tadao Kubouchi and Keiko Ikegami with John Scahill, Shoko Ono, Harumi Tanabe, Yoshiko Ota, Ayako Kobayashi and Koichi Nakamura. 2003.

Vol. 8 Joanna Bugaj: Middle Scots Inflectional System in the South-west of Scotland. 2004.

Vol. 9 Rafal Boryslawski: The Old English Riddles and the Riddlic Elements of Old English Poetry. 2004.

Vol. 10 Nikolaus Ritt / Herbert Schendl (eds.): Rethinking Middle English. Linguistic and Literary Approaches. 2005.

Vol. 11 The *Ancrene Wisse*. A Four-Manuscript Parallel Text. Parts 5–8 with Wordlists. Edited by Tadao Kubouchi and Keiko Ikegami with John Scahill, Shoko Ono, Harumi Tanabe, Yoshiko Ota, Ayako Kobayashi, Koichi Nakamura. 2005.

Vol. 12 Text and Language in Medieval English Prose. A Festschrift for Tadao Kubouchi. Edited by Akio Oizumi, Jacek Fisiak and John Scahill. 2005.

Vol. 13 Michiko Ogura (ed.): Textual and Contextual Studies in Medieval English. Towards the Reunion of Linguistics and Philology. 2006.

Vol. 14 Keiko Hamaguchi: Non-European Women in Chaucer. A Postcolonial Study. 2006.

Vol. 15 Ursula Schaefer (ed.): The Beginnings of Standardization. Language and Culture in Fourteenth-Century England. 2006.

Vol. 16 Nikolaus Ritt / Herbert Schendl / Christiane Dalton-Puffer / Dieter Kastovsky (eds): Medieval English and its Heritage. Structure, Meaning and Mechanisms of Change. 2006.

Vol. 17 Matylda Włodarczyk: Pragmatic Aspects of Reported Speech. The Case of Early Modern English Courtroom Discourse. 2007.

Vol. 18 Hans Sauer / Renate Bauer (eds.): *Beowulf* and Beyond. 2007.

Vol. 19 Gabriella Mazzon (ed.): Studies in Middle English Forms and Meanings. 2007.

Vol. 20 Alexander Bergs / Janne Skaffari (eds.): The Language of the Peterborough Chronicle. 2007.

Vol. 21 Liliana Sikorska (ed.). With the assistance of Joanna Maciulewicz: Medievalisms. The Poetics of Literary Re-Reading. 2008.

Vol.	22	Masachiyo Amano / Michiko Ogura / Masayuki Ohkado (eds.): Historical Englishes in Varieties of Texts and Contexts. The Global COE Program, International Conference 2007. 2008.
Vol.	23	Ewa Ciszek: Word Derivation in Early Middle English. 2008.
Vol.	24	Andrzej M. Łęcki: Grammaticalisation Paths of *Have* in English. 2010.
Vol.	25	Osamu Imahayashi / Yoshiyuki Nakao / Michiko Ogura (eds.): Aspects of the History of English Language and Literature. Selected Papers Read at SHELL 2009, Hiroshima. 2010.
Vol.	26	Magdalena Bator: Obsolete Scandinavian Loanwords in English. 2010.
Vol.	27	Anna Cichosz: The Influence of Text Type on Word Order of Old Germanic Languages. A Corpus-Based Contrastive Study of Old English and Old High German. 2010.
Vol.	28	Jacek Fisiak / Magdalena Bator (eds.): Foreign Influences on Medieval English. 2011.
Vol.	29	Władysław Witalisz: The Trojan Mirror. Middle English Narratives of Troy as Books of Princely Advice. 2011.
Vol.	30	Luis Iglesias-Rábade: Semantic Erosion of Middle English Prepositions. 2011.
Vol.	31	Barbara Kowalik: Betwixt *engelaunde* and *englene londe*. Dialogic Poetics in Early English Religious Lyric. 2010.
Vol.	32	The Katherine Group. A Three-Manuscript Parallel Text. Seinte Katerine, Seinte Marherete, Seinte Iuliene, and Hali Meiðhad, with Wordlists. Edited by Shoko Ono and John Scahill with Keiko Ikegami, Tadao Kubouchi, Harumi Tanabe, Koichi Nakamura, Satoko Shimazaki and Koichi Kano. 2011.
Vol.	33	Jacob Thaisen / Hanna Rutkowska (eds.): Scribes, Printers, and the Accidentals of their Texts. 2011.

www.peterlang.de

Ewa Ciszek

Word Derivation in Early Middle English

Frankfurt am Main, Berlin, Bern, Bruxelles, New York, Oxford, Wien, 2008.
141 pp.
Studies in English Medieval Language and Literature. Edited by Jacek Fisiak.
Vol. 23
ISBN 978-3-631-58372-2 · pb. € 27.50*

No comprehensive study of Early Middle English derivation has been published thus far. This book is an attempt to remedy the situation, at least to give a detailed analysis of one class of suffixes, i.e., seven suffixes forming abstract nouns. They are both of native (-dōm, -s(c)hipe(e), -hōd(e) and –nes(se)) and French origin (-āge, -(e)rīe and -ment). The analysis includes the semantics of the suffixes both from a diachronic and a synchronic perspective as well as their productivity and dialect distribution. The study is data-oriented, hence the analysis of linguistic facts is dominating. The analysed material comes from the *Dictionary of Old English* (A-F) based on the *Toronto Corpus of Old English Texts*, the *Toronto Corpus* and the *Middle English Dictionary on-line*. The unique features of the study are the account of the senses of the suffixes in Old and Early Middle English, and the semantic evolution of the native suffixes from Old to Early Middle English as well as the demonstration that some of the French suffixes were productive already in Early Middle English.

Contents: Historical word derivation · English historical word derivation · Historical word formation · Word formation · Early Middle English · Old English · Suffix

Frankfurt am Main · Berlin · Bern · Bruxelles · New York · Oxford · Wien
Distribution: Verlag Peter Lang AG
Moosstr. 1, CH-2542 Pieterlen
Telefax 00 41 (0) 32 / 376 17 27

*The €-price includes German tax rate
Prices are subject to change without notice
Homepage http://www.peterlang.de